Dedicated to Jer,
Ely, Liam, Tanya, Emet, and Kedem

Reclaim

PLaY

Avital Schreiber Levy

ReclaimPlay.com

Author's note

All children are designed to play. Independent play has tremendous benefits to children's development: physically, socially, emotionally, and even academically. It also makes parenting a lot easier. Unfortunately, play has declined so much in recent years, that now some children are living a childhood without play. Hooked on screens, clinging to parents and always discontented. That's a missed opportunity for the child and the parent. Reclaim Play will help you bring back this lost art and get your child playing for hours a day.

Preface

It's not like I hadn't been warned. Parents who went before me told me how it would be. Although they didn't need to tell me—I could see it in their eyes—the exhaustion, the utter overwhelm, the plea for help of any kind. Save me from the never ending bedtime. Rescue me from the remorseless screams. Aid me with the floor ridden lego. Please! Hold him, take her and give me a break. And at the same time, paradoxically: I love these little troublemakers more than you could possibly know. Only the initiation to parenthood itself will allow you into the club of those who love quite so unconditionally.

When I became a parent I understood. I understood that parenting will shake out whatever's not tied down: from your pelvic floor to your bank account. But also, more importantly, that this tiny human is like your own heart toddling around in someone else's body. It's a gut wrenching love.

It was mid-snowstorm in New York City when my third child was born. I found myself almost buckling under the pressures of parenting. Whilst our lives were privileged by every account, the stressors of the day-to-day grind were gnawing at my sanity. Managing volcanic tantrums, trying to stay "profesh" at my day job, keeping my house from looking like a crime scene and myself from looking like I had just survived a wolf attack. It was all just a blush too much to handle gracefully. My husband, bless him, was gone long hours, weekends, night shifts chipping away at a grueling medical residency... I was solo parenting most of the time. At some point the yells, sighs and resentment began to build up like my son's marble collection—it all threatened to tip me over into some unnamed abyss.

Change. Something needs to change.

"There must be a better way", a voice in my head began repeating.

"You're missing something." it said. "It shouldn't have to be this hard."

If I could go back in time to myself a decade ago, I'd tell myself to heed that voice: There *is* a better way. You *are* missing something. It *doesn't* have to be this hard.

So I set off to find that missing piece, that better way. As a designer, I rely on design thinking to approach clients' problems and come up with appropriate solutions. That's what I did for myself. I asked myself: Within the limitations of the situation, knowing what you know about yourself, your home, your family—what could make things easier?

There it was: staring me in the face. Some of my easiest, proudest, most joyful moments with my children are those times when I get to witness their creativity and imagination flourish. It's when they're not nagging, whinging, fighting, begging or generally creating mayhem in our home. It's when they are gainfully employed in deep, immersive independent play.

During those times I could potter around the house doing this or that, catch a quick rest on the couch with my newborn, take a phone call with my boss, get dinner started. In short: It was a breather. A relief. The second best thing to Mary Poppins herself showing up at my door.

That magic would occur from time to time. The wizardry of my son building elaborately with train tracks or planning out a show. The alchemy of my children being completely absorbed by the castle they were building and the little people that would live within its walls.

What was this sorcery and how could I make it last longer? Happen more often? More reliably?

I followed the rabbit hole—diving into all the research I could get my hands on regarding independent play. What I found fascinated and delighted me. Play was not only the secret to making parenting easier—it was also unequivocally fabulous for children's development.

7

So I set to work, using my own family as my lab. Leaning on my skills and training as a designer I experimented with tweaks to our physical space, to my own parenting approach and to the toys themselves—to see if I could encourage independent play.

It took trial and error but I learned that I could.

We now have five children of various ages and they all play independently for upwards of three hours a day. This has eased the inherent stressors of parenting tremendously. It has allowed me to keep my day job, start a side hustle and eventually scale my business. It has allowed my husband and I the space to have meaningful and important conversations, even when our children are around. It has meant that I was able to write this book, even without reliable babysitting help.

They play for hours a day and no, they're not special unicorns, although they're certainly special to us. The truth is that this is something that all children are designed to do. As you'll discover in this book—our children's play has been stolen, and you're about to learn why that's such a problem and what you can do to take it back.

How to Use This Book

Part One: Play in Theory

The first part of this book will give you context and insight into design thinking, the importance of play, and why it's been lost. Chapter 1 will give you the in-depth background to what Childhood Design is and how you can use it in your life as a parent. Chapter 2, What's the Problem?, explores the loss of independent play—how and why there's been a steep decline. Chapter 3, Why Reclaim Play?, will give you a thorough understanding of the benefits of play to your child.

Part Two: Play Prep

If you want to skip to the How To, the second part of the book is where you'll get highly practical steps to begin to reclaim play, starting today. Chapters 4 and 5, Babies Who Play and Scheming Toddlers, will set you up for Reclaim Play success with the youngest crew (yes, even from birth). If you don't have a baby or a toddler, you can skip those chapters and go straight to chapter 6, Busy Slayer, which will help you create *time* for play; and chapter 7, Declutter Boss, which will help you make *space* for play.

Part Three: Play Architecture

The most important concepts of the book can be found in chapters 8 through 16, where you'll learn all about how to set up your Play Zones and become a Play Architect and a Play Guru. In chapter 8 you'll learn how to become a Play Architect. Chapter 9 will introduce you to the Imagination Zone; chapter 10, the Messy Zone; chapter 11, the Movement Zone; chapter 12, the Quiet Zone; and chapter 13, the Focus Zone. Chapter 14 will help you become a Curation Diva and teach you how to choose the best toys and materials, and chapter 15 will disclose the secrets of being a Strew Pro—of keeping your toys fresh and interesting for your child—without purchasing more and more.

Part Four: Reclaim Play and Special Situations

After that, you'll find chapters on only children, on siblings, on screen usage—which you can sift through as they apply to your personal situation. Reclaim Play is applicable to every home, every family type, and every stage of children's development. With some key adjustments and experimentation, you'll find how you can apply it to your unique situation.

Part Four:
Reclaim Play and Special Situations

Part One:
Play in Theory

Chapters 1—3

Childhood by Design

Happiness . . . is not a destination: it is a manner of traveling. Happiness is not an end in itself. It is a by-product of working, playing, loving and living. **Haim Ginott**

How do we create an experience of childhood that both parent and child enjoy? Even if you are comparatively blessed with a comfortable life and a healthy child, parenting can stretch you beyond capacity. Pregnancy threatens to strain your back or your bank account or both. In the newborn stage, your marriage and melatonin come under barrage. Keeping a toddler from inserting peas into their nose is a full-time job. Add to that comparisonitis on social media, information overload that makes us consistently doubt ourselves, and the fast pace of modern life, and feeling overwhelmed, stressed, and frazzled seems a given. According to my informal surveys of thousands of families worldwide, the problems we face as modern-day parents fall under the following five Cs: chaos, conflict, clutter, clinginess and confusion. When children have a strong independent play muscle, many of the pressures that build up in the five Cs can be relieved.

Chaos

Parents feel frazzled. Rushed routines, busy schedules and feeling stuck in survival mode 24/7, with little sense of balance, order, and rhythm. That last-minute rush to sign up for summer camp before registration closes, or the gutting realization that you missed the dentist appointment this morning—over time, these mini-ordeals add up to a sense of helplessness. Sometimes it's your time management that's chaotic: meals blurring into snacks blurring into meals. Or bedtimes that go on seemingly forever, until you snap! When children can use the fallback mode of playing deeply for long stretches of time, you're allowed to find a greater sense of order and control. Sitting down to finish your coffee, sitting back on your sofa—in those lulls when they're playing, you can collect your thoughts and regain a sense of order.

Conflict

Many people experience high levels of conflict with loved ones, including in-laws, parents, partners, and children. Sibling rivalry between the kids, power struggles with the kids, and stress with your partner, not to mention the severe sense of judgment from our wider community, from neighbors to pediatricians. All this can lead to glaring isolation, leaving you wondering: What village?! When your kids play independently, there is less conflict—because they're happily absorbed for more of the time. This lessens the risk of burnout or resentment building between the partners. When they play, there's less chance you'll explode or nitpick or nag and an increased likelihood of enjoying quality time together. Plus, of course, children who play independently also allow their parents the time to have those deeper conversations that are needed to maintain their adult relationship.

Clutter

Modern living means materialism for many of us. While having many possessions can be a blessing, it can also become overwhelming. On average, people in the United States have 300,000 items in their homes, many of which are toys. It's too much "stuff" to handle. You might feel defeated by Mt. Laundry every day, uncomfortable with dopamine-dependent retail therapy sprees, and overwhelmed by the never-ending hamster wheel of mess-and-clean-up. One of the bedrocks of reclaiming independent play, as you'll soon discover, is that less is more. Through decluttering and setting up simple play zones (areas dedicated to specific types of play—more on that throughout this book), you'll find that you don't need as much "stuff." You'll start rejecting the mountains of plastic that find their way into your home and embrace a more minimalistic and orderly environment. When kids play for real, we don't feel driven to overcompensate or lure them with new toys and a never-ending barrage of "things."

Clinginess

Positive and healthy attachment behaviors (co-sleeping, breastfeeding, babywearing) can easily lead to the dark side: overattachment, where you begin to feel "touched out" and even resentful of your child. When your kids are overly dependent, needy, and clingy, you might feel smothered. If you're like most people—you'll look for an escape in better or worse ways; perhaps in the form of overeating, working out, a chat with a friend, a red wine habit, or a little harmless doom scrolling, we're looking to "get away" from our children's ever-present needs. Some of these habits may be good for us—but what's less great is the need to escape our day to day lives. That feeling of suffocation is born of too much proximity without enough space. Children who develop their independent play muscle are less clingy. They've been weaned off their addiction to constant attention and entertainment from their adult, and instead appreciate their own self-directed worlds of entertainment. In reclaiming independent play, you establish strong attachments during caregiving times, special time, and simple time enjoying each other's company. When you've filled up their love cups during those times of true presence, you are free to happily go about your business in parallel to their play, without constant intertwinement.

Confusion

Parenting in the digital age can be a double-edged sword. With easy access to more knowledge than ever, conflicting advice and paradoxical research can lead to confusion. Knowing a little bit about everything can make it difficult to trust your own intuition. Endless links to articles promising that a certain product, method, or insight is the ultimate solution to stress can leave you feeling overwhelmed and without a clear vision. Marketers often prey on parents' innate insecurities and fear of not being a good parent. This book offers practical tools to help you make your own decisions, rather than getting caught up in the noise. There is a lot of parenting information available, but one thing is clear: play is essential for children's development. By keeping this in mind, you can reduce the pressure to constantly entertain and occupy your children and trust that they can occupy themselves.

Design Thinking and Overwhelmed Parents

My career began as a graphic designer, and design thinking has informed my approach to many issues. I found that going through the process as though I were a designer who had been handed a "brief" with a problem to solve allowed me to see issues and solutions more clearly. The Hasso-Plattner Institute of Design at Stanford has proposed five stages of "design thinking," the process designers use to tackle and solve complex problems. To save time, I've whittled them down to three: empathizing, ideation, and experimentation. So, let's take a closer look at these three stages and how you can apply them to your family life:

Stage One: Empathizing

To do a good job of creating something that alleviates a problematic situation, designers must have a deep understanding of the human needs involved. If they've never been in a hospital bed, they may have a hard time designing one that improves patients' lives. Therefore, the first step in design thinking must be to walk in the shoes of the person with the blister—i.e., to feel what the negative experience is like. Empathy involves setting aside our assumptions and truly listening and observing with an open mind. To introduce more empathy to yourself you'll need to dodge the common tendency to berate yourself for your shortcomings, wallow in guilt and shame, and instead put on your designer's hat and get curious: How does it feel to be in my shoes? Where's the pain point and why is it significant?

Empathy is the ability to understand and share in someone else's emotions. But the curious thing is that we often don't give ourselves—or even our children—the empathy that we would automatically offer others. So if you're struggling in any area of family life, start by offering yourself a little bit of understanding and compassion. Feel the feelings, recognize the problem—that's the first place to start. As chapters two and three will outline in full, I empathize deeply with the plight of both parents and children in the modern world. There are very real and explainable reasons that lead to a burdensome feeling of stress and anxiety for today's parents, and there is no reason to feel shame over your challenges.

Empathy allows us to identify the core of the issue, the first domino. What is really troubling me—this will help us design an appropriate and effective solution. Of course, humans are complex and it's not always easy to identify the source problem—but accessing empathy for ourselves and others is a good way of peeling back the layers of behaviors that can obscure the deeper issue at hand. Empathy can also shift us out of the guilt and shame cycles. Guilt and shame may be useful emotions when they point us to ways we're not operating properly; however, staying stuck there is not a pragmatic way to solve problems. It blocks our creativity and we remain feeling sorry, or sorry for ourselves.

When you get upset, can you say to yourself: I see this is hard. I can totally understand where you're coming from and why this isn't working for you. I feel you. Let's get to the bottom of this and see the original cause of all this frustration. If you can, then you're ready for the next step.

Stage Two: Ideation

When we're struggling, we first need to validate our experience and empathize with ourselves. But it's important not to dwell on it for too long, as overindulging in self-empathy can lead to self-pity. Instead, let's brainstorm. The ideation phase is about coming up with creative ideas. Allow your imagination to take flight and come up with all sorts of solutions, from the obvious to the preposterous. Lots of ideas can come through at this stage; some are realistic, some are aspirational. Allow them all to pour forth.

To get your juices flowing, ask yourself some probing questions:

- How would I solve this problem if money was no issue?
- How would I tackle this if I had all the time in the world?
- What might I do if success was 100 percent guaranteed?
- What would I do if I knew no one would ever find out?
- How would my "higher self" (the best version of me) approach this issue?
- What would an architect, doctor, engineer, psychologist, politician, artist, and so on do with this problem?
- If I imagine myself twenty years from now, looking back at this time, what action would I be proud of?

The best solutions are often the simplest. Even if a solution seems obvious, it can be considered elegant for its simplicity. Convoluted, contrived designs are often superfluous—they try too hard. Throughout the action-oriented section of this book (chapter 4 and on) you will receive many prompts and ideas to get you started on all manner of solutions to help prioritize play for your child. I encourage you to view these ideas as a springboard for your own ideation. We are brainstorming together; this is an iterative process that can and should continue well beyond the pages of this book.

Stage Three: Experimentation
At this point, we want to choose one of our ideas and put it into action. We want to design a plan, perhaps put it down on paper and communicate it to the other people who are involved (partners, teachers, nannies, the kids themselves). The key to this phase is curiosity, an understanding that you don't have to get it right immediately, you just have to get it started. Prototypes

are never the finished product. They're just the first try, and as such, they're imperfect by definition. When you're trying to solve a problem like clinginess, you might be salivating for a quick fix. Not gonna happen. Everything that works well takes time to finesse. That truism is one hundred times more accurate when it comes to children, who are, by their very nature, changing by the millisecond.

No product is "perfect" when it comes out of the workshop; all companies create a beta product, test it, improve it and release the product to the market when it's "good enough." Even then, companies don't rest on their laurels. They gather customer feedback, fix bugs, make improvements, and offer upgrades.

The ideas presented in this book are invitations for you to experiment with what works for you and your child. Your unique, personal, and highly individual circumstance must always be the lens through which you examine any idea: "That's a nice idea," you might think, "Let's see if it applies to us." Take what works, leave the rest. Experiment like a mad scientist, and never take any of my ideas (or anyone else's) as dogma, until you've run your own personal batch of experiments in real life. The embodied experience of whether or not an approach works for you is the only meaningful thing.

Ultimately, you decide if and how you want to declutter (chapter 7), set up play zones (chapters 8 through 13) or become a play guru (chapter 17).

The Simplest Solution

Back to our five Cs: Chaos, Conflict, Clutter, Clinginess and Confusion. These problems seem disturbingly complex. How can there be one solution to all five? And how can it be something that is free, easy to come by, and also natural? I'll argue that there is one such solution to all of these problems, to some degree or another. And while there are many other steps we might need to take in due course, this one solution is a powerful catalyst to push us in the right direction. The first domino, you might say. So, what is it? Independent Play

In a way, this book is just one big mega-tip: prioritize play. Not just any play, but the type of play where children are independent, self-directed, and free. Take a moment to reflect: How well is your child engaging in play right now? Is your child deeply emerged in exploration, curiosity, imagination, and self-expression on a regular basis? How well is your home set up to support that play? Is there space in your schedule to allow for it? Do you yourself feel equipped to facilitate it? Are you even sure what it is or why it's important? If not, the answers will come in the upcoming chapters.

Reclaiming this type of play is crucial for children's development, and it's a fantastically effective stress-reduction scheme for parents. This is why it's one primary solution to the stress of parenting that I advocate passionately. In the coming chapters, it's my goal to take you on a journey of empowerment. We'll get über practical in design-oriented solutions that make parenting easier, more fun, and more effective. These solutions don't need to cost any money at all, and they don't take much time, but they do demand some intentionality on your part.

Many of us parents simply don't get to enjoy parenting all that much. We love our children, sure, but many of us succumb to the stresses of parenting. While there are tensions and complex issues built into any relationship and all of life, you're here to reclaim a sense of calm, connection, and joy. To enjoy your children, even while they're young. My goal is to help you not just love your children but to love parenting them as well. When you take the steps to reclaim independent play and design a childhood both you and your child enjoy, I believe you'll feel empowered and confident as a parent. And, as the research shows, when you feel confident as a parent, you'll enjoy it much, much more. Now it's time to get into the bread and butter of play—what it is and how it's going to solve some big problems for you.

Quick Summary: Childhood Design

Stage 1, Empathizing:

- Can I feel for myself and my child as I would a friend? Can I see myself as my own client and coach myself with kindness, compassion, and grace?

- How can I reframe any shame or guilt as compassion and empathy for myself and others?

- Going deep, what seems to be the core issue, the first domino? If I knock that one down, will it take care of the other issues?

Stage 2, Ideating (What are some possible solutions? Think of when/what/how questions here):

- How can we solve this problem? Come up with some wild and outlandish solutions—nothing is too crazy to brainstorm.

- What are some outside-the-box ways of looking at this issue?

- When can I experiment with this idea?

- How would I approach this if money, time, and energy were no barriers?

Stage 3, Experimentation (Let's put one of these solutions into practice, test it out, reiterate, and make adjustments as we go):

- Get into the mad scientist mindset—you're testing out prototypes, not expecting perfection on the first try.

- Try out a new way of doing things, a new timing, a new location, or new words put to a situation.

- Observe the results and keep what works, while editing out what doesn't.

What's the

Chapter

02

Problem?2

Children require long uninterrupted periods of play and exploration. **Jean Piaget,** *Play, Dreams and Imitation in Childhood*

My guess is that if I ask you to think back to your childhood, you might still be of the generation that can easily recall long hours devoted to play. These might register as your most cherished memories, like riding bikes with friends until the streetlights came on, building forts in the living room, and putting on a "show" for adults. However, I fear that today's children will remember hours spent in school or on homework, being drilled with new skills in organized activities, zoning out in front of the TV, or gaming on the computer. Self-directed, independent playtime is in short supply in the 21st century and it has consequences on children's health and happiness. Where has all the play gone? We might sum it up with the acronym: Our children's play was stolen.

S.T.O.L.E.N

S. Safetyism

The rise in parental anxieties and perceived responsibilities adds to the drastic cut in free time and the increase in parental involvement. In their book, The Coddling of the American Mind, authors Greg Lukianoff and Jonathan Haidt focus on the unintended consequences of a concept they coin as "safetyism," the idea that people are weak and should be protected from, rather than exposed to, challenges. The safety culture has the best of intentions: protecting kids from danger. However, similar to the failure of the "self-esteem movement"—which actually ended up lowering children's self-esteem as they learned to depend on others' praise for their self-concept—safetyism shapes children into delicate, fragile beings who have learned that they cannot withstand challenges, stress, or even uncomfortable situations without crumbling.

Reclaim Play

As Greg says, "Teaching kids that failures, insults, and painful experiences will do lasting damage is harmful in and of itself. Human beings need physical and mental challenges and stressors, or we deteriorate". In the name of safety, we are endangering our children's curiosity, sense of adventure, and independence. We are worried about leaving our babies to play in their playpens while we take a much-needed shower. We might be scared to let our four-year-old explore our enclosed backyard without constant supervision. We're frightened to let our eight-year-old use a hot glue gun to work on his creation. These limitations stunt children's creativity and development.

Lenore Skenazy, author of Free Range Kids, was crucified by America's media and crowned "Worst Mom in the World" (a label she then proudly adopted) when she allowed her nine-year-old to ride the subway alone—at his request and to great success. She has since begun a powerful crusade to free children to once again walk to their nearby playgrounds (without their parents being arrested by the police, which—yes—actually happens). Her work is profoundly important, and she helps parents find solutions and tactics to allow children more freedom within our safteyist culture. She helps us reframe what might be perceived as negligent parenting (allowing a nine-year-old child to walk to the playground alone, for example) as a strategy that actually keeps them safer in the long run. "We have to learn to remind the other parents who think we're being careless when we loosen our grip that we are actually trying to teach our children how to get along in the world, and that we believe this is our job. A child who can fend for himself is a lot safer than one forever coddled, because the coddled child will not have Mom or Dad around all the time, even though they act as if he will".

Our fears are not limited to physical dangers alone. Once the needs for shelter, food, safety, health, and education are basically met, parents don't stop worrying. Instead, we turn our worries to the realm of emotional well-being. I speak to many parents who are afraid that encouraging a child to play independently might cause psychological damage. What if they feel rejected? Abandoned? Traumatized because I wasn't available and interested? Will it harm our attachment? Will she believe I'm disinterested? Or my favorite: Why have kids to begin with if you don't want to play with them? These questions reveal a big misunderstanding of the importance of space in every relationship, the value of self-discovery and time for one's own thought, and the profound impact of trusting our children and ourselves to enjoy a fulfilling and secure attachment without being physically glued together.

As modern parents, we spend double the amount of time with our children compared to parents in the 1950s, even though we also work more. This can contribute to the rise in postpartum depression and parental burnout. Many mothers feel guilty about using screens or resorting to helicopter parenting, and sacrifice their own self-care for the sake of their children. Unfortunately, the past few decades have also seen a decline in free play for children, which is tragic considering the numerous benefits it has for child development and for parents. Independent play allows children to discover their own inner voice, ambition and direction, and also gives parents a chance to relax. However, too much adult attention can hinder this process, and make children dependent on external intervention and expectations.

Furthermore, such parenting can lead to burnout. In my practice, many parents share their sense of guilt at letting their children play independently: "I feel bad that I'm not giving him constant attention." Where did we get the notion that our children need us at every waking moment? If we're keeping them safe, cared for, and educated, why can't there be long stretches where we are uninvolved in the minutia of their activities? Burnout, or just plain old misery, is a very real risk that parents face. Not taking a few minutes to sit and enjoy your morning coffee, not saying no to a game of mermaids sometimes, or not feeling well within the healthy norm when you read a book on the couch as your child plays beside you. These types of thoughts and feelings can run through a parents mind, tuning you into an incessant track of guilt and exhaustion, and it has to stop. Constant attention is actually pretty terrible for children, and an almost surefire way to burn parents out, fast.

The unfounded and media-urged rise in our fears around childhood safety and anxiety around kidnapping in particular have led us to restrict the ways our children can play freely, especially unsupervised and outdoors. These growing concerns lead to a social norm of overprotection, over padding, and severe restriction of childhood play that removes all necessary and healthy risks, exploration and adventure from the realm of play. The focus on safety does not stay within the confines of physical risks but also stops children from taking emotional, social, academic, and creative risks that are foundational to independent play and to life success in general.

T. **Tech Addiction**

The meteoric rise in screen time over the past few decades, where children ages 8-18 spend an average of 7.5 hours in front of a screen for entertainment each day according to the CDC, has resulted in children spending more time being passive, sedentary, and glued to a device, instead of exercising their bodies and imaginations. Do younger children fare better? Slightly. Research shows that children under the age of two are averaging more than 3.5 hours per day in front of a screen, mainly the TV, a statistic that has doubled since 1997. Still pretty grim. I will address screens and their effects on play in chapter 19, it's not all bad news.

Excessive screen time can be detrimental to young children's development in several ways. It can negatively impact their physical health by leading to a sedentary lifestyle and reducing their opportunities for physical activity. It can also harm their cognitive development by limiting their ability to engage in creative and imaginative play, which is crucial for their brain development. Furthermore, excessive screen time can negatively impact their social-emotional development by reducing their opportunities for face-to-face interactions with adults and peers. Studies also suggest that excessive screen time can disrupt sleep patterns in young children, which can affect their overall well-being. Still, the negative effects of excess screen usage are perhaps most profound in what it takes away from—cutting into the hours available for free play.

O. Over Achievement

School-age children have faced a drastic cut in their free time compared to a generation ago. School days and the school year are longer; the homework load is greater and recess shorter; the little time left outside of school is spent in more structured activities, screen time, and "résumé building." Many children's lives today are busier than a termite hill, with little to no time left for free play. One would think that if school-age children are getting the short end of the play stick, perhaps the younger children are clocking the play that we think of as synonymous with childhood. But sadly, preschoolers' free time is not really free either; even little babies and toddlers are being primed for a structured, directed, entertained, and sedentary lifestyle.

"Since about 1955 ... children's free play has been continually declining, at least partly because adults have exerted ever-increasing control over children's activities," says Peter Gray, PhD, professor of psychology at Boston College. The rise in helicopter parenting—a style where parents hover over their children all the way to college—often means that children are never left to their own devices. This hovering can understandably begin at the vulnerable baby stage, where adults must be completely attuned to their infant, their very survival relies upon it. But even in the baby stage, incessant hovering and entertaining unintentionally disenfranchises babies from their own capacity to simply "be," without adult attention at every waking moment. If adults are always making themselves available to children, playing with them and even for them, children will not develop the skills associated with independent play. Instead, they develop an unnecessary dependency that doesn't serve them or their parents well.

Furthermore, adult intervention usually means adult direction. The adult chooses how the child should best spend time (Now we're going to do this puzzle!), which means that the adult crafts the schedule with socially sanctioned pastimes, often prioritizing adult-directed activities such as baby music classes, organized sports, or tutoring—anything that seems "productive" to our culturally conditioned adult minds. It's not our fault! We all want the best for our kids—but it's so hard to see how sometimes our adult eyes are oriented solely toward achievement and "success"—skipping over the beauty of the slow pace of childhood. The fact is that there's basically no industry that stands to gain monetarily from your child delving into long hours of unstructured play. It's free. Which is one reason why there's little awareness about the importance of free play and exploration. As parents, we often feel a sense of satisfaction and fulfillment when we invest our time and give our children ample attention and care. And fair enough. We feel a sense of privilege when we enroll our children in various classes and activities. We feel like we're doing the "right" thing when we spend hours on homework each day. What we sometimes don't realize is that there is such a thing as overparenting, especially when it comes to the kind of interjections that cut deeply into our children's free playtime.

Childhood has become less about developing mastery, confidence, social skills, emotional intelligence, independence, and resilience, and more about building an impressive resume to outpace competitors in the college admissions process. Children today, in comparison to decades prior, are being pushed earlier into academics, spend longer days in school, have heavier loads of homework, and participate in more adult-led, extra-curricular activities than ever before, with no evidence to suggest that any of these improve results for children; quite the contrary.

L. Loneliness

The normal development of human beings around the world and throughout millennia has included long stretches of independent play from very early ages. As D. F. Lancy explains, for many indigenous groups, play is not only the child's responsibility but also the gateway to their inclusion as active and productive members of their society. Jarawa (South and Middle Andaman Islands), Hazda (North-Central Tanzania), and Mbya Guarani (Argentina) children incorporate adult activities in their play. Adults believe that children learn best when unsupervised and assume that they will, of their own accord, begin contributing to the economy of their community when they are ready to do so.

Children in these and other indigenous groups are given great autonomy, not only because that's how they learn best, but also because adults realize that children have opportunities to earn social capital through "good deeds." If these are voluntary and not assigned, so much the better. In the Iatmul culture (Papua New Guinea), children are expected to contribute to the family's efforts, but they are not assigned chores. Instead, their autonomy enables them to offer assistance to others and establish lasting and valuable relationships. As part of a village, a parent has a network of eyes and ears to help keep an eye on their children's whereabouts. They also have the backing and validation of the community that collectively normalizes and encourages free and independent play as the expected behavior for kids. Additionally, there is a crowd of other children who can model this play and initiate group games.

However, when a parent is alone at home with their child and without this support, it can feel daunting, infuriating, and impossible to encourage such play. The child looks exclusively to the parent as the be-all and end-all answer to their entertainment. As one member of the Reclaim Play community, Valentina, wrote: "I often get angry at my son when he is whining constantly and clinging to me, pulling me to play with him. Often, I need to do something else like cooking, cleaning, answering emails, or using the bathroom. I know that he also needs my attention at that moment, but I get really frustrated because I can't finish what I am doing. Sometimes, I ignore him or even yell at him, which I truly never want to do." With the disappearance of the "village" it takes to raise a child, we're standing isolated and shoulders crumbling under the weight of the task. As parents, we are often alone, and usually lonely. Parenting has become a private affair; your challenges and wins are known to no one but you. Over-entertaining and over-involved parenting of children is bad for kids and it's bad for parents too.

If we adopted some of the well-established traditions of many indigenous groups, we too might look at independent play as an opportunity for kids to discover themselves, to find their voice and creativity—and to give us a few moments of hard-earned peace.

Children have moved indoors, away from their roaming friends. Nuclear family units have shrunk away from extended families, and into ever tinier circles. Parents are having fewer children than ever before, with less siblings and—eventually—less cousins around. In modern families, both parent and child often feel the sting of isolation. The child has no one to play with. The adult has no one to offer support and the proverbial village. When there is less support, less social acceptance of play and fewer play peers—play suffers.

E. Excess

Children today have more toys than ever before, yet this excess does not lead to more quantity or quality of play. In fact, when toddlers have more toys in their environment, it generally leads to less play. The toy industry sells upwards of 3 billion toys per year in the USA alone and parents feel pressure to keep up with others. The focus has shifted from providing a good quality, inviting environment for play and offering time and encouragement, to pumping childhood with ever more gadgets and toys. Many homes are flooded with toys but devoid of play. Research shows that excess clutter in the home leads to lowered levels of concentration and focus. Studies have shown that children with fewer toys are more likely to engage in creative and imaginative play. Additionally, research suggests that children with too many toys are less likely to play with any single toy for an extended period of time, leading to a decrease in the quality of play. Furthermore, Children, in particular, process incoming visual stimuli differently than adults. They absorb much more information all at once and have a challenging time filtering and making sense of it. They are particularly susceptible to cluttered environments and need less visual input, an organized space, and fewer toys and distractions to allow them to focus and engage in play.

N. Narration

Parents have received well-intentioned but misguided advice to constantly talk to and at their children. Recent parenting advice has mandated that the more words spoken to a child, the richer their vocabulary and the better their academic skills. This is based on the famous 1995 "30-million-word gap" study, which demonstrated that low-income children hear far less spoken language before their first day of school than their affluent peers, setting in motion dramatic differences in vocabulary and academic achievement.

This has led many parents into a well-intentioned frenzy, constantly talking at their babies, in an effort to ensure their child's academic success. But it's important to remember that this approach can have unintended consequences. Many of my clients come to me saying, "She's so dependent on me, she won't play by herself for five minutes." We should wonder, Who taught my child to be all that dependent on me? Usually, it's us, the parents.

When babies are raised with near-constant attention, entertainment, and narration of their lives (That's the blue block! You're looking at the plant! You touched your nose!)—they're conditioned to expect ceaseless interaction. It goes without saying that babies need interaction. But how much? How often? How consistently? Perhaps we've veered too far in the opposite direction, now talking to them too much rather than too little, which can exhaust us parents and leave no room for our children to appreciate a little bit of silence.

It is important to remember that while vocabulary exposure and conversation are important for a child's development, this does not mean that parents should be incessantly entertaining or narrating their child's every action. This practice can steal playtime away from both parent and child and also can create an environment of over-dependence on the parents' constant engagement. It is important to strike a balance between providing interaction and vocabulary exposure, while also giving the child the opportunity to explore and play independently.

The decline in play has devastating consequences for children's physical and mental development. And for family cohesion, joy and stability. In the past couple of decades we have even seen a sharp decline in children's creativity and a rise in all manner of childhood ailments like anxiety disorders and obesity. Our children's play was stolen, it's time to reclaim it.

Quick Summary:
What's the Problem?

- Children's play was S.T.O.L.E.N by Safteyism, Tech Addiction, Over Achievement, Loneliness, Excess and Narration.

- **Safetyism** — the urge to protect children from any risk whatsoever, rather than strengthening them as individuals and helping them face the risks wisely—has risen. This leads parents to fear the opportunities that would allow children to play independently, even in their own homes. There has been an increase in helicopter parenting—and with it, parental involvement in play, creating a dependency in children who are used to adult-led entertainment.

- **Tech addiction** — Children today are, on average, spending anywhere between 3.5-7.5 hours per day on screens. While screens may have their benefits, this time immersed in a virtual experience is, by definition, time they are not spending playing imaginative games in the physical world, with friends or outdoors.

- **Overachievement** — Children's free time has decreased dramatically, leaving less time for play and exploration. Childhoods today are more an exercise in "resume building" than they are a time to grow in independence, imagination, and creativity.

- **Loneliness** — Parenting has intensified—we're spending more time working and more time parenting than the previous generations. For many of us, our village has disappeared—which means both that we're more isolated and that we feel less encouraged to normalize and encourage independent play. Indigenous peoples around the world rely on independent play as a way of allowing children to learn naturally and keep themselves productively occupied. They have each other to help keep an eye out, to validate this parenting approach, and to model and learn from. We're far more isolated and less likely to see this as a healthy and normal part of human development.

- **Excess** — Children today have more toys than ever before, but this excess does not lead to more quantity or quality of play. Research shows that excess clutter in the home leads to lowered levels of concentration and focus in children, who are particularly susceptible to cluttered environments and need less visual input, an organized space, and fewer toys and distractions to allow them to focus and engage in play.

- **Narration** — Recent parenting advice has mandated that the more words spoken to a child, the richer the child's vocabulary and the better the child's academic skills. However, this well-intentioned advice has led to parents constantly talking to their children, which can exhaust both the parent and the child, and steal away playtime.

Why Reclaim Play?

Children do not play because they learn: they play because they play. **Magda Gerber, *Dear Parent: Caring for Infants with Respect***

Our focus on designing a world for our children will pivot around the concept of reclaiming play as the pillar of their lives. However, how do we even know what play is? How do we define it? Is it a child kicking a ball at soccer practice, a baby pulling on their mobile, a toddler slotting train tracks together?

It's important that as parents we hone our perception of play and learn to recognize the different types of play, differentiating the pseudo-play—fast-food play—from the hearty (or even gourmet!) play, the type of play that truly nourishes our children.

What is Play?

"Play is, first and foremost, an expression of freedom. It is what one wants to do as opposed to what one is obliged to do. The joy of play is the static feeling of liberty," says Peter Gray, PhD, a psychologist and thought leader who researches play, unschooling, and democratic schools and learning.

Gray teaches us that in order for play to qualify as play, it needs to be self-chosen and self-directed. This immediately rules out any adult-led activities. There are many, *many* benefits of adults interacting with children, teaching them skills and engaging them in various projects; however, adult-led activity is not independent play. It may be *playful*, and it undoubtedly has its place, but it isn't the child-led, self-motivated type of play we're reclaiming in this book and movement.

Think of it as the difference between being told to write an article by your boss and deciding to write a blog on your own. Both may be valuable, and following your boss's orders is necessary; however, our assigned work is rarely fueled by passion and rarely offers the satisfaction we experience when writing for the sake of it. Thus, self-initiation is a cornerstone of free play.

Have you ever lost yourself in a project? Perhaps you were trying out a new banana bread recipe and the sense of the passage of time simply faded away. Or you were playing the banjo and you were so immersed in tackling a new tune that you hardly noticed the garbage truck outside your window. Maybe you've felt the euphoria of being on a "roll" as you bang out a research summary on your keyboard or the state of supreme focus that comes with bird-watching. If so, you likely were in a state of *flow*.

Mihaly Csikszentmihalyi, a distinguished Hungarian American professor of psychology, named this psychological circumstance flow. Flow is a highly focused, productive mental state. There are nine core components of *flow*, as I outline them for you here, summon a mental image of a child immersed in play. How many of the nine components are present?

1. Challenge-Skills Balance

In order to be in a state of flow, there must be an equal balance between the level of skill and the level of challenge. When the challenge is too demanding, we get frustrated. When it's too easy, we get bored. In flow, we're fully engaged but not overwhelmed.

2. Action-Awareness Merging

When we're out of flow, we're often "time-traveling" in our mind—reminiscing or reliving the past and fretting over or planning the future. When in flow, we are completely present in the moment and absorbed in the task at hand.

3. Clear Goals

Often we find ourselves pulled in various directions throughout our day and unsure where to turn our focus next. However, when in flow, we operate with purpose and direction, with an intuitive sense of what to do next.

4. Unambiguous Feedback

When we're in flow, we know how well we're doing; we can tell if we're successful or if we need to make adjustments. We're not "shooting in the dark" and "hoping for the best"; we can see where we're being effective in real time.

5. Concentration on the Task at Hand

Flow requires high levels of focus that blur out any irrelevant information. When we're in flow, we're able to put all of our concentration on the task, and literally become unaware of any distractions, whether internal (thoughts) or external (noises or images).

6. Sense of Control

When we're in flow, we feel a surge of potency, authorship, and control over ourselves and the situation, as though we are able to accomplish what we are setting our minds to in this moment.

7. Loss of Self-Consciousness

Ego melts away as we flow. In contrast to our usual state, where we expend a lot of mental energy monitoring our appearance, self-consciousness disappears when we're in flow. We may even become immune to our own body's messages of fatigue or hunger because we are too involved in our activity to care.

8. Transformation of Time

As we flow, so does time. One might either feel it has slowed down or flown by. Two hours may go by without noticing the clock, or perhaps one senses that a portal of time has opened up. The time distortion signifies our alternative-reality experience.

9. Autotelic Experience

Anytime we're in flow, we're rewarded by the activity itself. The activity harbors an intrinsic sense of satisfaction and delight that needs no external praise or reward, and thus the activity of flow becomes autotelic, an end in itself, done for its own sake.

As I read through these qualities, I am struck by two meaningful and interrelated thoughts:

The first is that play equals flow. All of these nine components are fully present when a child is playing. Anyone who has ever had the great honor and pleasure of watching a child immersed in play *has seen* that the child is in a state of flow: oblivious to the outside world (and indeed, perhaps to their own bodies), sufficiently challenged, and intrinsically rewarded. They're in an intuitive trancelike state, while still being decisive and action-oriented; they know what to do and say next. Time stands still as they create their little worlds. No one needs to bribe them to go and climb the tree. They are completely present, action-oriented, and in control. Play *is* flow.

The second thought is the importance of experiencing flow (or play, for children) *daily*. This is a crucial element of mental health for adults and children alike, because it provides what Csikszentmihalyi calls the optimal state of inner experience.

The optimal state of inner experience is one in which there is order in consciousness. This happens when psychic energy—or attention—is invested in realistic goals, when skills match the opportunities for action. The pursuit of a goal brings order in awareness because a person must concentrate attention on the task at hand and momentarily forget anything else. These periods of struggling to overcome challenges are what people find to be the most enjoyable times of their lives. A person who has achieved control over psychic energy, and has invested it in consciously chosen goals, cannot help but grow into a more complex being. By stretching skills, by reaching toward higher challenges, such a person becomes an increasingly extraordinary individual.

Why Reclaim Play?

As time spent in flow increases, so does mental health.

In a state of flow, we create neuronal connections in our brains, learn new skills and establish them as second nature. We process traumas, make sense of the world, and expand our sense of self. We're lost in presence, truly experiencing creativity and alive-ness.

I've identified some core ways this type of flow-play state helps children. This is by no means an exhaustive list of the ways in which children benefit from play, but it offers a good start in understanding why we need to reclaim free play in a state of flow.

10. Benefits of Free Play:
Developing Motor and Academic Skills

As Jasmine, age two, tries to pick up pom-poms and put them in a jar, she is perfecting her pincer grip. As Abdul, age five, tries to balance on the arm of a couch, he's developing his core. Too often in our culture we believe there is work, which is meaningful, and then there is play, which you do when the work is done. This belief reflects a deep misunderstanding of how children actually learn and develop.

All mammals develop their physical skills and strengths through play: roughhousing with other young animals, climbing trees, digging for nuts. Monkey infants will challenge their bodies by swinging from small tree branches, slowly building up their muscles and coordination to tackle the larger leaps, and they'll continue to pursue these challenges all the way up through adulthood.

A 2001 longitudinal study by Wolfgang, Stannard, Jones and Phelps, measured the complexity of children's block play at age four and then tracked their academic performance through high school. Researchers found that the complexity of block play actually predicted kids' mathematics achievement in high school. In particular, those who used blocks in more sophisticated ways as preschoolers had better math grades and took more math courses as teenagers. The association remained even after researchers controlled for a child's IQ.

Their conclusion was that block play *itself* influenced the cognitive development of these kids. That's a big deal because that means that playing with blocks not only doesn't hinder our children's performance (oh, they're just wasting their time, playing), it actually *amplifies* their success.

As early as the mid-twentieth century, Jean Piaget (1945), a Swiss psychologist known for his work on child development, suggested that children can learn mathematical and geometric concepts (shape and size), create topological knowledge (above, below, larger than, smaller than), and learn patterns, categorization, matching and grouping . . . all through block play. Parents don't need to tinker with an already perfect thing. Yet today's toys are angling to *improve* simple block play, and us parents are pushing to "enhance" the play with our teachings and praise.

Consider a three-year-old, cross-legged on the floor, with a set of pastel-colored wooden blocks: she classifies them by grouping them by color, shape or size. She measures which are taller and shorter. She orders them by height or color gradient. As she counts them (sometimes using fractions), she gains number sense. As she creates her castle, she becomes aware of depth, width, length, symmetry, and space; she understands equivalencies and part-to-whole relationships. She develops her problem-solving skills and logical thinking. In other words, "the children's everyday experience forms an intuitive, implicit conceptual foundation for mathematics. Later, children represent and elaborate on these ideas, creating models of an everyday activity with mathematical objects, such as numbers and shapes, engaging in mathematical actions, such as counting or transforming shapes; and using mathematics to build structures. We call this process mathematization".

There is a firm cause-and effect relationship between the amount of time spent playing and academic success. This isn't only true for humans. In fact, throughout the animal kingdom, longer childhoods indicate a more intelligent species, with ravens being near the top of the intelligence chain, and with a long and playful childhood, especially in comparison to other birds. Young ravens fledge—take flight—at from thirty-five to forty-two days after hatching and are fed by both parents. But unlike other species, they stay with their parents for another six months or more after fledging. Fine, but what does that have to do with play? Ravens don't play, do they? Well, just search for a viral video of a raven snowboarding, a phenomenon that's been documented by scientists all over the worlds since, in 1999, Emilie and George Rankin saw eight crows doing so on very organic boards made of small pieces of bark . . . for over an hour. Play pays, no doubt about it!

The Top 10 Most Intelligent Species and Their Approximate Childhood Lengths

Raven—3 years	Pig—5 years
Chimp—16 years	Octopus—1 year
Elephant—9 years	Parrot—4 years
Gorilla—15 years	Dog—1 year
Dolphin—12 years	Raccoon—1 year

Take a look at Finland's education system, the best in the world. In Finland, 66 percent of students go to college, which is the highest rate in the European Union. Also, 93 percent of academic or vocational high-school students graduate. In 2000, tests by the Programme for International Student Assessment (PISA) showed that Finnish students were the best in the world when it comes to reading. In 2003, they achieved the best results in math, and in 2006, Finnish youth were first out of fifty-seven countries in science. According to the World Top 20 Education Poll, Finland shines at number one, while the United States lags behind, at number eight. Finland outshines the United States in test scores in math, science, and reading, and, in the long-term outcome, Finland's high-school and college graduation rates also surpass those of the United States (International Education Database 2019).

Counterintuitively, though, children in Finland don't start school until they are seven. They rarely take exams until they are teenagers and have only one standardized test, at the age of sixteen. It seems that less is indeed more. Play is a big element in their revolutionary educational system: elementary-school students enjoy seventy-five minutes of recess daily. That's almost three times the United States average of twenty-seven minutes. Furthermore, Finnish day cares don't focus as much on reading, writing, or math. Instead, they emphasize creative play. The main focus is on the promotion of health and well-being: the purpose of day care is to help children develop their social habits, learn to respect others, and create positive relationships. Also, a huge emphasis is on physical activity, as they exercise at least ninety minutes per day.

So many of the skills we force children to learn through textbooks and tests are seamlessly and naturally activated in play. Children will usually—and eventually—explore reading, writing and math—when they play freely. We have a predetermined set of images that indicate "learning" in our mind, and they usually involve a child bent over a worksheet at a desk. However, research has shown that through free play, children learn how to use the tools and utensils that are part of their culture, how to understand complex mathematical concepts, and even how to read and write. I'm not suggesting a completely hands-off approach to learning; I am suggesting a greater reliance on, and making more space and time for, the natural learning that occurs through long stretches of free play.

47

Taking Risks

Through play, children learn to take risks. They learn how to go to the edge of their comfort zone in any area, be it physical, emotional, academic, or social and push through the discomfort. By taking themselves to the limits of their abilities, slowly pushing those limits, they eventually master the skill they seek.

This is a natural response in all young animals. If you watch goat kids, for example, you will see them balance on a rock that's just at the edge of their comfort zone—just slightly too difficult—putting themselves in this risky position for the purpose of mastering that skill. Balancing on rocks is a crucial skill to adult goats who need to traverse treacherous terrain, thus they naturally begin practicing and building these muscles from their youth.

Unfortunately, when we see this in our children, we tend to have one of two responses: to push them further than they are ready to go, or to hold them back. When we push them before they are ready, they respond by protecting themselves. Children get defensive: no, I don't want to read; no, I don't want to climb the stairs; no, I won't go down that slide. When we hold them back (by saying things like, "Be careful," "That's too high," or "Here, let me do it for you") we don't allow them to take the risks they need to take.

If we allow them to take risks in their own time, children will naturally challenge themselves, as is required in a state of flow. They naturally push themselves. You'll notice this in most classic games like catch or hide-and-seek. These universally enjoyed games offer just enough danger for kids to push themselves. The game simulates an adult reality (which is genuinely scary!), such as being chased (tag) or getting separated from the group (hide-and-seek). These situations are realities in human life (thankfully less so in safe societies) and therefore children learn how to handle the situation by constantly playing it out.

Have you played a game of tag recently? You really do get nervous, feel the adrenaline pump, run away, and actually experience all of the same neuronal firings that you would in a real chase. The main difference is that you don't have to pay the price you would if you were being chased by a lion, for example. When children are chased by their friends, they are able to practice those same skills and learn about risk taking. They expand their edge, pushing past it to their next level. They practice and learn to run faster, hide smarter, and climb higher, and do so in a safe environment.

Through play, children will do something that's a little too hard for them. If the activities were led by adults, we would be dictating the level of risk tolerance, which doesn't offer children the internally led experience of attuning to their own risk awareness. Allowing them free play allows them to take those risks in a safe environment.

Scientific Exploration

Children are born scientists. They are born ready to explore and experiment. They like to pull and push things, mix different things together, and taste almost everything. Children want to see, look, and stare at the wonder of the world around them.

The problem is, we tend to hurry children along or stop their exploration.

"Don't touch that."

"Don't put that in your mouth."

"No."

"Why are you doing that?"

"Stop making a mess."

"Don't spill it."

"Hurry up, let's go."

We've all said these things (I sometimes say them on repeat all day). Instead of allowing them to follow their innate curiosities, we usher children along. What we fail to realize is that pausing on the sidewalk to stare at a snail or pulling at the end of the yarn to see where it leads actually is scientific exploration at work.

The great Albert Einstein himself said: "Play is the highest form of research." In fact, to him, all of his hypothesizing and research into quantum physics was *play*; he found it fascinating and simply followed his curiosity. That's child's play.

Allowing the time for children to go at their own pace, the ability to get messy as they explore, and the freedom to ask as many questions as they can think of is not always convenient.

Alfie Kohn, author of *Unconditional Parenting*, said: "When you come right down to it, the whole process of raising a kid is pretty damned inconvenient, particularly if you want to do it well. If you're unwilling to give up any of your free time, if you want your house to stay quiet and clean, you might consider raising tropical fish instead".

Convenience be damned. Allowing our children to be scientific explorers is going to set the stage for lifelong curiosity and discovery. And that's a beautiful thing.

Constructing Worlds

In play, children can be the masters of their own worlds. This is an *empowering* place for children.

Through play they get to direct what is going on in that world. They get to act out, plan, design, and produce the world they desire. They get to feel the power of manifestation, the power of bringing something they imagine to fruition. They can create a LEGO world, a Play-Doh world, a sticks-and-stones world—whatever they choose. They get to be the omnipotent god who runs the show. They get to have a sense of control. That is reassuring and hence builds self-esteem.

As adults, we too want to create our own lives and live a life we love. But we tend to get held back by voices in our heads that say:

Who are you to change the world?

Who are you to say how it should look?

Who are you to follow that dream?

Who are you to design that building?

Who are you to make the world a better place?

Children don't have those voices (yet!). They *know* that they are powerful creators. Through play, children learn that "I can create the image I have in my head and put it out into the world." This type of play sets children up for a lifetime of authorship, planting the seeds for an attitude that allows them to "be the change" they want to see in the world.

Attunement to Their Bodies and Physical Health

When children are free rather than stuck at a desk or trapped in a stroller, they tend to move—a lot. Have you ever watched a child at a playground? It's astonishing how they naturally work out and break a sweat. Even a six-month-old on the floor will exercise in a way that rivals any Pilates class. They're still at a stage in life where they naturally listen to their bodies' need to run, stretch, jump, and twirl or to simply lie down on the floor (yes, even in aisle 7 of the supermarket) and rest their bodies.

Unfortunately, we hinder this attunement by telling our children not to run or jump, and to sit still. The ramifications of this can be seen well into adulthood. As adults, most of us are no longer attuned to our bodies, we need doctors to scare us into working out and coaches to hype us up. We've lost the innate connection with our bodies' messages (Stretch! Run! Sweat! Rest!) and wonder why we have backaches, are overweight, or lack energy.

Imagine a world where (as much as possible) we didn't tell children to sit down and be quiet, where we told them that whatever their body wants to do, they should be doing (at least some of the time). Imagine how many physical ailments we could prevent if children maintained that attunement with their body through play.

While this book will focus on offering solutions to increasing *indoor* play opportunities, including those that involve movement, a book on play would be remiss not to mention the profound benefits of outdoor play. Outdoor play in particular—but any play involving movement—is crucial for children's health. According to an article in *The New England Journal of Medicine*, the rapid rise in childhood obesity, if left unchecked, could shorten life spans by as much as five years. It's shocking that for the first time in two centuries, the current generation of children in America is predicted to have a shorter life expectancy than their parents' generation.

Time spent outdoors builds physically healthier children. Outdoors, children *naturally* practice balancing, running, hopping, skipping, jumping, throwing, catching, pulling things, swinging, and climbing, all manner of physical movement that develops gross and fine motor skills. From carefully picking sticks and leaves to scaling a large tree, our bodies are appropriately challenged in nature. Studies show children burn more calories outdoors, helping to prevent obesity and strengthen bones and muscles. Playing in the sun is a natural way to build up vitamin D in the body, which means stronger bones and less likelihood of developing chronic diseases.

If the outdoor play involves peers, which are often found outside, it provides ample opportunity to problem solve and learn to cooperate, resolve conflicts, and invent imaginative games.

Exposure to the fresh air outdoors reduces stress levels. According to a Stanford study, outdoor light stimulates the pineal gland. This part of the brain is vital to keeping our immune system strong and making us feel happier. I'm sure you have experienced a stark improvement in your mood once you get outside. An added bonus is that children who identify with nature are more likely to grow up to be adults who appreciate and want to protect the environment.

Children who play freely regularly are more curious and self-directed, and are likely to stay with a task longer. Children who spend most of their time indoors with little exposure to activities requiring their own initiation and follow-through show less ability to initiate or participate in new activities. In fact, studies of children diagnosed with attention deficit hyperactivity disorder (ADHD) found that children with ADHD who spent significant time outdoors exhibited fewer symptoms.

The list of benefits goes on and on. Bottom line: we should foster free outdoor play for the sake of children and parents alike.

Artistic Expression

Have you ever heard a child say, "I have writer's block" or "I'm waiting for my muse"? No, right? Children aren't intimidated by a blank canvas; they know just what to do. They are able to express themselves fluidly and without any self-doubt.

Children can draw, paint, sing, and dance to express themselves with enviable ease. And yet, we hinder this process with adult intervention when we tell them how to draw or what to draw or that the way they are drawing is not the "right" way.

When we allow children to play their way through painting, singing, dancing, or, indeed, science, we honor what Picasso himself said: "Every child is an artist. The problem is how to remain an artist once he grows up."

Identity Exploration

Give a child a cape and she is a superhero.Role play is an important aspect of childhood development as it allows young children to experiment with different identities and explore different aspects of themselves. Research has shown that children who engage in role play are more likely to be comfortable with their identities in adulthood.

Kids at the ages of 3, 4 and 5 need to try on different identities. They need to be the fireman, the mother, the lion...

they need to dress up, put on that silly hat, prance around in the tutu. It's through this type of imaginary play that they develop empathy—by taking another's perspective. It's because they are fancying themselves to be a mermaid, or a zombie or a robber that they are actually making better sense of who it is they are. Parents often brush this aside as foolishness or a waste of time. Or they worry that dressing up as something is somehow akin to actually becoming that thing. However the opposite appears to be true.

Imaginary play, also known as role play, is a crucial aspect of childhood development that allows young children to explore different identities and understand their place in the world. When children are not given the opportunity to engage in imaginary play, they may not fully develop their sense of self and may struggle with excessive experimentation with their identities well into adulthood. This can lead to difficulties in understanding and navigating social interactions, and can be an indicator of mental health issues.

Research has shown that the lack of opportunity for children to engage in imaginary play can have long-term effects on their emotional and social well-being. A study published in the "Journal of Child Psychology and Psychiatry" found that children who did not engage in role play were more likely to have a negative sense of self and to be less comfortable with their identities in adulthood. Another study published in the "International Journal of Behavioral Development" found that children who did not engage in imaginary play had more difficulty regulating their emotions and had more behavioral problems.

In contrast, when children are given the opportunity to explore their identities through imaginary play, it is developmentally appropriate, temporary, and low stakes. This helps children to learn about themselves and the world around them in a safe and non-threatening way. It also allows them to develop their social and emotional skills, which are essential for success in adulthood. Adults who are excessively experimental with their identities are likely to suffer serious consequences to their relationships and general wellbeing, but in the context of early childhood play it is a normal part of development.

Social Skills

Playing with others—something that begins to evolve at the age of three or four—offers a most fertile ground for developing social skills. In an adult-led environment, we are continuously solving problems—or worse, avoiding them. You two are having trouble sharing? No problem, I'll take it away and *no one will have it.* You two can't agree on which game to play? *Monopoly. There, I decided.* We *think* we are helping children to get along, but *really,* we are robbing them of opportunities to learn crucial skills.

In fact, when children are allowed to play with each other *away from adult supervision and intervention,* they become fabulous problem solvers. They learn to negotiate, take turns and make amends. Consider the difference between an organized, adult-directed game of soccer and a pickup game of soccer initiated by the kids themselves. In the adult version, the kids don't get the chance to grapple with issues of unfairness, balance out the teams, or address claims of cheating. The adults make all the decisions, and the children are left impotent to handle such social challenges. In the child-led game, they have a very real incentive to work things out and to create a fair and fun play environment for everyone. After all, if you walk off because you don't like the way I play (and you *can* walk off, because this is self-elected and entirely free play), I just lost my play buddy. Realizing that intuitively, I'm going to work extra hard to make sure you're having fun too, so that the game can go on.

I also want to ensure that you'll play with me *again* in the future. So if I lose, I'd better not be a sore loser—and if I win, I'd better not be a sore *winner*. After all, it's more important to me that I know you'll want to play again tomorrow. *That's* a *real* incentive to play fair.

Pretend play has also been correlated with two crucial skill sets: the ability to self-regulate (impulses, emotions, attention) and the ability to reason counterfactually. Kids who engage in frequent pretend play have stronger self-regulation skills. That's a win for any parent.

Free play with others is what lays *all of the groundwork* for children to learn how to handle conflicts, rejections, squabbles, and disagreements. If we take this from them, how will they learn?

Emotional Processing

During the horrors of the Holocaust, did children play? As their families were carted off to gas chambers, as piles of bodies amassed in their neighborhoods, as starvation took root in their empty bellies, did these kids . . . *play?!*

Yes. Dr. George Eisen, author of *Children and Play in the Holocaust* (1990), reveals that Jewish children ages two to fourteen in concentration camps and ghettos during World War II spent their few idle moments playing games. So did they play games that would offer them a reprieve from their dreadful realities? Did they play fairies, musical chairs, or hopscotch? No. According to Dr. Eisen's research, they played games such as:

- **"Gas Chamber"** — children would imitate the screams of the people being gassed
- **"Burial"** — children would play dead, and others would roll them into shallow graves
- **"Doctor"** — a child would take food rations away from children pretending to be sick and refuse to help them without a bribe.
- **"Blockade"** — children would reenact being sealed off from their families by Nazis.
- **"Seizing the Clothes of the Dead"** — children would steal clothes off those who played dead.

Children living through one of humanity's worst possible nightmares did not play games that would help them escape their misery. They instead enacted what they saw happening in their surroundings.

Why?

Play is not escapism; it is a very real and necessary part of development. It is not the opposite of work. It is not the opposite of learning. It is synonymous with learning, work, flow, and, equally important, emotional processing or *healing*.

During the Holocaust, children were processing the death and destruction surrounding them while also practicing necessary survival skills. But we needn't go to such an extreme and, hopefully, isolated example. After all, every single child will face challenges, no matter how prosperous and healthy their family life may be. Whether dealing with external or internal adversity, play can help process, digest, and metabolize challenges in healthy ways.

Children who have gone through a challenging divorce in the family will act it out with their dolls. Even overcoming something as mundane as a doctor's appointment can be processed through play.

Trauma research teaches us that no matter the external reality of the anguish and pain, whether or not it solidifies as a trauma in the brain depends on whether we can tell its story. Dr. Daniel Siegel, pioneer of Mindsight, teaches us that in order to overcome any trauma, big or small, we must tell *and retell* the story, making chronological sense of what happened. Until it is integrated into our brain as yet another story that makes *sense*, even if we don't like it, we understand and hence can process what happened.

This is what children naturally do through play. If we yell at them one morning, we might hear them yelling at their dolls that afternoon. If they feel powerless in school, they might put on a superhero cape and exert *extra* power at home. If they feel rejected and socially outcast in their neighborhood, they might become the "queen" of their stuffed animals. Much of the work adults pay good money for in therapy—talking to an empathetic ear, engaging in role play, mindset shifts, and reframing challenges—children do naturally through play.

Quick Summary:
Why Reclaim Play?

- Play is self-directed, self-motivated and, by definition, fun. Whatever is learned through play is learned without the downside of feeling like you've done "hard work." When learning is forced upon us or feels arduous or arbitrary, it's harder to retain the lessons we acquire and easier to abandon the learning altogether. And it's hard to achieve a state of flow, the psychological experience of being totally, and happily, immersed in what you are doing.

- Play is an obvious gateway to the state of flow. Playing freely is *synonymous* with being in a state of flow with the characteristics of intrinsic motivation, losing oneself in time, and being appropriately challenged and meaningfully rewarded by the activity.

- Play has huge benefits to children, including developing motor skills and academic skills, learning to take risks, and explore scientifically. Through play children construct worlds, attune to their bodies, express themselves artistically. They get to explore their identity, improve their social skills, and process difficult emotions.

- There is empirical evidence that kids treat play as a tutorial for coping with real-life challenges. Play is a form of practice. All around the world, throughout history, children engage in free, unstructured, undirected, independent, imaginary play that simulates the sorts of activities they will need to master as adults.

- Play is crucial to childhood, and we absolutely *must* reclaim it.

Part Two: Play Prep

Chapters 4—7

Babies Who Play

Chapter

04

If a child has been able in his play to give up his whole loving being to the world around him, he will be able, in the serious tasks of later life, to devote himself with confidence and power to the service of the world.

Rudolf Steiner, *The Education of the Child and Early Lectures on Education*

How Imaginary Play Changes When Kids Grow from Babies to Preschoolers

Babies don't dress up, don't construct train tracks, and don't build with LEGO. For babies, play looks a little different, but it is no less crucial.

The Fourth Trimester

"A fourth trimester of cuddling is the birthday present your baby really wants!" says Harvey Karp, MD. "You may think your peaceful nursery offers your new baby the perfect environment, but from her point of view your home feels like it's part wild Las Vegas casino . . . and part dark closet!". During this period your baby may not seem like they are able to play at all—they're just gaining an understanding of their most basic bodily functions—eating, sleeping, burping, pooping. Their entire experience is made up of adjusting to life outside the womb—the light, the noise, the sensations.

Everything is brand-new to a newborn baby. Obvious-town, right? But why, then, do we feel the need to entertain them? Why are newborn babies gifted rattles and poster boards? And why are they propped up in front of baby mobiles? To interest them, train their eyes to focus, or soothe them? Strangely, many parents "treat children more like they're brains they must train, rather than gentle spirits needing to be nurtured".

For a baby, watching the flicker of a shadow on the wall is as fascinating as observing the colors of the pillows on your couch. They're making out shapes, colors and textures, movement,

Doing it for them

Non stop entertainment

Being buckled in A LOT!

Overstimulation

sound and sensation. In the words of Susan Brink, "what a baby needs to grow and develop during the first three months is all right there. Let him feel the chenille on his chest as he notices the contrast of, say, a dark-and-light leaf pattern on a bedspread. Let him touch your face as he looks at you and hears your voice. Help him begin his lifelong exploration of the world by first becoming familiar with the sights, sounds and textures from the home he has entered."

Beyond your smiling face and cooing voice, they don't need any form of entertainment. So why offer it?

What's the harm in a mobile?! None. It's fine to have sweet decorations for your baby (and you!) to delight in. The point is: do not to fall prey to a mindset that babies need entertainment. That simply being on the floor, with themselves and their current surroundings, isn't enough. Believing their child needs constant stimulation, "parents feel guilty for not doing enough, or for talking on the phone with a sister or friend instead of 'stimulating' junior". And this mindset matters because it's the foundation of how we view our children's needs for entertainment and input for years to come.

Babies are born to soak up the world around them. That world, just as it is, fascinates them.

Three Months and Beyond

As babies graduate from their fourth trimester, they start accelerating their exploration and the use of their bodies. How to move toward an item, how to operate these awkward limbs called arms, how to wrap fingers around a block, grasp it, and bring it to their mouth. But by the time they're a year or so, they may delight in knocking over a tower, in practicing their pincer grip as they place one block on top of another, or even in jabbering to and hugging a doll.

However, if they've been trained in passivity from the earliest stages—acclimated to being strapped in, watching other

Less is more!

Simple & Chewable

← *ADULT* →
nearby

TRUST & Patience

things move and sing—they might not feel the call inside them to be the movers and singers themselves.

If babies aren't given sufficient free (!) floor time to simply be with themselves and their surroundings, how do they stretch, roll, and eventually learn that pushing one knee and the opposite hand forward propels them towards that ball they're trying to reach? Why crawl if Mom always brings it to me anyway? Why find my feet if the bouncy chair rocks me all on its own? That's why in the view of Deborah Carlisle Solomon, author of *Baby Knows Best: Raising a Confident and Resourceful Child, the RIE Way*: "When considering equipment such as bouncers, walkers, slings, baby carriers and backpacks, the question is 'Whose need is being served?' Very often these devices serve the adult's need to hold the baby captive so that they can make dinner or take a shower... But none of these devices are ideal, because they inhibit your baby's free and natural movement."

An important caveat here is that serving your needs, as the parent, is totally valid and in fact, crucially important. The odd bounce in the walker or lulling swing can be heaven-sent for a parent who has a colicky baby or needs to fix dinner or finish a conference call. Doing so should not be a source of shame, it's just pragmatic sometimes. Bouncy chairs and swings have their place, and if using them gives you a short break, feel free to do so. However, in this book I want to offer an alternative. In lieu of constricting entertainment, I have always used another 'contraption,' known as the Yes Space, and it's saved my sanity many times.

The Yes Space

Once a baby begins moving and exploring, suddenly he's into everything! How do we support their independent play, keep them safe, and keep our home from being ransacked? How do we do this in a peaceful, respectful way?

Some parents, and some schools of parenting methodology, suggest that parents begin by saying a harsh "No!" when babies or young toddlers touch dangerous things such as sockets (or simply things we don't want them to touch, such as light switches). The idea is based on a behaviorist theory that suggests reinforcing desired behavior with praise and reinforcing undesired behavior with negative feedback.

There is a lot of conflicting information regarding disciplining children in this age group. Much of it involves parenting from the fear that we can't keep our children safe. Methods involving shame and punishment such as spanking and yelling (as in the "blanket method," where babies are placed on a blanket and admonished if they crawl off) put a damaging amount of stress on the developing young brain and have other serious drawbacks.

When you stop and think about it for a moment, taking this approach puts immense pressure on us adults to continuously watch everything our child is doing and catch them in the act of doing something wrong. It models a continuous flow of "No!" which will ricochet back to us quicker than you can say "toddler's parrot." And worse—a barrage of limitations does little to create an environment that supports and *encourages* the exploration babies were designed for.

A disciplinary approach to young kids (or any kids!)

- bases your relationship on fear,
- might not work and you're still responsible for your child's safety,
- is likely to create pushback, especially as he grows,
- will cause the toddler to model saying "NO" and being contrary,
- doesn't respect their innate need to explore.

Instead, we could and should Yes Proof — create a safe space that offers a great opportunity for the baby to play independently.

This is an area of the home that is 100 percent suited to your baby's age and stage, an area where they cannot get into mischief, even if they tried. The Yes Space is a term I learned from RIE (Resources for Infant Educarers), a school of thought founded by Dr. Emmi Pikler and made popular by Magda Gerber. As Gerber said, "What infants need is the opportunity and time to take in and figure out the world around them."

Deborah Carlisle Solomon explains the Yes Space as follows: "For your baby or toddler to have the freedom to move freely and independently, it's essential that he has a safe space in which to do it—one where he can move whatever way he likes to without risk of injury. If you take to heart the RIE principle of providing a safe play area, your baby will be free to move where and how he chooses, and you'll be free to relax, knowing he's safe."

Do we want to teach our babies that the world is a forbidden, dangerous place? Or that the world is safe and loving and that they are allowed to be free in it? Providing a Yes Space involves reframing our approach to involve disciplining with love. It means considering the true meaning of the word *discipline*. Think "disciple," who is a student, and when you think this way, learning takes center stage.

A Yes Space liberates both adult and child from constantly saying no to each other. A one-year-old's job is to explore, touch, taste, feel, climb, grab, smell all of the things they come across. These sensory experiences influence the way the brain grows and develops. "The sensitive period begins when the embryo begins to stretch and move. It continues from the moment of birth, with the baby turning his/her head, grasping objects with the hands and feet, putting them into the mouth, rolling over, crawling, sitting, standing and finally walking. This is the height of the sensitive period, and the ability to walk facilitates exploration of a wider environment". It is our job to make sure that the things they come across are safe. And so, in true Montessori style, rather than manipulating the child, we manipulate the environment.

Countless Reclaim Play students I meet regale their regrets at not starting down the independent play path earlier. Sarah, a Spanish Reclaim Play student who now lives in South Africa, shared that the difference in play between her eldest and younger child is significant. She discovered the Reclaim Play philosophy when her eldest was three; she had to help him "unlearn" some of his dependencies. Her younger child, on the other hand, started off with independent play as a baby, and as a result has become a deep player, even as a young toddler.

Magda Gerber said: "Every baby moves with more ease and efficiency if allowed to do it at his own time and in his own way, without our trying to teach him. A child who has always been allowed to move freely develops not only an agile body but also good judgment about what he can and cannot do." Of course, how long and how deeply children play is dependent on countless variables. But whatever your child's temperament, it's never too early to cultivate independent play.

As you look to set up your Yes Space, consider the following:

A mat or comfortable rug on the floor
Make this a lovely spot for baby to roll around, crawl and attempt to walk, but not too fluffy, to minimize dust and maximize easy breathing. Carlisle Solomon says: "At RIE we cover a foam play mat of braided rug with a cotton sheet tucked underneath; this provides a smooth, clean surface for young babies who are not yet crawling. A wooden floor is best for crawling babies and toddlers who are beginning to walk because it's firm but also has some give to it".

A gated-off area, playpen, or completely baby-proof room
Or indeed, rooms. When my babies are still putting things in their mouths, we section off a part of the house for the *older* kids

to do their LEGO or painting, and let the toddlers roam free. You could also section off any dangerous areas such as the kitchen, stairs or a fireplace—and make whatever is left (the living room and/or dining area, perhaps) into a Yes Space.

Absolute 100 percent safety

Simply baby proof this space properly, so much so that you can take a shower, go and cook dinner, or change the laundry and know with full confidence that (while she may not prefer you gone) your baby is fine without you.

Some open-ended toys

Babies and toddlers do best with simple objects they can mouth, throw, roll, and explore. My favorites are silk scarves, simple blocks, and a variety of balls. Teethers, pots and pans, wooden spoons, spatulas, and stainless steel or wooden bowls are favorites, too. Along with a few musical instruments such as shakers or rattles. "Open ended materials and toys can be used for any purpose. The only limit is the child's imagination". In my own personal lab—my family—I have found all of my babies to be far more interested in household objects—a bunch of keys, a remote control, or a few measuring spoons—than baby toys. So I prefer to save my toy budget for the time when my children actually engage with imaginary play, which is just around the corner.

A climbing opportunity

As babies start to crawl and cruise, something relatively small and safe, yet challenging, can be a wonderful play opportunity. "A heavy sofa cushion or bolster that's not too thick can serve the purpose quite well. When they start to pull up, they will need something stationary to pull up on." A small climbing dome, a wooden rocker or a Pikler triangle may be right for your home. Or a simple, low step stool or two. We've also been known to fill a play yard with balls (I love the transparent ones) as a makeshift ball pool that our young toddlers have loved. An unbreakable floor mirror can also be fascinating for your baby.

Soothing and understimulating walls

Rather than rendering our walls shaggy with artwork, Post-its, postcards, kids' creations, banners, garlands, and all manner of ABC posters, a few, well placed, well considered pieces of beautiful art (beauty is in the eye of the beholder) will do. While bright walls may be your preference, consider a color that is calming to the eye, given your baby will be staring at it for long stretches of time (think *not red*).

THE YES SPACE

some greenery

natural light

something to play music

Somewhere near the adult

Natural colors and materials

mirror on the wall or floor

Safety Plugs

Books

open ended chewable toys

soft rug or mat

Something cozy to sit on

Something to climb

Soft music

Add in some lovely melodies, playful pop songs, or classical music to give baby something to listen to. No, it won't turn them into baby Mozarts, but who doesn't enjoy beautiful music?

Natural light and natural elements

Do everything you can to have your baby spend the majority of their indoor time with access to natural light (although we prefer almost pitch-black for sleeping). "Scientific research has found that although a baby's circadian rhythms will not become fully established until 12 weeks of age, babies who are exposed to natural light patterns from birth are generally faster to adapt to the 24-hour cycle and differentiate between night and day". And while spending long stretches outdoors applies to babies as well, bring nature in for those indoor stretches. A gorgeous bouquet of twigs, a beautiful fiddle plant growing overhead, a flower arrangement, placed where the baby can see.

Time with you and without you

I'm a big believer in being continually responsive to baby's cues, building secure attachments and holding, nursing, or helping babies to sleep on demand. We also practiced part-time elimination communication and babywearing, which means we were aware of our baby's ongoing signals. In addition to all these beliefs of responsiveness and attachment (and alongside them) sits the belief that babies and their mamas and papas need breaks from each other throughout the day. They needn't be long, and they needn't be forced. Independent play happens in those natural lulls when you're busy with your stuff, and baby happens to be content. It also happens when you need to go to the bathroom, fetch the laundry, or make dinner, which is when you need to put a (happy, fed, clean, alert) baby down for a while.

Your baby might not always be happy to be put down, and you'll need to do it anyway. Sometimes you'll pop them into a carrier to soothe them, and sometimes you'll allow them to overcome their frustration and find contentment and exploration on the floor. Both are valid choices, and they depend only on your intuition at any given moment. But remember, a baby who is never given time to be on the floor never flexes their exploration muscles—just as a baby who is never put down doesn't develop the coordination needed to crawl. "Independent play makes for highly productive, happily occupied kids, which in turn makes for happier, calmer parents. It's natural—the desire and ability to create play is inborn. So, to activate your baby's "independent play" mode, leave the Yes Space from time to time—gradually, gently, and respectfully. This might cause some frustration on your baby's part. To me, the independence and strength gained for babies who are encouraged to enjoy a few minutes alone in their Yes Space is priceless.

I need to clarify that this is not about pushing babies into independence. It's not about "growing them" up quickly, getting any kind of developmental upper hand, or advancing them in haste. The motivation to develop their independent play is not about milestones and measurements, graphs, charts, or future "success." It's about honoring their abilities and capabilities. Not belittling them, coddling them, or making them smaller than necessary. It's about being the wind beneath their wings and encouraging them to fly when they are ready—and not a moment before.

Elimination communication, mentioned earlier, is a method by which we notice babies' signals that they need to pee or poop and take them to do so hygienically in the potty. Before I heard about this method (when my first was six weeks old), I was under the impression that babies had zero control over their bodily functions and peed with no awareness they were doing so. It hit me like a ton of fascinating bricks to learn that, in fact, babies (all babies) intelligently communicate their needs, just like all mammals do—from birth. Ingrid Bauer explains: "Babies experience the world with a keen sensitivity. Experiences, feelings and stimuli flood their senses. They don't need to learn to feel their elimination sensations, because they are already present. They are aware of them from birth, among all the other amazing impressions that make up their inner and outer environment. However, it's only when these sensations and signals are responded to, when there is communication about them with the parent, that the awareness of and communication about them is validated and strengthened."

Before we understand babies as highly communicative, intelligent, aware, and strong individuals, we might look upon them as people "waiting to happen." As cute little pre-people who just need to be kept alive until they become actual people who can walk and talk, and all that jazz. But when we learn to see babies through fresh eyes—eyes more sensitive and attuned—we notice they are potent communicators, avid explorers, and people of immense agency. Supporting their independence by allowing them time to play (i.e., learn, express themselves, and explore) alone, is one powerful way of honoring their sovereignty.

Some babies are born with a natural propensity to be content playing by themselves; others will seek constant touch and closeness. Observe your baby and experiment with different voice cadences, communication styles, time of day, location, and toys. Every time you leave the space, let your baby know—with simple language. They may not fully understand each word, but, as Janet Lansbury teaches us, they often understand far more than we imagine. This is as much for us parents as it is for our children; it will get us into a "respectful communication" frame of mind.

Simple communication works. "Ella, I'm going to heat up the soup. I'll be back in a few minutes." If your baby seems to do well with short bursts of independent play, you might gradually increase your increments of time spent away. You might stay close by but not engaged in the play itself, picking up your book instead. Such spaces "encourage uninterrupted, self-directed play

Staring at a Plant

Eating their toes

Listening to music

Rolling around

by offering even the youngest infants free play opportunities, sensitively observing so as not to needlessly interrupt and trusting that your child's play choices are enough".

And there are other times when sitting on the floor and engaging with your baby serves you both. You feel the pull of your heart wanting to spend precious time with your precious little—and you have the space and time to do so. Climb right in. Observing our babies play must be one of the most magical privileges of parenthood. Rolling a ball toward a crawling baby, singing nursery rhymes, stretching out their bodies in little baby yoga poses, reading to them and generally delighting in their yumminess—these are yours to claim multiple times a day. There is no such thing as spoiling a baby with touch, love, and attention.

A great mindset and loving energy

Joanna lowers Heidie onto the floor in her Yes Space and gathers a few balls, a small pot, and a wooden spoon, placing them within arm's reach of Heidie, who is just beginning to army crawl in an attempt to grab at an interesting object.

"I'm going upstairs to get my phone," Joanna says calmly. "I need to call my sister." Heidie, five months old, looks up at her mother and begins to whimper. "Don't go!" she's saying. But Joanna remains calm, and confidently tells Heidie she'll be right back. Heidie senses her mother's ease and clarity, and it's almost as though she were thinking, *She believes I am safe, perhaps she's right.*

Our energy is hugely powerful in influencing our babies. They are looking to us for cues and clues on how to interpret the world and conduct ourselves within it. When we are stressed, anxious, and worried about our babies, if we're feeling guilty or uncertain (as we're all prone to be from time to time), our babies "catch" that energy and mirror our emotional state.

However, when we send them the clear, encouraging (subconscious) message that we believe in them and that all is well, they too are at ease. Of course, there are endless

Grasping a household object

Trying to reach a toy

temperaments, and some babies are highly sensitive, but all babies can benefit from our strong belief in their capabilities, and our loving energy toward them—and us. "Every time we do that, we show our child that we are a separate person taking care of their own needs, so that we can be the best parent for them. And that sometimes we have to be the priority for a moment or two when our child is safe, fed, physically comfortable. And we welcome them to have their feelings about it, whatever those are".

When you let your baby play, do so out of love and support, encouragement, and acceptance rather than from a place of fear or anxiety. Not only will it feel much better but it will have far greater efficacy as well.

Independent Play, Baby

So, if you've successfully set up your Yes Space, you may be wondering what independent play looks like for babies. It can be obvious or subtle, a flash in the pan or prolonged. Here are some things to look for:

- Lying on their backs and staring at the ceiling
- Playing with their fingers, holding their feet or toes
- Stretching, kicking, rolling or attempting to roll
- Following you around the room with their eyes
- Making different facial expressions—blinking and opening their eyes
- Pushing themselves up to all fours, or hands and knees
- Any movement or crawling attempts
- Pulling themselves up to stand and trying to walk
- Reaching for and grabbing objects
- Mouthing and biting toys or teethers
- Listening intently to music or to your voice

Reclaim Play

Please don't use this list (or any other in this book) as a checklist to measure your baby's progress. There are endless additional manifestations of play that might be the way *your* baby does it. There's no right way. Really, there isn't. The point is to expand our own definition of play, not to usher our little ones into tight, predetermined ideas of what it is and isn't.

Your baby will go through bouts of teething, growth spurts, fevers, and times when they just really need to be held. You won't know why, and that's okay. Resist the temptation to rationalize, as in "It's because I let him cry" or "It's because I couldn't breastfeed." While sometimes this type of thinking helps us learn something useful, usually it's speculation, or worse: brazen and pointless self-chastising.

Troubleshooting Babies' Play

If it sometimes seems like your baby simply does not like being in their play space, look around and ask yourself why. Is it too cold or hot? Too bright and overstimulating or not stimulating enough? If you're unsure what might be missing from your Yes Space—and to double-check its safety and comfort—go ahead and get on your tummy, on all fours, and on your back. Test it out for yourself and you might just notice something you could add or subtract to improve its "playability."

Remember, as your baby grows, so too will their play spaces. In no time, they'll need their "play zones" (these are areas of the home you set up for specific play purposes). We'll explore those throughout the rest of this book. But before we get there, let's explore toddlerhood and how babies' play transforms as they start toddling and getting into, well, *everything.*

Action Steps

- Set up a Yes Space for your baby: a space where they can play safely in a contained manner, without you worrying or hovering.

- Include simple, open ended, chewable toys for your baby to explore.

- Consider adding something to climb on.

- Try to set it up near the adult action, in an area with natural light.

- Add some greenery, some gentle music, and perhaps a nonbreakable floor or wall mirror.

- Let your baby play. Remember that a happy, alert baby who is simply eating their toes, rolling around, reaching for an object, or staring at a shadow is playing. Don't interrupt.

Scheming Toddlers

Treat a child as though he already is the person he's capable of becoming. **Haim Ginott**

Hands On

Gracie, nineteen months old, rocks an auburn mohawk and an amber teething necklace. She has those creases in her forearms that don't correlate to either the wrist or the elbow, but somewhere in the middle, the telltale sign of true-blue baby pudge. Alyssa, a Reclaim Play student, and I are watching Gracie as she loads shells from the beach into her bucket and dumps them, repeatedly. She doesn't bore of this activity; in fact, her focus is enviable. Just a few feet from her, clad in nothing but his birthday suit, Carter is spinning around tirelessly. He collapses in a dizzy whirl onto the soft sand, only to collect himself back up, spring-load his stubby arms and begin twirling again.

Toddlers. Why do they do the things they do? Why do they empty our sock drawer, just as we finished putting the clean laundry away? Why do they send little toy cars zooming under the oven, jammed there for eternity? Why do they *insist* on receiving a grown-up cup of water, only to dump it into their freshly cooked oatmeal and all over themselves in the process? Why, why, *why?*

There is a reason. Inconvenient as these repetitive and often destructive behaviors may be, they're actually a crucial part of our children's development and learning process. They are both natural and necessary. These patterns of behavior are known as schemas, a concept I happened upon when my first child was already three years old.

I had become pretty obsessed with learning about parenting at the onset of my first pregnancy. Even with well over fifty parenting books under my belt, when my eldest hit three, I still had never learned this term. When I discovered it in a blog post by Nature Play UK, my eyes were glued to the screen. I later shared the new concept I'd just learned in one of my videos, and it quickly became one of the most popular I'd ever done.

It turns out, toddlers aren't "jerks," no matter how many parenting memes, frustrated mama blogs, and sarcastic comedians paint them so. I get it, really, I do. Their unruly tantrums, compulsive behaviors, and imaginary friends are all somewhat alien to our grown-up selves. But when you peel back the onion layers of childhood behaviors, you find insight into your child, a mutual understanding born of decoding years of evolutionary development.

Jean Piaget proposed the idea of schemas as patterns of behavior that are linked through a theme and that form the basis of exploration and play for young children. Chris Athey developed this idea much further through the Froebel Research project and applied it to observation of children's play. In Athey's words, "a schema . . . can be described as a pattern of repeatable behavior into which experiences are assimilated and are gradually co-ordinated. Co-ordinations lead to higher and more powerful schemas".

Coordination implies that schemas allow children to express and explore the most basic ideas and actions in human behavior through play. Through play! It's a genius code, programmed into our littlest people, that helps them develop the skills they need to construct meaning. "Through repetition and exploration, they become coordinated with each other and grow increasingly complex as children develop and learn". This means that as kids mix the enveloping schema (wrapping a doll in her blanket) with the transporting schema (putting it in a stroller and pushing it around the dining-room table), for example, they make sense of their world and are able to interact with it ever more effectively.

When toddlers feel this innate, instinctive urge to explore a certain schema, they do so with an insistent gusto, putting their body and mind into engaging learning activities that help them to demystify the world around them. "They are in a special state. They are concentrating and are eager to continue with the

make a pee

check in with mom

change clothes

Play trains

Put on a mask

Build a masterpiece

Paint a Jackson Pollock

Pull the cat's tail

Eat a snack

TODDLER TO DO LIST
(TWO MINUTES PER TASK)
(REPEAT ON LOOP)

activity. They feel intrinsically motivated to carry on, because the activity falls in with what they want to learn and know i.e. their exploratory drive." This is what Ferre Laevers calls involvement, which is key for children's development. And the reason is simple: "Children (and adults) who are in a state of well-being, feel like 'fish in the water'. . . . They adopt an open, receptive and flexible attitude towards their environment. A state of well-being results in a fair amount of self-confidence and self-esteem . . . They have unhindered contact in their inner selves."

Through independent play, toddlers develop a methodical, systematic, and logical collection of facts. They do so through their senses and movements and mostly their hands. Testing the velocity, weight or speed of an object. Speculating about the properties, temperature, or texture of a substance. Predicting the stability of a tower, the volume of the cup of water they pour, the bounce of a ball. The trick then, with toddlers, is to observe their schematic play patterns and support their individual interests, catapulting their natural instincts into a powerful learning opportunity.

Here's why it is so important to learn about schemas and to understand their function: approaching childhood behavior through the lens of schemas can help adults respect toddler's play exploration and make sense of a child's play behavior. For instance, a child absorbed in his "transporting" schema may move objects from place to place. From an exclusively adult point of view, the child is "messing up" the environment by putting toys and objects where they don't belong. From the child-oriented perspective, he has a clear purpose and is learning.

Rather than tearing our hair out or posting crying-toddler-revenge memes on Instagram, we can turn our creative efforts to catering to our kids' needs and watching as our whole home breathes a sigh of relief.

Let's look at the most typical schemas and ways we can support them:

Trajectory

Think of trajectory as any time your child moves something through the air. Babies begin by swinging their arms and legs— eventually their entire bodies will rock up and down. Toddlers will kick, reach as high into the air as they can, and as their gross motor skills grow, they'll swing their entire bodies through the air as they jump off the couch. Trajectory includes throwing objects too: a ball, a vase, a little sister... Clearly, this is a schema that often causes parents to yell "Noooo!"

But before we rush to stop it, let's take note of all that is being learned. In the trajectory schema, your toddler is learning that a pebble *drops* to the floor, but a feather seems to *float*. She's noticing that a ball might *glide* through the air when you throw it hard, but *spin* on the floor when you *roll* it softly, and *bounce* when you hit it in a downward motion. She'll learn that one firm push of the swing makes it *swing fast* back and forth for quite some time, but that eventually it *slows* down. Notice just how much Newtonian physics goes into these experiments!

Still, we don't want our three-year-olds throwing rocks at the window, even if they are exploring objects in motion. So how do we support the trajectory schema? When we catch our child beginning to throw something that isn't safe, we redirect them to throw something that is. When they're about to throw their bodies off the couch onto the hardwood, we pad the floor so that they don't get hurt. As we notice our children's interest in throwing, we provide ways for them to do so safely and celebrate their exploration.

For *Trajectory* Ninjas

- A basket of soft balls, pillows, or rolled-up socks for throwing, flicking, and squeezing
- A large empty container (such as a laundry basket) to throw things into
- A wand for blowing bubbles—catching giant bubbles is amazing!
- Paper airplanes or kites
- A trampoline or soft play area at home with a rubber mat or interlocking tiles for jumping on
- An indoor swing (particularly a Raindrop), rope ladder, or trapeze swing

- A box of feathers, silk scarves, or tissue paper to blow on
- Water guns and targets, Velcro dart boards or a beanbag toss game
- Paints and paper for action painting, Jackson Pollock style
- Ribbon sticks to dance with
- Skittles (could be empty water bottles) and a small ball for bowling
- Pendulums, yo-yos, or any object tied to the end of a rope or yoga strap
- Cars and vehicles for racing along a track
- PVC pipes, turkey basters, and pipettes for moving and squirting water

85   Scheming Toddlers

Transporting

Transporting is all about moving items from place to place, and often it's about the children moving themselves. When your child fills their pockets to the brim with acorns, fills a bucket with sand or plops themselves into a wheelbarrow, they are expressing the transporting schema. Now, there's logic behind the apparent madness. According to Tina Bruce, "objects look different when scattered about or heaped together, but they are of the same quantity even though their appearance changes. The transporting schema leads toward the concept of quantity."

In this schema, the key is to offer your child a workable container, perhaps with wheels, for transporting their objects. Working on transporting, Emilia notices a row of jars that are *empty*. She begins by *opening* the jars and *scooping* dirt into them. She notices when they're *half full* and continues *filling* them to the brim, taking care that they are not *overflowing*. She wants to *close* them, after all. Once her jars are well *stacked* in her wheelbarrow, she can *push* them across the play yard and *unload* them on the other side. Remember, these are the early makings of a child who is able to prepare their backpack for the day ahead or an adult who is able to get their shopping from the supermarket to their car.

For *Transporting* Enthusiasts

- Laundry baskets full of clean (unfolded) laundry to push around, dump, and refill
- Clothes with pockets, or a fanny pack for collecting found objects

- Wheelbarrows, trolleys, carts, shopping cart, cardboard box with rope attached, diggers or trucks that can transport balls, tissue paper or blocks.

- A basket of natural objects to transport: acorns, pinecones, leaves, twigs, gravel, sand, pebbles
- Buckets, scoops, pipettes, measuring cups, funnels, and shovels for kinetic sand, water play at the kitchen sink, or a sit in the tub
- Trays on which small worlds can be built with animals and blocks—and moved from one place to another
- Bags, suitcases, purses, backpacks for transporting things up and down the stairs or from one room to the next
- Tupperware boxes or nesting bowls from your kitchen
- Stacking and sorting toys, ice-cube trays, teapots, pans, and cups that can be filled with rice or beans on a large, walled tray
- Recycled boxes, jars, plastic, or paper containers

Have you ever spun yourself *dizzy*? Become mesmerized by a *spinning* top? Enjoyed *twisting* ropes again and again and then watching them *unravel*? Then you, my friend, have visited the rotation schema. This schema is all about *twisting, flying, spinning, turning, rolling* in *circular* motion. It is the 360-degree *dizziness* that has been a meditative practice of the Sufi whirling dervishes for centuries.

If your child loves doing her pirouettes, watching her tutu lift into a *twirl*, that's rotation. If your child loves *spinning* his yo-yo up and down (it's all in the wrist, you know), that's rotation. And for the toddler glued to the washing machine, enjoying the never-ending *pattern* of blurred soapsuds and clothes, that's rotation too. Unfortunately, there has been a decrease in the rotation "allowed" to our children. Merry-go-rounds have been disappearing from playgrounds over the past decades, and teachers can often be heard saying, "No spinning!" at recess. However, spinning is an important part of developing our children's vestibular system and keeping their inner ear fluid liquid, thus improving their balance.

For Dizzy *Rotational* Schema Buffs

- A 360-degree swivel hook placed on an indoor swing to allow the swing to spin on the spot for hours of dizzy fun
- Toys like kaleidoscopes, yo-yos, spinning tops,pinwheels and dreidels
- The washing machine or dryer, and perhaps spinning it while it's off and open
- Merry-go-rounds and Hula-Hoops
- A salad spinner
- Cookie dough (or paint) to stir or cream or smoothies to whisk or blend
- Shells, coils, springs to promote exploring circular patterns in nature or man-made objects
- A pencil sharpener and pencils to spin; a spiralizer to make zucchini spaghetti
- A screwdriver to drive screws into cardboard
- Reels, cylinders, spools, rollers, wheels of all sizes, CDs, balls, marbles

Olivia *joins* train tracks together, Hillel *knots* two ropes, Dyllan *zips* up the doll's dress... These children are *connecting*. They're learning how things come together and separate. They're learning how to physically make connections between objects, from puzzle pieces clicking into each other to snaps or buttons closing on a coat, to holding hands with Mommy. In order to connect items, toddlers need to see whether they can stretch them to reach each other. Are they flexible or rigid? They need to see how to construct something that is strong, not fragile. They need to get creative in exploring new ways to fuse these objects to each other. Threading? Tying? Taping? Gluing?

The flip side of the connecting schema is, of course, the disconnecting schema, where children are learning to dismantle the connections they or others have made. "As the connecting schema evolves, disconnection sometimes becomes as important as connection, untying as important as tying and, as children begin to explore the idea of separating things, they often demolish items they have previously constructed, or take toys apart". Thus, a child who is picking at the hole in their seam is *disconnecting*. So is the child who is knocking over a tower of blocks or demolishing their sibling's train tracks. Disconnection can look like purely destructive behavior until you examine it more closely. Disconnection often precedes connecting and is a way of understanding how *strong* connections are. So if your child is still firmly in the disconnection phase, it may be helpful to create a series of things for them to disconnect, such as towers to *knock down*, buttons to *open*, lids to *pull off* Tupperware containers.

Activities for the *Connector* **and** *Disconnector*

- Train tracks
- Tape, glue, or paperclips to connect bits of scrap paper
- Slime
- Buttons or beads to thread on thread or shoelaces
- Ribbons, belts, yarn, jute or thread to tie together
- Any toys that connect using suction, magnets, or by interlocking
- Pieces of scrap paper or natural materials to use in weaving
- Snaps, zippers, and buttons on clothes

Imagine your children *building* a living-room fort. They *position* the chairs *next* to the couch so they can stretch a bedsheet over the *top,* creating a *roof.* On one *side* they block the *exit* with a stack of pillows, and on the other side they create an *entrance.* They crawl into the space and divide it into *smaller spaces* within, using pillows to delineate *rooms.* Then they *cover* themselves in a blanket and *unwrap* their snack *contained inside* a *small* box. Throughout this experiment, your child has been considering the *positioning* of things—on *top, underneath,* or *beside.* They have been taking into consideration the *size* of the items they're using—*large* bedsheet, *small* pillows, *medium*-sized chairs, *long* couch.

When children explore the enclosing schema, they're often creating a structure of some shape—fences, walls, or even lines around an object.

"The enclosure schema enables children to order, combine, place and bridge things to form enclosed spaces. They may also be exploring how things will get in and out of their enclosures. Some children make enclosures for farm animals but leave an opening so the animals can get in and out, or build a big enclosure with smaller ones inside. Children who are interested in enclosures may also arrange objects or food around the edge of a table or run or ride bikes round and round an enclosed space".

Consider this a territory-marking schema: creating borders around their creations or marking separation between what's theirs and what's others'.

For the *Enclosing* Schema

- Tunnels, cardboard boxes, or dining-room tables—anything that can enclose a child
- Living-room forts made by draping sheets and blankets over couches and chairs
- Climbing domes (often covered in a sheet) or large play parachutes or silk scarves
- Backyard or living-room tents

- Painter's tape for creating shapes on the floor (square, circle, rectangle, hexagon)
- Boxes, baskets, or trays of all sorts to create small worlds in
- Ribbons, bangles, bracelets, necklaces, crowns, Hula-Hoops, scarves to mark areas with

Positioning

Have you ever watched a child carefully line up toy soldiers in a row? Or organize their markers in the order of the rainbow? Or carefully arrange their plate so that foods don't touch each other? One word for you: Positioning.

In this schema, "a pattern that involves children in positioning, ordering and arranging objects of their own bodies", children give special attention to where objects, or parts thereof, are placed in relation to each other. It can look a little obsessive as they categorize their animals into families, and they may become irate if something disrupts this arrangement. This is (perhaps the only) schema that breeds order and attention to detail. Children exploring positioning might berate you for putting the red block *next to* the orange one, rather than *behind* it. They might demand that their Noah's Ark lineup be preserved for months to come. Or they might file a complaint that the order of the peas on their plate is incorrect.

For the *Positioning* Schema

- Blocks or cups to organize by size, shape, color
- Toys and dolls to categorize by subject or type: animal families, professions, and so on
- Objects to stack and unstack by size
- Hide-and-seek, spot the lady, or "what's missing?" games
- Balance beam made by a two-by-four on the floor for items or themselves
- Friends to organize for turns or in teams for games
- Patterns, mandalas, tangrams, or other shapes

Enveloping

When children explore enveloping, they tend to *cover*, or *wrap* something or themselves. They may cover their heads with a balaclava, wrap a cloak around their shoulders, or throw a sheet *over* their entire bodies, ghost style. They may take some plastic wrap or aluminum foil and wrap items such as pencils, keys, or a snack *inside*. Or they may create a space in which to be *enveloped*, such as a living-room fort or den. They're learning about *hiding* things and *exposing* them, about being *visible* or *invisible*, about the *order* of items in view, and what makes something *cover* something else and hide it.

For the *Enveloping* Schema

- Bags, pillowcases, socks, or gloves to put things in
- Puppets for enclosing little hands in
- Nesting toys, stacking boxes, shape sorters, or Russian dolls
- Sheets, blankets, silk scarves, small rugs to roll or wrap things in
- Posting games, box with slit for posting, piggy banks
- Containers to be filled with pasta, sand, pebbles, or beans and emptied
- Pass the parcel; packages to unwrap or open
- Wrapping paper, newspapers, aluminum foil, plastic wrap, clear tape, bandages
- All manner of dress-up items: gloves, hats, scarves, cloaks

95   Scheming Toddlers

As children hang upside down, they're getting a new perspective on the world. Literally. You and I know what it feels like to see the world from upside down, because *we too* explored orientation as children. When exploring orientation, kids will turn, twist, roll back and forth, do rolly-pollies and cartwheels, and hang upside down however they can, feeling the blood rush to their cheeks and seeing things in the room they may never have noticed before.

I vividly remember my wonderful *bubi* ("grandmother" in Yiddish) singing the German children's song "Hoppe, Hoppe Reiter" as she bounced me on her lap, only to push me, head back, into a backbend at the end of the song. I'll spare you the song's translation. Like many nursery rhymes, it's pretty gruesome. "Again! Again!" I would squeal. A tradition that has continued with my own children. Today, as I work hard to maintain my wheel pose, my handstand, or any other yogic inversion, I can see the draw of this children's song. There's a flexibility and an invigoration that comes with inverting ourselves, and as nature would have it, children seek this out naturally.

For the *Orientation* Schema

- An indoor trapeze or Raindrop swing (surprise, surprise!)
- Rock-climbing walls, indoor domes, monkey bars
- A place to do cartwheels or rolly-pollies
- Space for human wheelbarrows or handstands and headstands
- Floor mirrors—for a new perspective

Transformation

In this schema children learn about the properties of substances and materials. Do they absorb liquid? Do they get soggy? Do they change color? Temperature? Consistency?

Consider the child mixing Play-Doh colors together to find new colors emerging. Or mixing their juice with their cereal. When toddlers mix materials, they're being scientists and chefs: discovering ways to transform flour and water into cookies, or red and blue into purple.

Activities for the *Transformation* Schema

- Play-Doh in various colors; add (skin-safe) essential oils, flowers, twigs, and leaves for additional exploration
- Ingredients to mix together for baking so that children can watch what happens when they're heated
- Ice cubes in a bowl to explore the freezing feeling—and the process of melting

- Bubbly water, cups, spoons, funnels, pipettes, and turkey basters
- Finger paints, face and body paint, watercolor, sponges, paintbrushes
- Slime, glue, glitter, kinetic sand
- Bath bombs, bath color tablets, ice cubes in the bath
- Wands for blowing bubbles and giant bubbles

Redirecting Schemas to Avoid Power Struggles

Providing for our toddlers the support they need in meeting their urges to explore is a crucial step in developing their independent play muscles. If toddlers are stopped, controlled, and restricted throughout these formative years, they may learn to suppress their curiosity in order to stay in good standing with Mom and Dad. Or their explorations might become ever more forceful and anger charged.

We want to avoid being that cliché of a parent locked in a power struggle with a toddler. Instead, by understanding their schematic needs, we can come alongside them as their mentor, guide, and play buddy, understanding their natural needs and catering to those as they arise. Not only does this make the toddler years more bearable; it also makes them magical, and it honors the continual process of individuation and playful exploration that began as babies and will continue as life-long playfulness.

Action Steps

- When your toddler engages in enraging behavior like dumping fresh laundry, mixing juice into the pasta, or hanging themselves off the side of your bed, think, *Schemas!*

- Avoid unnecessary and unwinnable power struggles by providing them alternative and acceptable ways to meet this natural urge.

- Look for repeated behaviors to notice which schemas your toddler is currently exploring. Remind yourself that these behaviors allow children to express and explore the most basic ideas and actions in human behavior through play.

- Look out for the most common schemas, including trajectory, transporting, rotation, connecting, enclosing, positioning, enveloping, orientation, and transformation.

- Arm yourself with throwable things like balls, socks, or cushions.

- Collect things that can be contained, dumped, and enveloped, like toilet-roll tubes, silk scarves, baskets, boxes, little carts, buckets.

- Find sensory opportunities like baking, playing with mud, Play-Doh, or sand.

- Consider setting up a place where your toddler can climb and hang upside down, such as a swing, a climbing dome, or a Pikler triangle.

- Redirect your toddler away from dangerous or mischievous explorations by supplying a safe and acceptable way to explore the same schema or pattern of behavior, like throwing, spinning, or mixing.

- Remind yourself that you are encouraging their independent play rather than dampening it from the start—this can set them up for independence throughout their childhood.

Busy Slayer

Chapter

06

How we spend our days is, of course, how we spend our lives. What we do with this hour, and that one, is what we are doing. **Annie Dillard,** *The Writing Life*

Kim John Payne, author of *Simplicity Parenting*, shared that children's schedules today are busier than ever, "as some parents may push their kids into activities driven by a desire to see them achieve or by a need to have them occupied while they—the parents—are at work". He explained that childhood has become a rush for ever more, faster, bigger. He wrote the book in the early 2000s, and if I had to guess, I'd say there's only been an increase in kids' screen time, scheduled activities, and homework since his book was published.

According to the University of Michigan, kids are now spending between 4 and 4.5 hours in front of a screen per day; similarly, the Common Sense Media Report found that children up to age eight spend an average of 2 hours and 19 minutes every day on screen media, but tweens, ages eight to twelve, spent an average of 4.5 hours per day with screen media and 6 hours with all media—including reading and listening to music. There's quite a wide variation of screen time reporting from various sources—but they're all reporting multiple hours a day even in toddlerhood, and more as the child grows. This is after the 6.8 hours of school, homework, and three or four extracurricular activities per week. The weekends are not much better, with structured sports activities and even more hours of TV.

If you're feeling the race of childhood, you're not alone. The rise in depression and anxiety among kids today indicates that our children are crumbling under these pressures: "In every aspect of our lives, no matter how trivial, we are confronted with a dizzying array of things (stuff) and choices. The weighing of dozens of brands, features, claims, sizes and prices, together with the memory scan we do for any warnings or concerns we may have heard; all of this enters into scores of daily decisions. Too much stuff and too many choices. If we're overwhelmed as adults, imagine how our children feel! . . . Today, the 'real world,' in all of its graphic reality, is available for view anytime, anyplace, via the Internet".

If we want to reclaim play, we're going to need to reclaim our time, reclaim our *children's* time. Childhood is but a short season of life; let's continuously remind ourselves that we don't get second chances at these early years. That doesn't mean we should spend energy on guilt or worry about the lack of play or the overscheduling that's already happened, but it does mean we need to take stock and make changes *now* so that we can free up the majority of our children's time for free play. "Children really need that time to lie around, play more freely and have periods where they are side by side with their parents in the same room, being 'alone together,'" as Dr. Young-Eisendrath declared in an interview with the *New York Times*.

You might be reading this and shaking your head, feeling like you have the opposite problem. Too much time on your kids' hands, which seems to lead to a dissatisfied sense of boredom and impatience, sibling rivalry and near constant bickering, or the clinginess of a "Velcro baby." If your children are at a loose end and spend too much time climbing the four walls, remember that getting outdoors can do wonders. And of course, some scheduled activities can be useful and fun. However, in those stretches of *indoor* time, there is so much you can do to facilitate healthy, productive play. More on that will follow in the chapters to come. If you're spending all of your energy handling your children's messes, complaints, and sibling spats, independent play is one answer that can help ease *all* of those.

If we work outside our home, we often feel frazzled and overstretched because we're trying to get out the door for the morning rush, trying to look presentable for work, remember all the minutiae of our children's backpacks, and then we feel pressured at the other end of the day as we hustle to find something for dinner, get through homework, and navigate post-preschool tantrums. And then we somehow need to wrangle our entire family into a restful night's sleep, only to start the whole shebang again in the morning.

If we're staying home with young kids, we often feel frazzled and overstretched because throughout the day there are endless demands on us to continuously prep and clean up snacks and meals (is there a famine coming?!); to wipe surfaces, noses and tushies; and, most of all, to handle the big "bad" feelings and emotional meltdowns (our own among them).

Of course, these are pictures drawn in broad strokes that may or may not resemble your own daily grind—you may recognize yourself in these struggles, or you may face additional responsibilities such as PTA meetings, running your own business, infertility or adoption processes, caring for an aging parent, a crumbling marriage, or financial pressures. No one ever said adulting was easy, right?

The harsh truth is that the harder it seems to make space and time for play, the more crucial it is that you do. "When a child is constantly busy, bouncing from one thing to another, it is hard for them to know what they 'want to do.' First of all, nobody's asking. Their schedule, responsibilities, plan and parents are driving them". If you and your children are experiencing high levels of stress, the call for you to reclaim time for play is ever louder.

Remember, too, that having your children interested in and drawn to independent play will release some of your time to tend to your daily chores and, hopefully, squeeze in some self-care. It might make it easier for you to manage your team, to plan an event or to schedule doctor visits. Whenever I need to send a few emails, get dinner going, or reorganize our wardrobes, I can usually rely on my children busying themselves in play. That is a priceless life upgrade for an overwhelmed parent.

Whether your sense of busy-ness is born from chauffeuring your child to never-ending classes, your own work, your household errands, or from chasing your own tail all day with a toddler, let's consider some ways you can slay that busy.

Extracurricular Activities

I absolutely love extracurricular activities. Many people of the simplicity, minimalist or slow living movements have shared their thoughts that classes in martial arts, robotics, guitar, or LEGO club are the culprits that rob children of their childhood and stress parents out. I don't find that to always be true. Some well-placed activities outside the home are a precious opportunity to connect with other families, to have a place to go, and to broaden our children's educational horizons. While music or gym classes for babies are certainly not necessary for their development or social skills, they can sometimes be necessary for Mom's development and social life, which is no less important. Plus, particularly if you're homeschooling, having classes to go to can be a huge supplemental aspect of your child's education—and a breather for Mom or Dad to put their feet up while someone else is the "on" adult for the hour.

However, if *you* find the extracurricular activities in your schedule to be too much, then it's too much. Dr. David Elkind, PhD, author of *The Hurried Child* says, "Often, this overscheduling of structured activities is more the result of parental anxiety than for the needs of the child. Parents feel that because they're working or busy with their own hectic schedules, they need to keep their children occupied. But children don't have need to be in *any* organized activity before age 6 or 7, any earlier than that is really not age appropriate".

As with all parenting issues, choices depend on your budget, lifestyle, temperament, age, and resources. The point isn't to identify an age at which it's "okay," a fixed number of classes or the type of classes that "count"; the point is to be aware of your and your child's needs and, if either of you are feeling overwhelmed, to feel free to reduce your scheduled activities. "My rule of thumb is there should be no more than three activities—one sport, one social activity like Scouts, and one artistic endeavor like music lessons or art class," Elkind says. "And they should only go for an hour or so to each one each week. It's really inappropriate for elementary school children to go to daily practices". I promise you, your child won't "miss out" or "fall behind." If anything, they'll be gaining a calmer parent, and time to play.

"I'm Bored"

Once you have freed up ample time for free play—hopefully a few hours per day—you may find your children at a loose end, "climbing the walls," or complaining of boredom. This is an excellent sign. It's the phase of planting in which we are digging the hole in the ground. It feels like we're destroying something—ruining it. Everything was ticking along perfectly, and we came and dug up perfectly good soil—and now there's nothing there. But, as you already know, this is how we sow seeds. Or, as Sherry Turkle puts it, "Boredom is your imagination calling to you."

When my children whine "I'm b-o-o-red!" my answer is always the same: "Okay. It's fine to do nothing. You'll have an idea when you're ready." With an answer like this, it'll become clear to them that not only are you not going to rescue them, you're also not going to entertain them, you're not a bit interesting, after all. You're boring. Off they'll go. I don't want them to grow up thinking that it's never okay to have nothing to do. I know so many adults, like myself, who feel deeply uncomfortable with any small unclaimed slot in their schedule. It's the urgent feeling that they must cram their time full of "productivity" or else they're wasting it. But this is a question of framing. As Thomas Szasz says, "Boredom is the feeling that everything is a waste of time; serenity, that nothing is."

Play Cycles

As Olivia closes her eyes to settle into sleep, she's drowsy but easily woken. Her body jolts about as her muscles relax, only to suddenly jerk into a momentary awareness and drift back into a dreamlike state. Soon, her heart rate slows, her brain waves slow, and her eyeballs settle into a lull. Finally she enters a deeper sleep; it would be difficult to wake her up now, and if we did, she would be groggy. As she dreams, her body is still, but her eyes begin to flutter. She's transported to another world. She completes the sleep cycle; her sleep lightens once more, and her eyes begin to flutter. Perhaps she wakes up, perhaps she begins another sleep cycle.

If you're wondering why we need *so much time* dedicated to play—why we need to "slay the busy"—play cycles are one important reason why. I have no scientific evidence to back this up. But, from my own observations, I believe there are Play Cycles that are akin to sleep cycles. Stages of play, if you will, that one must progress through in order to reach the really "juicy" play. In sleep, science has discovered that one must go through the stages in order of progression, and that each stage has a distinct purpose and set of characteristics. I believe the same is true for our children's play.

I'll share my observations of my own children's play cycles, but they are very likely to be different for yours and just as likely to change based on their age and stage. However, in my own personal work of sinking into creative flow, I've found a similar pattern. I like to imagine there's a universal structure at work here, and that one day, we'll have the same clarity around the stages of play that we have around the stages of sleep.

Stage One: *Searching*

As in sleep, stage one is the lightest stage of play and the one most easily disrupted. In this stage, a child who is basically comfortable (alert fed, clean) is restless in that they're looking for something

with dis-interest

There's plenty to do...

offer a choice

to occupy their attention. This might look like wandering about the house, tinkering with things, climbing on the sofa or making a mess. It looks like aimlessness. It looks disorganized and most of us are extremely uncomfortable with this stage. It's at this moment that we say, "If you can't find something to do, I'll give you something to do," and make a mental note that our children need more structured activities to stop them from climbing the walls. This is the exact stage where Strewing—setting out toys as prompts and invitations to play—becomes so powerful (we'll visit this concept in chapter 15, Strew Pro).

The challenge of stage one is to allow our children to go through it and get to stage two. If we swoop in there and turn on the TV, give them a project, or strap them into the car for a round of errands, they never discover self-agency in finding their own projects and entertainment. Of course, there are times when we simply need to direct them onto the next activity of our own choosing, but if we want to strengthen the independent play muscle, we need to allow our kids to move through this stage.

If our children seem at a loose end, or complain of boredom, we might be wise to sometimes do nothing in response, and instead reframe our own mindset that this is, in fact, a problem. It's not. Just as a child trying to fall asleep might complain that she "can't sleep," she really just needs a little more time. "Now I'm not saying we only go to sleep because we're bored. Your body does need sleep for you to function properly but the time when your body chooses to shut off is very specific. For our bodies, "shutting down" is a process. First, we become inactive physically. Then we become content with our thoughts and fall asleep". Same with the interplay of boredom and self-directed play. It will happen eventually. If we quickly offer them something else to do, we sabotage the possibility of playing at all.

Stage Two: *The Challenge*

At this stage our children zero in on a challenge, problem or conflict that draws their attention long enough to engage. A toddler might see a pile of blocks that looks ripe for knocking over. A four-year-old might identify a particular teddy bear that looks thirsty for a hot cup of tea. Or an eight-year-old might notice a pile of LEGO figures that seem displaced and need to be organized into a school room.

In this second stage, they find the prompt that ignites the play—the sand that beckons to be fashioned into a castle, the dolly that shouldn't be wearing that dress, but rather the other one. This is like the writer who has finally found their muse, and they're ready to commit—for a time—to *this* story. It's the hiker who has chosen his trail. The chef who has selected the recipe to pursue. It's about staying keen on life itself—engaged, alert, rapt.

Stage Three: *The Plan*

As in sleep, stage three is where we get the real healing benefits. It's where we practice skills, solve problems and process ideas. This is where the toddler actually grapples with the fine motor skills it takes to build a tower. It's where the four-year-old "makes" the tea and serves it to the bear. It's where the eight-year-old builds the walls of his school, designing a world after his own imagination.

In stage three, our children are in the depths of play. A deep state of flow. It's during this time that the "outside" world disappears. What is left is only her and her bear. Him and his cards. It is the child who has *become* the doctor and is comforting his doll as he administers the medicine. It's the child who has an architectural blueprint in her mind and is in the throes of constructing her palace. It's the child who sees only her brushstrokes, who has eyes only for his marble run, or who is fixated on the train tracks. It's the child who is swinging on their rope ladder repetitively, with no mind for the clock, mastering

ok, what ideas do you have?

Help brainstorming

I'm sure you'll figure it out

With trust

their skill of climbing it to the top. It's the child who is lost in a fort, a series of cartwheels, or threading the beads on a necklace.

Stage Four: *The Resolution*

Stage four is the successful completion of their project (My necklace is done!), the resolution of the conflict (Teddy is happy now!) or a solution to the problem they tried to solve (I can climb to the top!). Stage four might also be a sense of completion in their endeavors, without any clear triumph or verdict. A sense of satisfaction (I have knocked over enough blocks for today) or perhaps frustration (I can't click these train tracks together, I give up!). To put oneself in a state of flow proposed by Csikszentmihalyi, the activity at hand can't be too challenging, causing anxiety, or too easy, making it understimulating or boring. What generates the flow channel leading to enjoyment is the balance between the complexity of a challenge and the skills we possess and can develop to face it. If a child has successfully reached stage four without being interrupted or distracted in the previous stages, they might settle back in for another "cycle" or may "wake up" from their play and be ready to interact with us once more.

These cycles may go quickly, cycling through all four stages in a matter of minutes, only to flutter on to the next challenge, with a visit to the searching stage first. Or they may take hours of engrossed play in one particular challenge before emerging, well rested, from their adventures.

The point is not to see these stages as prescriptive or rigid, but rather to begin to notice how they might play out in your own child's life. notice that, although one stage might feel uncomfortable, perhaps going through it and allowing it to pass like a wave, will bring about a new stage, where deeper and more meaningful play can occur. Perhaps we need to get through that initial boredom—as we need to get through the light stages of sleep—without being jolted out, in order to sink into the deeper, restorative play.

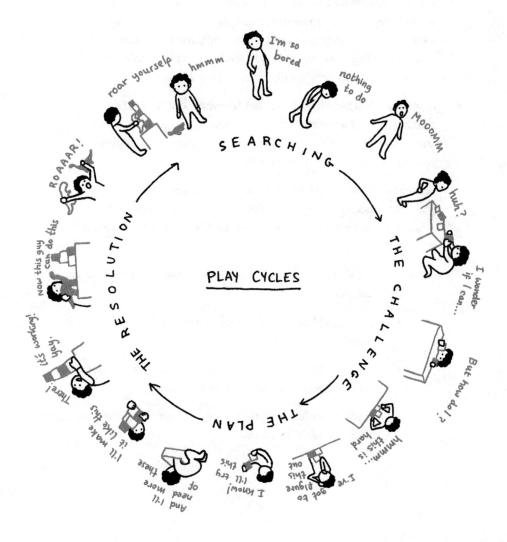

Action Steps

- Find the right balance of extra curricular activities for your unique family's needs. Sometimes some well placed activities can be a wonderful way to connect to a community and to get a break while our children are being taught some interesting skills. Just be aware when it becomes too hectic and dial it down.

- Remember that boredom is ok, healthy even—and always the starting point of a creative endeavor. Resist the urge to swoop in and fix the boredom with novelty and excitement—this allows your child to develop that agency themselves.

- Perhaps deep, independent play operates similarly to sleep—where one must proceed through specific cycles before one gets to the rejuvenating, deep states. Allow your child the time to go through these stages:

    - Searching for their next activity of interest. (*I see playdough—that looks fun.*)

    - Finding a challenge that they're excited about. (*I know, I'll make a dinosaur out of playdough.*)

    - Making a plan to meet that challenge and overcome it. (*Hmmm, it's not easy to make a dinosaur. I'll do it this way.*)

    - Finding resolution in their play and beginning the cycle again. (*There, I made it. What's next?*)

Declutter
Boss

We should be choosing what we want to keep, not what we want to get rid of. **Marie Kondo**

I looked around Jenny's basement and literally could not see the floor for toys. The stuffed animals alone could have filled my minivan to capacity. The dolls in this room had more accessories than I do. And there was a distinct crunch of orphaned puzzle pieces, train tracks and LEGO figures underfoot.

Jenny's not the only "victim" in hurricane Clutterina. In 2018, toy purchases accounted for 21.57 billion dollars in the United States. That's a lot of plastic we're moving (and of course some other materials too).

Take a look around your child's play space. Is it brimming with toys? Is it bursting at the seams with whatnots, old favorites, singing alligators, flashing pianos? Do you hyperventilate when it's time to clean up?

So, been there. This #firstworldproblem is a classic symptom of our society's endless chase for more, bigger, faster.

It's not entirely our fault that we buy a lot of toys. We are being bombarded with marketing messages that might as well say:

This toy will magically make your 2-year-old read Proust (in French, of course), dance ballet and put herself to bed for a 14-hour nap! It will also keep her so engrossed, that you can go on vacation and she'll be none-the-wiser!

Another message that we keep getting is: *Without this toy your child will suffer social penalization. She will never be cool if she doesn't own this.* Not to mention: *The stuff you buy your child shows you love them. More is more.*

As philosopher Alain de Botton puts it, "Advertisements would not work so well if they didn't operate with a very good understanding of our real needs. We hunger for good family relationships, connections with others, a sense of freedom and joy, a promise of self-development, dignity, calm and the feeling that we are respected. Advertisers understand these needs so very well, and that is why they have so much emotional pull."

The good news is, we do not have to accept these messages, because they're not just false, they're potentially harmful. Flooding your children with more and more toys will actually lead to less and *less* playing. A cluttered, brimming, and bursting playroom lends itself to distraction, frustration and overall agitation. "The brain has a limited capacity to process information," says Marie S. Davenport, "to filter out extra stimuli and focus on what we're trying to achieve at any given moment, the top down and bottom up attention mechanisms compete. By mutually suppressing each other, brain power is exhausted, and ultimately, we lose focus." So, in the end, having too many toys isn't more fun, it's more confusing.

To illustrate this point, imagine coming to your desk one morning to find you had five different laptops, three tablets and seven smartphones to choose from. Not to mention printers, scanners, cameras, pencils, pens, paper ... you get the idea. It's hard to get to "work" when you're paralyzed by too much choice.

Having too many toys also sets children up for a materialistic outlook on life. Research shows that "kids can recognize logos by eighteen months, and before reaching their second birthday, they're asking for products by brand name... Upon arriving to schoolhouse steps, the typical first grader can evoke 200 brands. And he or she has already accumulated an unprecedented number of possessions, beginning with an average of seventy new toys a year... American children view an estimated 40,000 commercials annually. They also make approximately 3,000 requests for products and services each year". It further separates the haves from the have-nots. We want to step out from the endless race to more and the pester-power given to children, both aimed at getting us to spend money on what eventually translates into more junk.

Perhaps we can send our kids a different message: *In this home, we're not keeping up with the Joneses, we're satisfied with what we already have. While we enjoy what life has to offer, including new things from time to time, we're mindful about which things we consume, how, when, and why.*

This is a message I need to hear from time to time, myself. (You should see my shoe collection!)

Toys that are there for entertainment discourage independent thought and play. In the short-term, entertainment works—we want little Johnny to be busy with something, and this flashing-singing-flying ninja will obviously do the trick. But for how long? And at what cost? What is it *teaching* Johnny to do for himself? Not very much. In the long run, if children are used to being entertained, they are not practicing the skill of entertaining themselves with their own imaginations.

Imagine, if you will, turning your child's play space into a safe haven that invites imagination and creativity *and* helps to lay the foundation for years of exploration and self-motivated play. But before you rush to get your garbage bags, know that in order to successfully declutter, you'll need to overcome any mindset blocks that are holding you back. Thoughts such as *What if I need this one day?* or *But isn't that a waste?* can derail all your efforts. So let's address them.

In my work with parents designing play spaces for their children, I've come across every resistance in the book. Here are the seven most common mindset blocks that counteract decluttering toys, and a few tips to counterbalance them:

1. "The toys I have bought for my children represent my love for them."

When we buy toys, it is often an act of love. We imagine our child so tickled, so pleased, so excited about this new shiny item, that they will most definitely know how much we love them. Gift giving here and there is lovely. But gift giving backfires if it becomes the love language we use regularly to show how much we care for our children. Our children begin to feel a sense of entitlement, expecting physical gifts when a hug or hair tousle could (read: *should*) have sufficed. Caught in the trap we've set ourselves, we begin to actually feel guilty for saying no to more toys. We eventually cave in and indulge them yet again, so that our love for them is not called into question. The long-term effect of this dynamic can be disastrous. "Showered with gifts, toys, and tokens of love as they grew up, the indulged expect blessings to be bestowed on them in adult life without effort on their part. Bored and restless with life, they seek continued indulgence without recognizing how their own effort can create internal satisfaction and contentment with life". Is this what we want for our children? If not, we're right on time to make changes.

One way to step back from this overindulgence is to quit, cold turkey. You may choose to commit to buying new gifts only two or three times a year (such as birthdays, Christmas, Hanukkah, Eid or graduations). Instead, you might direct your efforts on learning new ways of expressing your love. The most classic example is a hug and the simple statement "I love you." You could also write a note, spend special time together, or list all the ways you adore your child. But make every effort not to use gift giving to convey your love, except once in a while.

2. "The toys my children have represent special people in their lives."

Sometimes we hold on to an overwhelming number of teddy bears, gadgets and gizmos, dolls, books, and vehicles, simply because these were gifted to us by someone important.

But when toys no longer serve our children, or don't serve their best interest, that gift becomes a tiny little ball and chain you're carrying around, constantly tidying and organizing it, until, as in Jenny's case, your home is literally buried in the rubble of all these well-meaning gifts.

When people give us a gift, they do so (hopefully) to show their love for us. If they ever imagined the item would become burdensome, one hopes they wouldn't want us to keep it anyway. Now, this is a normal human behavior: "Without attachment to the people you love and the memories you cherish, your stuff would simply be stuff." But you need to "distinguish your attachment to your belongings from your belongings themselves".

To alleviate the guilt and unlink the stronghold of attachment, you could take a photo of the toys that are meaningful but that you don't want to hold on to anymore, that you have no room for, or that don't align with your philosophy. That way you can add them to your family album and hold them in your memory (not your home) forever. If there are some really (truly) special items, decide what makes them keepsakes, keep those, and make sure they have a special place (like a dedicated shelf or display). For the rest, donate them with your blessings and gratitude for the time they spent in your home and the way they lit up your children's faces. Remember that "your stories turn a house full of stuff into a home full of memories," but while "your heart can never be too full, your house can!".

3. "The toys we have represent the promise of prodigy, or at least education."

From Baby Einstein CDs to Leapfrog reading machines, every toy on the shelf seems to improve your child's memory, logic, reason, number sense, spatial awareness, fine and gross motor skills ... and the list goes on. And where do those toys find themselves just a few weeks later? You guessed it, underfoot.

It's high time we stop believing that a toy is the thing that will make or break our children's future career. A toy aisle in any big box store reads like an Ivy league college application: "meaningful mentoring", "enhanced instruction", "engaging learning opportunities". It's overwhelming. "Skills learned include math, logical thinking, concentration, problem solving, and geography and environment". (this on EduQuiz Basic Set from Best Learning). I've literally copied these phrases off toys aimed at three-to-five-year-olds.

But, despite these promises from well-meaning (I guess) toy manufacturers, I urge you to keep it simple. Any "thing" that promises to teach your children, improve their skills, or expand their minds might be promising too much. And it's playing into our vulnerability as parents. Of course we want the best for our kids, but when it comes to expanding the minds of children, there are no shortcuts for sale at Target. Learning and development happen through relationships and time, not objects. The way these very appealing promises hook you is by subconsciously claiming that you—or rather your kid—would be missing out if you don't buy the toy. Will your boy be at disadvantage if he doesn't own this or that set of building blocks? Will your girl be forever socially rejected if she can't develop her skills through that board game or interactive doll? While toy manufacturers want you to believe that the answer is yes, the answer really is no. Children truly learn through consistent, committed, connected relationships And exploration. Glamour and flashing lights are not necessary. Are there some lovely tools and toys out there? Of course. But you don't need them all. Just a few solid choices that stand the test of time. Remember that toys are optional. "The history of play is largely a history without toys for children" as Sutton Smith noted. Millions of children have grown up without manufactured toys and have done just fine—more than fine.

4. "The toys we have are a status symbol that proves I'm providing prosperity for my children."

This sentiment is the plain ol' keeping up with the Joneses, but with a twist: We're keeping our children up with the Joneses' children. Just because the kids around "all have one" or because your friends rave about it (read: *gave in and bought it*) doesn't mean you have to. Your children will benefit much more from a more orderly, manageable, and streamlined home than they will from yet another Shopkins or fidget spinner. Really.

Plus, they'll benefit from experiencing their parent as a confident leader who does not buy things simply because others do, but who stands their firm, empathic ground and is true to their values. When I used to say, "But Zoe's mommy . . .", my mother or father always responded with "Well, I'm not Zoe's mommy." What drove me crazy back then, I utterly respect now.

Rather than following every trend, we can begin to cultivate a mindfulness about what's driving your urge to buy a particular item. Is it really necessary? Is it well made? Will it stand the test of time? Is it going to serve constructive play? Are you buying it so that someone will see your child has it? Be brutally honest. And. Step. Away. From. The. Cash. Register (or checkout page!).

5. "The toys I buy serve as a 'behavior modification' trump card."

It's true, the promise of a new toy can smother even the wildest tantrum and bribe even the shyest child into posing for a photo with Grandma. New toys are alluring for adults and children alike, and we're willing to jump through some pretty uncomfortable hoops to secure them. But unless this is used sparingly, it's a dangerous and corrosive message. "If you do this (insert thing the child doesn't want to do) for me, I'll give you this." I don't need to elaborate on how that type of conditioning can manifest in the future. While we're all susceptible to the occasional bribe, the transactional nature of this is not a good lesson in healthy relationships.

Usually we bribe because we feel powerless as parents. We don't "own" our authority. We're not clear in the conviction that our child can and will cooperate with us. As long as our requests are reasonable and appropriate, and our child feels sufficiently connected and nourished, our requests can be complied with. Instead of believing they will cooperate, we worry we'll be "shown up" or that they're uncontrollable otherwise. Or we're afraid of big feelings.

"But he'll have a meltdown!" clients say to me. "Great!" I reply. "An opportunity to express his pent-up feelings is never a bad thing."

If bribery has been your go-to, then you may have unintentionally created a relationship monster: a situation where your child expects to be "paid" for any cooperation. With the monster already created, the trick now is not to feed it. I'm sure you don't want the threat of a screaming tantrum lorded over you for one more day.

Learn to set empathic limits and hold them with consistency and confidence, bribes notwithstanding.

6.   "I don't want to waste them now that I've bought them."

Often we hold on to things simply because we bought them. The logic goes: "Well I've already spent money on this, and even though I now hate it and want it out of the house, I'd better keep it so I'm not wasteful." Here's how I respond: Don't pay for things twice. Just because you made the "mistake" of buying it the first time doesn't mean you should now pay for it a second time with your energy and precious real estate.

Check this out: Ann Zanon, a certified professional organizer in Norwalk, Connecticut, calculates the cost of space per square foot and uses that to inspire her clients to clear out unused stuff. For example, a family that bought a two-thousand-square-foot home for 300,000 dollars typically spends nearly fifteen dollars per year for each square foot. "It doesn't sound like a lot," she says, "but that's fifteen dollars every year to keep a toy your child isn't playing with.". Zanon estimates the average household could free up 20 percent of its space by getting rid of items that are not needed or used.

Let go of the guilt and shame of having spent money "unwisely." Those moments and choices are in the past. And if you declutter these items, they will be out of your life and bring joy to someone else. Remember: Just because you're keeping it doesn't mean you're not wasting it. Give it to someone who can use it.

the vicious cycle of

Decluttering

WITH KIDS

7. "What if they need them again in the future?"

Look, this is legitimate. If you're not done having kids, hold on to your baby toys. If you're seriously considering moving to a snowy climate, keep that sled. But if you're holding on to things that *you know* you will never use again (flower press, anyone? Bread maker? Plastic pirate ship that lights up and spins?), please release them to the next lucky person who actually might have a use for them. In the wise words of Marie Kondo, "When you come across something that you cannot part with, think carefully about its true purpose in your life. You'll be surprised at how many of the things you possess have already fulfilled their role. By acknowledging their contribution and letting them go with gratitude, you'll be able to truly put the things you own, and your life in order. In the end, all that will remain are the things you really treasure."

Remind yourself that if you really end up needing this item in the future, you could probably borrow one or buy a new one. But what are the chances of that actually happening? Don't think that holding on to useless items now doesn't cost you. It does. Items we hold on to end up holding on to us.

Ultimately, the relationship we have with our stuff mimics the relationship we have with ourselves and the world.

- Do we feel fearful of scarcity, fearful that we might someday be wanting or hungry, so we need to stock up?
- Do we feel inferior, as if we can't keep up, and need to constantly compare ourselves to others?
- Do we feel compelled to "please" and appease?
- Do we feel powerless and unheard, compelled to gather ammunition we can use to manipulate and bribe?

When we feel secure, confident, and crystal clear with our goals and boundaries, then every single facet of our lives begins to reflect this. Our jobs, weight, relationships, health, thoughts, and of course, our stuff begin to mirror our best selves. So, with that in mind, let's proceed.

Where to Start so You Finish

When decluttering, it can be tempting to go at it all at once. You're in the mood! You've got energy! Let's DO this, right? Wrong. When you bite off more than you can chew, you end up giving up halfway through, just at the messiest mark of all. It becomes so difficult to get your mojo back to declutter, because all you've experienced is "failure."

To begin your decluttering journey, I want you to have at least one success, no matter how small. Then you can build on it and tackle your next category. If you don't take a project to completion, if you give up halfway, chances are you took on too much too fast. And then your brain gets the "fail" signal and files away a note: *Do not attempt this again.*

You may be wondering if you should declutter *with* your kids—I will answer that question in depth after I outline the decluttering process.

Begin by Choosing a Category to Declutter

To ensure your success, start small—really small. Choose just one category from the list below (or make up your own) to take to completion this week (yes, all the way through to donation). Then you can rinse and repeat for other categories once you've shown yourself you can do it.

After that, you can begin to take on other categories altogether, such as kitchen utensils, cables and electronics, or even the much-feared paperwork.

The categories of toys below are ordered by level of challenge. Start at the top!

Beginner	Intermediate	Advanced
Dress Up	Characters	Books
Pretend Play	Animals / Dolls	Puzzles
	Construction/ vehicles	Games

Gather all of the toys that are in the category you've chosen to begin with and complete the following process through to donation, then repeat with the next category. This will make each decluttering effort short and effective.

Select a Donation Destination

You've chosen your category—congrats! Before you dive into decluttering, decide where you'll be donating these goods once you are ready to part with them.

You really must do this; don't leave it till later because that can sabotage the endeavor and derail all your efforts. You'd be surprised how a little thing like putting off calling the church to arrange a drop-off time can stop you from actually getting rid of your clutter, and you'll find it back underfoot within a few weeks.

I'm sure you already have some ideas of where you might donate your pre-loved objects, but here are some ideas and prompts to help you decide. Remember, you're choosing where to donate the rejects from one particular category, not from all your future decluttering forever and ever. Keep this as simple and easy as possible.

Do you have anyone in your life who would appreciate hand-me-down toys? Friends? Siblings? Cousins? Neighbors? Anyone who works for you or services your neighborhood somehow? It can be most satisfying and meaningful to pass on toys to someone you know who wants them. Warning: Waiting until the next time you happen to see your cousin who lives one and a half hours away is not a good plan of action. So please only choose this option if you have a plan to see them within the next week.

Are there institutions nearby that would love some toy donations? Chances are you have a chapter of the Salvation Army, a local charity, school or preschool, or a religious institution that would be happy to use or distribute toys that are in good shape. If you've found a place you'd like to donate to, call them up immediately to arrange a time for drop-off, within three to four days.

Are there pick-up services operating near you? A quick Google search should tell you if there are charities operating locally who would be happy to pick up your unwanted toys. If so, call them now and commit to having them come within three to four days. Having this deadline and knowing they will show up at your door expecting a bag of goodies will help kickstart your decluttering action.

Are there drop-off bins near you? Many towns have drop-off recycling bins for clothes, books and toys. This is an easy and quick option that requires no scheduling.

Can you sell these items? Christi, a Reclaim Play student from Canada, was able to make a whopping three thousand dollars selling the excess toys she had at home and was able to more than fund the dreamy organic wooden toys she never thought she could own. Perhaps you have some extra money lying around the house in the form of unloved toys, furniture, or clothes.

Choose the Easiest Labeling System to Stay on Track

Now that you have your category picked out and your donation location identified, you're ready to prep your decluttering process like a boss. You'll need two or more medium-size bins and about four garbage bags.

Label your storage bins with an erasable chalk label. One will be called "Toy Rotation." In the rotation bin you will place all the toys you love but have gone "stale"; in other words, your kids have not shown interest in them for a while. They'll be going out of sight so that they can be brought back out in a few weeks or months, and your kids can get excited about them again. (Pssst: if you're using see-through storage bins, try putting the toys in pillowcases or bags so that they can't be seen and asked for by your little ones).

In a bin or bag labeled "Toy Donation" you will put anything you're giving away.

In a bin or bag labeled "Selling" you'll put the stuff you want to sell. If you don't sell it within a week or so, it goes into donation.

The "Garbage/Recycling" bin or bag is for broken, dangerous, or otherwise unusable items. Depending on the materials, check out your local recycling options.

The "Display" Pile is for the toys that get the "all clear" to be out, displayed, and played with right away. These are in good shape, have all their pieces, and are toys you and your kids love. You can put these into your play space immediately and rotate them out when you bring out your rotation box next time.

Keep a small "Travel Toys" bin with random little toys that your kids might enjoy but that you don't mind losing. Things that aren't precious or special but are perfectly okay—like little animal figurines or a bouncy ball. If you have them all together in a particular place, you can just grab them when you need to go on a long car ride, to wait at the doctor's office, or if you're traveling for a while.

Pump It Up and . . . Sort

It's time to sort your category into the bins. So, for example, if you've selected dolls, you'll gather all doll-related items into one pile, decide which items are for the trash, which go to donation or for sale, which can be stored and then reintroduced later, and which are being played with excellently right now. Once you've done that, you'll gather your next category (say, animals) and go through this again.

How to know which bin to sort it into? Just follow this simple guiding principle, and always trust your intuition. You can't get this wrong; it's whatever works for you.

- **Donation:** We don't like it and it has no resale value.
- **Sale:** We don't like it, but it has resale value.
- **Rotation:** We like it but haven't touched it for a while.
- **Garbage/ Recycling:** We don't like it and it can't be used anymore.
- **Display:** We love it and play with it all the time.
- **Travel:** We like it but could live without it, and it's small enough to take along.

Which toys should I absolutely get rid of? As I mentioned earlier, please apply your own intuition and common sense here. There is no right or wrong. These are general guidelines based on Kim John Payne and Ross's seminal book, *Simplicity Parenting*. I've adapted them slightly over the years, but what's important is making them work for *you and your child*. Don't get rid of your children's prized possessions, even if it is a singing, plastic, flashing, ugly Spider-Man model. Beyond that, here's a guide of toys to cut out.

Broken Toys

Toys that are broken can sometimes be used for collages, but often they're not touched because they are broken. If games or puzzles have missing pieces, they're usually not fun—or even possible—to play with. Bless them and bag them.

The one with an
identity crisis

The one that
gives you a
headache

The one that
gives you
nightmares

Ultra-Specific Toys

Toys that can't be imagined into something else, like an ultra detailed helicopter. Sometimes these toys are worthwhile, if they still encourage creative, imaginative play. However they are less adaptable and offer less bang for your buck—because they're often really only used for one, specific thing.

Toys That Play by Themselves

Magda Gerber taught: passive toys make for active children. If your toys flash lights, sing songs, move and entertain your children, consider replacing them with toys your child manipulates.

Annoying Toys

You just really don't like it and can't explain why—toys that seem to provoke your child to play in an irritating way or have features like whistles or drums you find unpleasant. You actually *can* get rid of them: problem solved. If a toy represents a potential trigger for your anxiety and bad temper, it has no business in your home.

Advertisements for Products or TV Shows

From Winnie the Pooh to Scooby-Doo, entertainment companies have their copyrighted characters all over our homes. Our kids can enjoy an ad-free environment where their ideas come to life—not a reenactment of someone else's designs and imagination. I know this sometimes rubs some people the wrong way, and as with all these ideas, you do not have to be dogmatic about it. If your kid is attached to their Paw Patrol characters, hold on to them. The suggestion is simply to try to avoid choosing items that are commercially driven and are the products of another person's creativity. Instead, make space for open-ended and creative exploration so our children can connect to their own inner Walt Disney.

Passing Fads

Tamagotchi anyone? Pokémon cards? I know, I'm showing my age. But that's the thing: passing fads don't make for time-tested toys. We want to imagine whether our grandparents or grandchildren could play with an item before evaluating whether it has earned the precious real estate in our homes and hearts.

Duplicates

Doubling up is some parents' answer to "sharing" trouble, and in some cases it may make sense. If it's truly an item both kids play with often, I get it. But in general, you don't need to have the same item twice—especially since learning to take turns is a valuable experience.

Ugly Toys

What goes into your sacred temple—your home—matters. Your visual experience of the space around you is built of all its elements, and if you have a bunch of toys that are eyesores, feel absolutely free to get them out of your line of vision.

Take a moment to imagine your child's play space as a soothing environment that invites imaginative and meaningful play. Give your child the gift of an uncluttered, inviting space to fill with their dreams and ideas.

Aggressive or Violent Toys

This is not so much about the toy itself, but what it brings out in your child. Guns, swords and other war or fighting themed toys can actually be healthy for play—more on that in the Curation Diva chapter—however there may be a toy in your home that your child always seems to use in destructive or aggressive ways. Good news: you can get rid of it!

The one that didn't make it

The one that lost its soul

The one that's all wrong

Should I declutter with my kids?

Now that we're clear on *which* toys to get rid of and on *where* they should go, the next most common question is: Should I declutter with my kids? My short answer is: It depends (kind of like all of parenting decisions—ha!). Some children can understand and appreciate the concept of decluttering. They can get on board and even enjoy it. They like the idea of giving their old, unused things to someone who can enjoy them, and they love the idea that they're making space for more joy and more of the things they do love.

For these children I would use language like this: "Darling, we seem to be a bit overwhelmed by our toys taking up so much space. To really enjoy what we have, it will feel better when we have more room to store it and play with it. There are lots of toys in our home that we don't play with anymore, and another child could really enjoy them. Let's sort through and decide which things you no longer need!"

Explaining the process and the fact that a minimalist environment feels better, while encouraging and appreciating their help will work wonderfully for some kids. Others may feel resistant to the idea of decluttering their belongings. The moment you start organizing, these kids are worried that you'll take their favorite things and give them to other children.

In this case, I would advise decluttering without your children present (while they're sleeping or out), but letting them know you'll be doing so. I let my children each have a box where they can keep any special things—even random junky things— and they're off limits for me. But, if it's outside of the box, it may get cleaned up or donated.

Of course, I never donate toys they enjoy greatly. I don't recommend getting rid of anything your child is currently playing with and loving it, even if it falls into the "declutter" category (as listed above).

The ultimate goal is deep play, and so it doesn't serve us to get rid of the tools of your child's play, even if they aren't our favorite toys. When they lose interest in those toys, you can take them to donation.

When you're decluttering without your child, here's some language to explain: "It seems like we've got too much stuff in here and it's hard to see what we have. I'm going to tidy up one day this week so that you have a clear, easy space to play in and lots of room for your creations. I won't get rid of any of the toys you love to play with, but I'll clear out the ones we don't use anymore. If there's anything that is special to you, let me know and I'll be sure to hang on to it. I'm excited for you to have a really lovely area to work in!"

Once you begin, it can be tricky if you leave the job half finished; that's just when your children will rediscover the items you're trying to part with. Finishing is the most important part, hence I suggest to go by category.

That said, if you need to stop in the middle, pile everything together, including your bins and bags, and get back to it as soon as possible. Leave it in an inconvenient place (like on your bed or your kitchen countertop) so that you can't ignore it much longer.

If you're feeling overwhelmed and wondering how you can make this easier, I want to remind you that much of this is in your mind. I find decluttering fun because I see it as an act of self-care, not something I have to do, but something I get to do. Something that makes my home and life so much more enjoyable. Something that my children and I *deserve*.

Action Steps

- If you're feeling down, remind yourself that you're not alone if you're overwhelmed by clutter. You've been sold the message that toys are vital for kids' development and happiness.

- Before you declutter, address your mindset blocks by understanding what these toys "represent" for you. Are they the love you express to your children? The promise of education? The connection to the loved one who gifted the toy?

- Choose *one* category to begin the decluttering process, so that you're sure to finish and experience success.

- Identify where your clutter is going. Where can you donate, sell or recycle?

- Decide whether or not you'd like to declutter with your children. Prepare them either way by reiterating that you'll be clearing out the space so they have more room to play, but remind them that you'll never get rid of the things they love and use.

- Get rid of toys that are broken or missing pieces, that are ugly, passing fads, don't "earn their keep" or that are advertisements for brands.

- Sort your toys, of that category into six bins or bags: Donation, Sale, Rotation, Garbage, Display or Travel.

- Celebrate your success and rinse and repeat the process with the next category!

Part Three: Play Architecture

Chapters 8—16

Become a Play Architect

The first aim of the prepared environment is, as far as it is possible, to render the growing child independent of the adult. **Maria Montessori**

When you enter a supermarket, you typically see a large retail space with aisles and shelves stocked with various food and household items. Cash registers and a customer service desk can be found at the front of the store. The store is usually well-lit and organized, with clear signage to guide shoppers to what they are looking for. The design of the supermarket helps you stay focused and complete the shopping process efficiently. From the proportions of the space and the signage to the color scheme, materials, and layout, everything is designed to prompt you to take a cart, walk up and down the aisles, collect items, pay, and leave.

Contrast this to walking into a church. While there may be an aisle, it is clear that the intention is not to pace around, but to sit down, reflect, listen, and pray. The design and proportions of the space, with features such as high ceilings, natural light, deep earthy tones, and natural materials like stone, marble, glass, and wood, are carefully chosen to evoke a sense of awe, wonder, and connection to a community that acknowledges something greater than themselves.

A casino is designed to create the illusion of an alternate universe. With no easily accessible exits, clocks, windows, or natural light, the space is meant to be disorienting. Psychedelic patterns on the fabric, frenzied lighting, and plush, cushioned seating aim to transport you to another realm, suggesting that there are no real-world consequences for what happens within these walls. The design invites you to stay and play.

A spa, on the other hand, is designed to provide comfort and relaxation. Its purpose is to make you feel special, deserving, and worthy of luxurious treatment. In a spa, you'll find elements like candlelight, intimate spaces, natural materials, water sounds, and meditative features that are meant to encourage you to relax and unwind. This atmosphere is in stark contrast to that of a supermarket, casino, or church.

Let's focus on our homes now. Our homes also follow established expectations for the functions a family needs to fulfill in their living space. In the kitchen, the smooth, shiny, wipeable countertops, stove, sink, knives, and fridge all instruct you that this is a place for food preparation. It's acceptable to use water, knives, and fire in this space.

In the bedroom, the soft fabrics, layout, and cozy features like a carpet signal that it's not a place for lighting fires or using knives. It's a place to rest, relax and sleep. Meanwhile, the bathroom conveys a completely different message. By simply looking at the room, we understand its purpose and what is appropriate in this space, which is not the same as what is appropriate in the living room. This room is about privacy, self care and hygiene.

So what instructions is your child receiving from your home? The message that a child receives from a playroom overflowing with toys spilling out of a jumbled chest is not a positive one. Rather than feeling inspired to play, a child may feel overwhelmed, frustrated, or even inclined to scream or walk away. Understanding the power of our home environments to influence behavior is a key aspect of becoming a play architect.

By creating designated play areas, parents can ensure that each type of play is only appropriate in the environments designed for that activity. This helps to reduce confusion and conflict between siblings, and supports the development of positive play habits. By designing defined play spaces—the play zones—parents can make their home a more effective co-parent. It not only helps to foster a sense of order and responsibility in the child, but it also makes clean-up go smoother and quicker.

In short, becoming a play architect can lead to a more relaxed and enjoyable parenting experience, by using the home

Become a Play Architect

environment to guide and support the development of healthy play habits in children.

Why Zones?

Remember the three stages of design: empathy, ideation, and experimentation. Play zones emerged from this process.

So what exactly are play zones? They are areas of the home designated for a particular type of play.

When you set up a zone system, you're operating from the belief that the sensory exploration a child gravitates to when they claw at the mud in your front yard is necessary and worthy of a station, just as your own work and cooking and sleeping needs a place to "live" within your home. You're respecting the fact

ALL FIVE ZONES CAN BE POPPED UP OR HIDDEN AWAY - IT'S ENDLESSLY ADAPTABLE AND FLEXIBLE

quiet zone - resting and snuggling on the couch (or bed)

movement zone can be stored when not in use

dining table doubles as a messy zone and focus zone

imagination zone can be pulled onto any floor anytime

that children need the space to play and that your home should be fertile ground for their imaginations. You're acknowledging the idea that "play is the work of childhood," as Jean Piaget so famously said, and that the home is the friendliest environment for them to meet their natural urges and needs.

Having zones also makes parenting much easier, because rather than practicing "hope" parenting—hoping that your kid doesn't take a marker to your freshly painted walls—you can be proactive in directing their behaviors to the appropriate spaces.

According to psychologist Diana Baumrind, when children inevitably are drawn to activities like dumping out the clean, folded laundry or exploring their trajectory schema by throwing their sippy cup to see what happens, most parents tend toward one of two categories:

- Punitive: they shout "no!," reiterate house rules, emphasize that those behaviors are *not allowed* and will *not be tolerated*, and follow up with consequences such as time-outs or loss of privileges.
- Permissive: they shrug it off because, what can you do? Kids will be kids. Dealing with their meltdowns and tantrums, when they've set a limit, is too daunting.

By designing spaces that are specifically cater to those schemas, urges, and needs, you're allowing yourself a third option:

- Redirecting the exploration to the appropriate location where it's acceptable, contained, and even desired.

You're neither banning messy play nor permissively allowing it to run down your home. You're proactively designing a designated space for it. You're not forbidding jumping, swinging, running, and rolling, but as you may not want those things happening on your couch either, you're effectively answering the child's legitimate need through design. You're not prohibiting LEGO,

"We only need ONE chair. This works. For sure."

"We're minimalists in a maximalist kinda way."

but you don't want them taking over the house either (we've all stepped on that one gosh-darn-it 4-by-4 piece at 3:00 am), which is why there's a zone for that.

This goes beyond simply making a space where things are allowed to happen, it actually shows your children that you *support, facilitate, and encourage* their play. By making space for it in our home, we're showing our children that what's important to them is important to us.

Warm Minimalism

As we look to designing play zones, let's keep ourselves loosely committed to a minimalistic approach. We've already spent considerable effort decluttering and parting ways with those items that don't "spark play." Maintaining a light, airy space is key to supporting a child as he or she sinks into deep flow.

As you set up the zones, whatever size home you live in and whatever your budget, reign in any hoarding tendencies. More is not necessarily *more*. Excess will inevitably seep into the zones and call for a continual decluttering practice. That is normal and unavoidable, but as we set up play zones, don't fall prey to the temptation of stuffing them with extras. Keep it simple. Err on the side of sparse.

Some strategically planned "white space" is sometimes the birthplace of more imaginative play than any toy-filled-box. What is white space? It's emptiness, nothingness, void. It's a naked surface, an unfilled bucket, a bare shelf. Leave a *lot* of breathing room around each item for the magic to occur. In the world of design, white space is often referred to as negative space; the portion of a page left unmarked, such as margins, columns, or the space between letters and lines. There's a consensus among designers that it's the parts left *unmarked* that are often the most important. Likewise, it's often what is *absent* from a play zone that gives power to what is present.

Imagine walking into a playroom with a giant bag of LEGO on the floor; next to it is a mini trampoline, and on the other side a Barbie dollhouse, complete with all the toppings. Closer to you, a pile of wooden blocks and some stuffed animals hang in a hammock overhead. There's a mini red piano and percussion toys off to the left, and in the far right corner is a giant bookshelf, oozing card books, comics, and picture books of all kinds. What should you focus on? Where should you start?

Now imagine that same room with only the bag of LEGO on the floor. Just that bag, opened out on the floor with a lot of space around it, nothing else filling the room. Where does your focus go now?

When we use white space, we create clarity and direct our children's attention to the *one* invitation before them to play, liberating them from information overload and decision fatigue.

An overly bare space might feel cold—and that's where the "warm" part comes in. Warm it up with earthy tones, with plants, with natural light, with artwork you cherish—not with more and more stuff.

The minimalist Police

The Palette of Play

His eyes dart around wildly, trying to find something to focus on. Look at that string of letters and numbers floating overhead. Wait! There's the ABC poster, he can find the M! Or should he sit on this bright rug with the map of the world—*he knows where America is!* Adrianne is confused as to why her four-year-old son Mason becomes so agitated when she drops him off at preschool. He has so many friends there and a true bond with his loving teacher, Ms. Harper, so what's going on?

Of course, many things might be going on emotionally for Mason, but the influx of visual stimuli surely doesn't help. Consider how you feel when you go into a supermarket. So many packages! So much to look at, read, and consider! Beyond the obvious choice paralysis (too many options), you're also

"If I can't see it, I don't own it!"

experiencing visual overload (competing colors, messages, shapes). In places like casinos or arcades, where a multitude of flashing lights and messages compete constantly, our eyes dart nervously from one focal point to the next, never resting. It's exhausting.

In nature, powerful colors like red and yellow are used sparingly. They usually signify danger (such as a poison dart frog), and it seems our brain has learned to take special note and be drawn to bright colors, because an awareness of danger helps us survive. As such, many toys and play spaces, preschools, and day-care centers use bright primary colors (red! blue! yellow!) liberally. These colors are sending our brains into overdrive trying to keep up with the "alerts," impacting our entire nervous system.

"Overstimulation can trigger physical or psychological changes. On the physical level, breathing or pulse frequencies can be affected: blood pressure and muscle tension may increase" **(Meerwein, Rodeck and Mahnke 2007, 4).**

So, when choosing colors for your play zones—the chairs, tables, rugs, wall art, or storage systems—consider going for a neutral palette. Despite our cultural dictate that children love things with vibrant colors, I invite you to take a leaf out of the pages of Maria Montessori, Regio Emilia or Rudolf Steiner, and create more of a "white canvas" on which your children can imprint their own colorful creations. In other words, go for the creams, grays, browns—soft and subdued colors (often borrowed from nature)— over the bright ones. Or, if you have a special affinity for vibrant hues, use them sparingly: in a cushion on the couch, a poster in an otherwise neutral room, or a bright rug in a white space.

At the risk of sounding clichéd, I'll share that my absolute favorite material for a play zone is wood. Nothing new here, but the earthiness, warmth, and organic nature of wood feels incredibly grounding and calming. When designing your space, consider the qualities you're introducing with the materials, shapes, dimensions, and colors. For bright, airy spaces we want white (or at least light) walls, light grains of wood, thinner and lighter pieces of furniture (extra points if they're on legs or wheels and expose more of the floor), and, most important, natural light.

Light Play

Some of us live in homes with a basement, and it's become typical in suburban homes to dedicate this space to the playroom. My clients ask me, exasperated, after spending thousands of dollars refurbishing this carpeted basement with the best toys and the cutest wall murals, why their children never go down there to play.

There are two core reasons kids don't go to play in the basement for long stretches of time. First, children naturally seek proximity to their caregivers. It's an evolutionary survival tactic that has served us well throughout millennia: stay close to mom or a saber-toothed tiger might eat you. We would do best not to fight with this innate survival mechanism but instead surrender. Setting up play zones right there in the kitchen, living room, or bedroom, where mom is within earshot and eyesight will ultimately produce a much more satisfying independent play experience for both parent and child.

Second, humans thrive in natural light. Most of us intuitively prefer spaces with large windows that allow lots of light to spaces that are lit by fluorescents (which have been linked to depression) or even warm artificial lighting. In the words of Louis Kahn: "So light, this great maker of presences, can never be . . . brought forth by the single moment in light which the electric bulb has. And natural light has all the moods of the time of the day, the seasons of the year, [which] year to year and day for day are different from the day preceding."

Natural light is probably so attractive to us because of its innumerable health benefits. It boosts our vitamin D, our productivity, improves our vision, and elevates our mood. Sounds like just the type of environment we want for our children! So, when setting up your play space, opt for the coveted near-the-window spots over the sprawling basement. Of course, you can create zones in both areas, but I think you'll find that the darker the zone, the less it is used regularly.

Planting the Seeds of Play

Another quick win, and another reason you'll prefer natural light, is bringing nature into the play zones. We all know that getting out into nature is linked to reduced stress levels and tension relief. But even on those indoor days, we can capitalize on some of that juicy goodness by bringing nature in. Some well-placed greenery brightens a room, purifies the air, and creates a more relaxing, restful ambiance.

Rooms with plants aren't just Pinterest worthy, they have a proven effect on our mood and even our health. In 2008, a Dutch study found lower stress levels and higher healing rates in patients who had indoor plants in their rooms, compared to those who had none.

Research also demonstrates that the presence of plants in university classrooms and workspaces creates a more comfortable learning environment and has a positive impact on student performance and on their perceptions of the course and their instructor. Students at universities show a 70 percent increase in attentiveness when they're taught in rooms with some leafy plants, according to a study at the Royal College of Agriculture in Circencester, England. In fact, even attendance was higher for lectures given in classrooms with plants.

In our own homes we're trying to increase attentiveness, lower stress levels, and even increase attendance in a way (by beckoning our children to stay and play for longer). So, let's scatter houseplants around our homes and particularly in the play zones, so our children can enjoy the effect of focus, elevated mood, and purified air.

In addition, caring for the plants—watering, weeding, feeding, pruning—can be a meaningful and enjoyable job for little hands. Of course, while your child is still at the oral-fixation stage or exploring the filling and dumping schema, keep those plants on high shelves. Ask me how I know.

Find some easy-to-care-for houseplants to complement any play zone. My personal favorite is the fiddle-leaf fig, for its gorgeous look, and golden pothos, for its cascading leaves and easy care (crucial for me, as my thumbs are anything but green). Other great indoor plants include the aloe plant, rubber tree or snake plant, which are also strong survivors of plant killers such as me.

Aroma-Play-Therapy

Walking into a shoe shop of high-end stilettos, pumps, and flats, you eye a pair of beautiful sandals. They are really gorgeous and look like they'll be comfortable too. Score! Slightly out of your budget for shoes just now, you decide to sleep on it and revisit the store the next day.

As you walk in the following morning, you're struck by an even *greater* excitement to purchase them. Suddenly, budget be damned, you whip out your plastic and you're back on the street, wearing your new wedges before you can say Steve Madden.

What happened? Why the sudden clarity? One reason might be patchouli.

Researchers at Chicago University have an answer for you. They compared shoppers looking at shoes in a room with no odor with shoppers doing so in a pleasant-smelling room and found that 84 percent of shoppers were willing to spend ten dollars more on shoes in a room that smelled nice. They also found the shoes more attractive.

As you look to create a multisensory experience that attracts, calms, and focuses, reflect on the potent yet underutilized potential of aroma. Smell cells in the nose are linked to the limbic system, the oldest part of our brain, which governs emotions, behavior, and long-term memory. In evolutionary terms, it's thought that the effect of smells on the brain are a relic of the life-and-death significance smell had for early man's survival.

Children no longer need to sniff out their environment to test for safety, and we're now running with far fewer smell receptors than other mammals and primitive man (humans have around 5 million, dogs around 200 million receptors), but a powerful subconscious association between smell and behavior remains.

Research shows that what we smell impacts almost everything—stress, pain, memory, concentration, dreams, and emotions. The scent of eucalyptus boosts alertness, stopping to smell the roses lowers blood pressure, a whiff of lavender makes us happier and releases feel-good hormones.

Aromatherapy and essential oils have been receiving a lot of attention over the last decade, and we'd be wise to include them in our parenting toolbox as well. Consider including an essential-oil diffuser near your play-zones (although out of reach of little fingers!) and diffusing pleasing aromas that relax, rejuvenate, and stimulate. Peppermint, for example, is a natural stimulant that

CITRUS	FLORAL	HERBAL	SPICY	WOODSY
Bergamont	Neroli	Rosemary	Clove bud	Cedarwood
Orange	Rose	Peppermint	Cinnamon	Sandalwood
Grapefruit	Jasmine	Tea Tree	Ginger	Juniper
Lemon	Ylang ylang	Eucalyptus	Patchouli	Pine

has been shown to increase concentration and energy levels and to boost your mood. Lemon, which energizes and calms, clears the mind and decreases anxiety. There are many dreamy scents to choose from: cinnamon, frankincense, rosemary, grapefruit, ginger, or jasmine. Note that these are unregulated and need to be from a reputable company. In addition, some oils are not safe to use around people or pets.

The Sound of Play

Remember, the first phase of design thinking is empathy. When we want to influence someone's behavior—and let's just admit it, as parents, we do—we need to put ourselves in their shoes and experience the world as they do. This includes all sensory experiences: what they see, touch, smell, taste, and hear. Sounds, their qualities, association, pitch, tone, frequency, and volume, have a huge effect on our children, who are designed to prick their ears and be alert to any incoming information that might keep them alive.

Just like the preferences for various fragrances over others, children will vary in their comfort level with respect to sound. And just as some adults *need* music and background noise in order to concentrate (Crazy! I know!), others require absolute quiet in order to focus their minds (my kind of people). Some children fall asleep only with a fighter jet sound machine a-blasting in their ears (although this may well have damaging effects, I have some such children in my family), and others will nod off even in front of the television. Get to know your child and experiment with sound.

For example, try playing music—classical, kid pop, or nursery tunes. Remember that playing is similar to the creative process of writing a novel in that it requires a certain *atmosphere*. But there's no one-size-fits-all. Still, there are some core principles that are likely to be applicable to all children. Having the TV or radio (so nineties) on in the background is a no-no in my book. I don't know any writer who can create when exposed to an input of random information and conversation. An adult who's on the phone nearby may be very distracting to some children, while others take it as a cue to tune out. And some children do very well with an audiobook playing, connecting with the story and including it in their imaginary play, while others will sit, mesmerized and listening, but unable to play.

I love audiobooks, and we listen to them every day, but one of my sons will have an audiobook with earphones on as he plays LEGO, while the other one thrives on quiet or gentle music.

Of course, there may be sounds beyond our control, such as a baby sibling screaming or Roxie barking, but let's focus on those disturbances and channels of input that we can control. One audio interruption is most definitely disruptive to a child's process: adult intervention. Talking to a child about their work, commenting on it, and asking questions will pull them out of their flow. My recommendation therefore is to *tiptoe* when your children are playing. We will revisit this concept in the chapter on becoming a Play Guru.

Storage Systems

In every play zone you will need some form of storage. It might be pen pots for crayons, baskets for dolls, or a large lie-flat drawstring bag for LEGO. Try to choose a modular, interchangeable system that serves you for as many purposes as possible. Not only will this mean you have fewer choices to make but it will also offer greater flexibility. When choosing your system, simpler is better. But before you run out and clear the shelves at the Container Store, remember to build slowly. If we overstock, even storage containers can become unwanted clutter. I recommend setting up the zones one at a time so that you can see what you're using and attempt to first use what you have on hand before rushing out to buy more. Perhaps you'll need less than you thought in one zone, and you can use left-over storage in the next zone.

Testing Your Play Zone

"Ugh, he never seems to want to stay in the imagination zone for any length of time," I complained to my husband. "I'm not sure why, but every time I take him in there, he quickly gets restless."

I put on my detective hat and rallied to figure out this puzzle: Why did my eighteen-month-old not enjoy playing in our lovely, inviting play space? I got down on the floor and looked for clues. Suddenly, a blast from the air-conditioning vent smacked me in the face and I let out a legendary sneeze. "Oh my God, it's *freezing* down here!" I exclaimed, both miffed at how I had missed this and ecstatic that I had an explanation as to why my son wasn't enjoying his time there. He was cold! Some furniture shuffling later, I worked the angles and was able to make the imagination zone a toddler-friendly temperature.

From our giant, adult perspective, we may be missing something that could make or break our child's experience in any one of our play zones. To avoid repeating my misstep, as you set up each of your zones, try getting down to your child's level and look at the zone through *their* eyes. First, check for any safety snafus you may have missed from your towering perspective, such as exposed sockets or splintered panels. Next, imagine how your child might perceive this space. Is it inviting? Is it comfortable to sit or stand and work here for long stretches of time?

Action Steps

- Prepare to set up your play zones; doing so shows your children that you *support, facilitate,* and *encourage* their play.

- Make each zone as much of a Yes Space as possible. The more babyproof, spill proof, accident-proof a space can be, the freer you are to let your child explore unrestricted.

- Practice benign minimalism and use white space. That way we direct our children's attention to the *one* invitation before them to play, liberating them from information overload and decision fatigue.

- Opt for neutral and soothing: contrary to the popular "pops" of primary colors in children's play spaces, create a relaxing environment by opting for a palette of neutral, light colors and natural materials with sparing splashes of vibrant hues.

- If possible, avoid the basement and try to maximize natural light, which is attractive to children and holds innumerable health benefits.

- Add some plants: a splash of green from indoor plants elevates the mood, purifies the air, and adds a dose of Zen to any play zone.

- Infuse some great aromas: Certain smells can increase focus and calm. Diffusing pleasing aromas such as peppermint, lemon, or lavender can have a meaningful effect on children's behavior.

- Experiment with your soundtrack. Deep play requires a certain *atmosphere*, which can be amplified through music.

- Test your play zone from your child's eye level. As you set up each of your zones, look at the space through their eyes. Is it attractive? Is it comfortable?

Imagination Zone

Let the child be the scriptwriter, the director and the actor in his own play. **Gerber and Greenwald, *RIE Manual***

This zone is the space where imaginative play occurs. Of course, all play is stirred by the imagination, but while other forms of play are rooted in physical, sensory, scientific, or academic exploration, this zone is dedicated to children directing their own theater and becoming the architects of their own worlds.

Benefits of Imaginary Play

"Rah! Rah! I'm gonna get ya!" I heard my five-year old's muffled voice from our imagination zone and tiptoed closer to listen (and to ensure he wasn't talking to his little sister). Through the crack in the door I watched, enraptured, as he lifted his LEGO pirate figure into the air and chased it after a robber figure who had apparently stolen the pirate's treasures. Witnessing my children play in this manner never fails to beguile.

Imaginary play, pretend play or make-believe—call it what you will—involves acting out scenes or stories that include multiple perspectives, such as my teddy bears and me enjoying a tea party, or my Playmobil firefighters saving the cat stuck in the tree. These narratives, while made up by the child, are often based in reality, books, media, or movies and reflect social situations that are emotionally charged, at least for the child. A baby crying, hungry and in need of a diaper change. A police officer chasing a bank robber. A troupe of ballerinas preparing for a big performance. Throughout the past century, theorists and researchers have identified the values of such imaginative play and crowned it as a vital component to the healthy social and emotional development of a child.

By virtue of acting out scenes and creating worlds, children develop empathy, perspective, language, communication, and problem-solving skills. For instance, Brian Howe and Katherine Hovel argue that "experiences in role-play… foster both intellectual and ethical development. Role-play in small groups can increase the child's self-esteem [as] each member has the opportunity to contribute. Less able students have an unusual opportunity to experience success [while] gifted students have an opportunity to express their creativity. These experiences validate the importance of all children to themselves and to each other, and help each child gain a positive sense of self and personal agency."

When they take on these varying points of view—as they do when dressing up and role playing or playing with dolls or action figures—they develop the all-important Theory of Mind. They're able to understand that another person's knowledge, beliefs, emotions and intentions differ from their own, and then apply that understanding to successfully navigate social interactions. It's what allows many children, at around the age of three or four, to "get" that even though they don't mind having water sprayed in their face, their baby brother might.

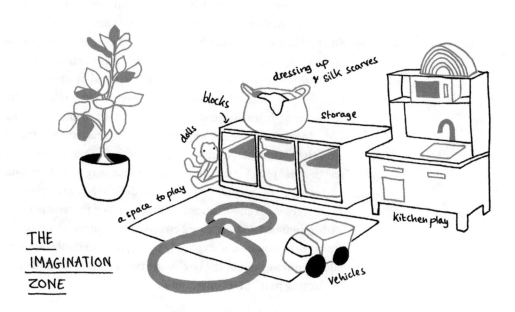

THE
IMAGINATION
ZONE

The construction of a Theory of Mind implies the development of the executive function, "which includes the ability to plan, organize, inhibit responses, think abstractly and reallocate mental resources . . . necessary to complete tasks that require complex behavior or multiple steps". With it comes the ability to regulate thoughts, feelings, and actions. It's what—sometimes— helps a child hold back when the impulse to whack a friend's head with a lightsaber strikes. Self-regulation in the face of an onslaught of powerful emotions is a cornerstone of maturity. Luckily, this too can be nourished through pretend play. As children are given license to assume a variety of roles, taking on these different roles allows them to collect "data" on the different angles and experiences that a single situation involves, which then translates into a better ability to stay calm during real-life challenges.

Imaginary play also encourages creativity. As children flex their storytelling muscles, they enhance their cognitive flexibility, which can be defined as "the disposition to consider diverse context-specific information elements while deciding on how to solve a problem or to execute a task in a variety of domains and to adapt one's problem solving or task execution in case the context changes or new information becomes present". This strengthens their adaptability, confidence, and awareness of self, environment, and others. So, as my five-year-old is chasing the robber away from the pirate's loot, he's simultaneously *running* away from the pirate. He's holding both perspectives in tandem. He's alternating between considering both the best route of escape *and* the best plan for the chase. And he's coming up with twists and turns to his plot that surprise and delight *him* as he goes along. In fact, research shows an actual link between pretend play in early childhood and increased creative performance later on in life, since "being aware and explicitly taking into account the context allow thinking 'out of the box' while consciously and deliberately neglecting particular constraints".

Linked to but not synonymous with pretend play is constructive play: the building of worlds with blocks or LEGO or creating train tracks and dollhouses. Children famously *love* to create little worlds and then play God. They get to inhabit, manipulate, and eventually destroy these worlds at their whim.

Construction play is a powerful way for children to learn core concepts such as . . . well, gravity for one! They learn about mass, shape, surface, height, and size and concepts like heavy and light as well as spatial positioning such as above and below, next to, and far away from. They explore patterns and sequence, symmetry and asymmetry, balance and depth. These are all the building blocks (pun intended) of later success in numeracy, literacy, math, and divergent problem solving.

So the imaginary zone is a space in our home that is dedicated to constructing worlds and inhabiting them, whether the children themselves are the inhabitants (dressing up and acting out a scene, which usually begins at around age three) or they're using toys—dolls, action figures, animals—to act for them.

This type of play is incredibly healing. Children can "step outside the restrictions of their real lives and explore meaning free from the constraints of what's possible for a child". Think back to when you last had a truly uncomfortable encounter. Perhaps your boss criticized you unfairly in front of your colleagues, or the supermarket checkout lady was rude, or your mother-in-law berated your parenting skills and offered your children candy without your consent. When we have emotionally charged interactions, most of us replay the scene over and over in our heads. If we're honest, we'll admit that we sometimes even speak it out loud, rehearsing what we *should have said* or how we *wish* we had reacted or what we *intend* to do next time. If we're in touch with our feelings, we might journal about it, dance it out, sing it out, or take it to our kickboxing class. If we're talkers, we'll tell (and retell) our husbands, sisters, or soul friends about what happened—how unfair, shocking or scandalous it was. This is how we process as adults. This is how we play out scenes from our real lives, trying to make sense of them through story telling and reenactment.

Kids are doing all that and more through imaginative play. That's where they're exploring the scary, icky, confusing, or exciting themes in their lives. This is what is happening when your three-year-old pretends to be the doctor, giving their stuffed elephant a shot just days after she received a vaccination. They really don't need much stuff for imaginary play. What they need instead is a few tools to project the scenes they want to reenact and process.

Toys for Imaginary Play

The toys, or *tools* as I'd rather we think of them, for this type of play fall into three main categories: construction, small world play, and role-play. Construction demands some type of building block in order to create the symbolic reference to the house, the castle, the hospital, the school, the fire station, the pirate ship, or whatever "world" your child wants to inhabit.

Construction

This type of play makes use of any toy with which a child can build a symbolic world, from raw, unpolished wooden blocks—a fan favorite—all the way to the intricate pieces of highly detailed Lego sets and everything in between. Think of train tracks, various shaped blocks, arcs, planks, domes, pyramids, cylinders, and spheres. Magnetic tiles, stacking rainbows or rubber blocks can all be used to create worlds.

Small World Play

Small World Play involves figures that inhabit the world the child has constructed. People or animals, vehicles or any other item that can be anthropomorphized, or imagined as having

humanistic characteristics. This allows children to project their own perspective on the small world inhabitant. Trains, for example, may inhabit the train tracks the child constructed and hold social interactions and human emotions such as jealousy, ambition, or generosity, as in *Thomas the Tank Engine* or the *Little Engine that Could*.

Role-Play

Role-play may require items that allow children to dress up and temporarily transform ourselves symbolically into someone else. This can range from simple Waldorf-esque silk scarves to a full no-detail-spared, bling-bling Princess Sophia costume, complete with lilac silk elbow-length gloves and her famous amulet necklace. Simple silk scarves can be imagined to be anything and never lose their pliancy to become whatever a child imagines (A pair of handcuffs! A waitress's apron! A doctor's scrubs!).

A dress-up box that offers a range of hats, scarves, jackets, and accessories such as glasses, gloves, and bags can offer hours of imaginary play. I recommend using items that were discarded from your own closet or Grandma's, rather than the readymade costumes sold by the dozen every Halloween. Pieced together individually (as opposed to a complete, and perfect, package brought to you by Disney), the self-made costume offers the child an opportunity for creativity and self-expression. That said, we do enjoy the Princess Sophia purple sparkling flamboyance I described earlier.

Doll play is dramatic play as well. In my own attempt to maintain some minimalism in this zone, I do not purchase single-use toys such as a dolly bed or stroller. Instead, you might use a simple cart as a stroller, and any toy basket—or even a large Tupperware container—as the doll's bed, a cardboard box as her table, and so on. In other words, let your kids improvise and use the household items they can find rather than outfitting their doll play with specific accessories available for sale.

The nature of role-play requires that children move around when acting out a ninja scene or a hostage-in-distress rescue. So dramatic play likely infiltrates all the play zones. If your child is going through a mermaid phase, for example, she may remain dressed up even when she plays with Play-Doh later, or she might *need* to make some Play-Doh shell friends *for* her mermaid play. As we later explore the movement and quiet zones, you'll find that dressing up and getting into character can happen *anywhere*, as it should. My four-year-old spent the better part of a year dressed as a pirate, something I thoroughly supported, recognizing this crucial and healthy developmental stage.

However, having a place for all things, and for all things a place, is key to keeping a decluttered, streamlined environment. So, I suggest that, at least at the end of every day, all dress-up items return to rest in their spot. If space is too tight for a large container in the imagination zone, relocate this particular container to the quiet zone or the movement zone. Your choice.

Setting Up Your Imagination Zone

In my experience, children spend most of their time in the imagination zone. Therefore, it is best to locate it close to where the adults spend most of their time. Usually this means near the kitchen and/or living room. A corner of your living room or a den or enclave nearby might be the perfect location for your imagination zone.

You'll need a surface on which to build small worlds, a place to store the construction toys and the inhabitants, and a container for your dress-up items. If space allows, you might also add a play kitchen or pretend workbench.

In Montessori and Reggio Emilia schools, all materials are typically displayed and available in open shelf units or baskets. This allows children to manipulate their storage systems on their own. However, at least in a Montessori environment, where materials are not seen as toys to be played with any old way, this only works with a staff who continuously ensures the "correct" usage of such materials and helps the children to tidy up. It also works only if there's an appropriately minimal number of items available.

Personally, I prefer most of our toys to be in closed containers, with few open baskets. This makes cleanup easier and discourages dumping all toys out at once. It also helps children focus on the toys they're working with rather than being distracted by shiny objects everywhere.

My favorite storage system for toys is the Ikea Trofast unit, which provides both a perfect surface to work on and a set of bins of varying sizes to store toys. It ticks all my boxes: it's wooden, has white bins and is very inexpensive. If you have more than one child, it may be helpful to have more than one of these units. Each child needs their own surface to work on and you'll likely want more toys when you have more children, although if space doesn't allow for it, don't squeeze. The key is to ensure that each child has the space to build their worlds, be it a classroom out of Magna-Tiles with Playmobil people nervously attending their first day of school, or a castle out of LEGO where knights fight off dragons.

You can experiment with a table and chairs in this zone, but I find them unnecessary. Children work best sitting on the floor without having to manage the balancing act of sitting on a chair, or they work well standing up. Avoid overly fluffy carpets in this zone; they're not conducive to balancing block towers, and it's all too easy to lose a LEGO firefighter helmet in a shaggy rug. If your rug is too fluffy for train tracks, roads, or castles, place a large tray or a sanded wooden board on the floor to help stabilize structures. A large tray is also a wonderful tool at clean up time, should your child not be ready to dismantle their masterpiece yet. Just pop the tray on a shelf and save it for tomorrow.

Speaking of, it's particularly inspiring to have a few shelves with some well-placed items. A shelf could be the perfect spot for that essential oil diffuser and a cascading plant or the proud

acting

screen writing

architecture

cinematography

directing

haute couture fashion

Creativity

Engineering

cuisine & hospitality

Child rearing

urban planning

saving the day!

empathy

Confidence!

zoology

display for any prize constructions your child wants to share with the world. It's also a great spot to place some items that remind you of your own values and the energy you want to infuse into this space.

Small Imagination Zones

If space is tight, you could try using your coffee table or side table and double their function as an imagination zone. Rather than having adult items in the living room, clear out the coffee-table books and use that spot for a basket of figures or blocks. If you have a TV console in your family space, move it as far back as possible (or get rid of it altogether) and use that spot as a surface for imagination play. You could also have the TV mounted on the wall to free up the footprint underneath. If you do have a TV in the area you want to dedicate as the imagination zone, cover it with a tablecloth during the day so that it doesn't pose a distraction.

If you have no surface to dedicate, repurpose a container—the wider and flatter the better—or a shallow cardboard box. A large shoe box, for example. Store the play items in the box and simply close it and store it under the sofa or bed when not in use. Remember, the goal of this zone is to offer the opportunity to design worlds, build them, control them, manipulate them, and act out plots and scenes within them. Kids do not need much space to accomplish that.

I've had clients who are able to create on-the-go imagination zones even in a caravan or trailer while world schooling (traveling the world and educating children through life experiences). All this requires is a lie-flat drawstring bag with some blocks and figures inside. Lay the bag flat on a tray, the table or the floor, create a world, and play to your heart's content. When you're done, pull the string to store. Easy as pie.

Action Steps

- Set up your imagination zone. This is the area in the home dedicated to children building small worlds and inhabiting them with people, animals, or vehicles.

- The imagination zone is the place for construction toys (such as blocks), dramatic play toys (such as dolls or work tools or dress-up items like silk scarves or discarded hats), and small world inhabitants (such as animals, vehicles or people).

- The imagination zone requires storage for the toys and a surface on which to work (which can be the floor), and would benefit from a shelf (which is a space saver) where you can display your children's masterpieces.

- Remember that imaginative, pretend, or make-believe play is crucial to children's social and emotional development. It fosters empathy, problem-solving skills, self-regulation, and communication.

- Support your child's imaginative play by offering tools for role-play and dressing up and for playing with dolls or with small figures—anything that involves acting out a narrative of the child's choosing.

- Keep all of these toys in your imagination zone: imaginative play and construction play blend well together as children engineer their worlds and then act out scenes within them.

Messy Zone

Chapter

10

Art has the role in education of helping children become like themselves instead of more like everyone else.

Sydney Gurewitz Clemens, *Art in the Classroom*

Benefits of Messy Play

Have you ever felt the squish of mud between your fingers? Sifted sand through your toes? Or impressed your painted handprints onto a blank piece of paper? Manipulating the materials around us—whether natural or synthetic—affords us a literal experience of authorship. We notice that when we squeeze the Play-Doh, it takes on the form of our palms. When we pack the sand with water, it fashions itself after our bucket. We find physical evidence that our actions shape the world around us.

When children are allowed to get messy, they develop curiosity and imagination, and they strengthen their natural urge to explore and discover the world. Rather than reigning in their inquisitiveness, messy play capitalizes on their natural tendencies, offering plentiful opportunities to learn and grow. The aim of the messy zone is to provide a space where children are allowed to explore through their senses and express themselves visually and tacitly.

Creativity and Self-Expression

There are endless ways in which creativity expresses itself in the world—poetically crafting words together, mathematical prowess, movement and dance. Messy, sensory play such as painting and sculpting is but one such opportunity for creativity, not the epitome of it. We'd be wise to depart from the dualistic thinking that some children are "born talented" and others aren't, based on how lifelike and realistic their depictions are. As Picasso said, "All children are born artists. The problem is to remain an artist as we grow up."

The opportunity to express ourselves artistically by creating drawings, paintings, sculpture, sandcastles, or Play-Doh soups is not about the end result. It's about the process, the act of shaping, molding, mixing, and brushing. In these inquiries we probe our own agency as creators and find fascination in our capacity to influence the world around us, delighting in our ability to make something where nothing existed before.

"Look, Mommy! Grayson's hand looks *just* like a turkey! Good job, Grayson!" squealed Miss Arielle as she presented Megan, Grayson's mommy, with the mandatory hand-shaped-turkey decoration to adorn their refrigerator at Thanksgiving.

"I just don't get it," Megan relayed to me on our coffee date. "Both she and I know clearly that Grayson didn't make that turkey picture. She must have sat there moving his hand or sticking the pasta on *for* him. What's the point? I didn't sign him up for preschool to teach *her* to color in the lines."

Megan got me thinking. Why *do* we collectively seem to force kids' art into something we recognize as "good"? Do we parents so badly need some kind of "proof" that our children are doing well that we're willing to settle for a thinly veiled lie? Do we think that only those creations of our tiny humans that are immediately recognizable are valuable?

Sure, there's a time and a place for learning to follow instructions, color in the lines and create art that others can easily interpret. And some children may need more support in reaching developmental milestones in their handiwork or hand-eye coordination, but what if we were to cherish and honor our children's creativity, exactly as it develops, naturally? What if we were to find value in what they express, without measuring it up against a "what your four-year-old should know" chart (pincer grasp, check!).

If we are to encourage our children in their creative endeavors, we'd do well to learn from Carol Dweck's notion of a growth mindset. As Dweck puts it, "In a growth mindset, people believe that their most basic abilities can be developed through dedication and hard work—brains and talent are just the starting

I'm noticing...
I see that...

I'm curious about...
Tell me about...

point. This view creates a love of learning and a resilience that is essential for great accomplishment."

One of the core tenets of Dweck's thesis is that our children benefit when we focus on the process rather than the outcome. It's true for math, for learning to swim and for artistic expression. When we look to create a zone for our children to express themselves, we must understand this isn't a space for creating masterpieces. We're not trying to push our children into "productivity" or "résumé building" or being a "prodigy." Instead, we're allowing them a space for exploring tactile, messy materials—if something thought-provoking comes out, then so be it.

With this in mind, it won't serve our children to push, reward, punish, cajole, manipulate or even praise artistic "talent." Talent is something that people foster through hard work and deep intrinsic interest and motivation, not through being coaxed or labeled by their loving grown-up. Adding a layer of parental involvement inhibits this internal drive to create. Stay interested and supportive but also slightly detached emotionally.

So, what should you do when your child is busy creating? Sit on your hands and zip your lips. Or better yet, go and treat yourself to a homemade facial in the bathroom. In other words, buzz off and let them play. If your child shows you their picture, Play-Doh mound or sandcastle and wants your feedback, smile, encourage, take interest, and celebrate them without praising. Here are some sample scripts:

- Take note of specific choices they've made: "I notice a pink sky! That's an interesting choice. Can you tell me more about it?"; "I see a beautiful mountain, is it from your imagination or from a memory of hiking?"
- Tell them how it makes you feel or ask them how it makes them feel: "I feel surprised when I see that bear inside the ocean!"; "I feel happy when I look at that big smile you

drew on the horse!"; "How do *you* feel when you look at your sculpture?"

- Point out their process, and the choices they've made: "It was hard to get the clay to stay in that shape, but you focused on it and succeeded!"; "You really wanted to make her fur look fluffy, I saw you copying that photograph so carefully. It looks so lovely and fluffy!"; "You're mixing it round and round"; "You're pinching it and letting it go!"; "You're really working hard on that."
- Ask them how they feel about it and what they are thinking of, as they make it.

You're reaching all the way to the top!

I see a lot of red and purple!

If you can't resist the urge to praise, Dweck suggests you refrain from person (or trait) praise: "If children are often told that they are "good at this" or "smart" when they succeed at tasks, they may become more interested in performance goals than in new learning when faced with challenges." However, when they do fail, then they conclude they are not as smart as they were told, which will undermine their self-perception. So if you're bursting from the inside out to offer some compliment to your little Van Gogh, focus on process praise—feedback that praises the effort they have expended at formulating problem-solving strategies— so that your child might become more interested in learning goals, knowing that improving their competencies will gradually allow them to deal with more complex challenges. Yet, keep in mind that art is not a problem to be solved. There are no right or wrong answers when it comes to artistic creation. Truth be told, there isn't even a consensus on the nature or definition of art. There are no universally accepted standards to evaluate what makes a good or valuable work of art. So, if the quality of productions by Jean-Michel Basquiat, Jackson Pollock, Damien Hirst or Ai Wei Wei are still controversial among experts, who are we to judge the work of our innocent kids?

169   Messy Zone

Sensory and Scientific Exploration

Children need to get messy in order to make sense of the world around them. Young toddlers, in the oral fixation phase (up until around eighteen months) will put everything in their mouths, including mud, soccer socks straight from the dirty hamper, and that cat furball they found under the couch (those little chubby fingers, gosh darn it). It can be incredibly inconvenient. However, in the words of Sue Gascoyne, "There is a danger that we judge the external appearance of mess, chaos and disorder, rather than recognizing children's systematic, ordered and purposeful investigation and underlying sophisticated thinking. Comparable to judging Newton by his overflowing wastepaper bin rather than his theories that forever changed our understanding of the world, if we are too focused on the appearance of disarray and mess, we may miss the signs of a genius at work."

Through feeling of things, mouthing of things, rolling around in things, they learn. They learn temperature: Is this hot, cold, warm? They learn texture: Is this rough, smooth, bumpy? They learn volume: How much of this can I fit in my hand? Shapes: This has a sharp edge, whereas this is rounded. And consistency: Is this liquid, solid, somewhere in the middle?

Those little fingers are scrutinizing everything and absorbing useful information about the way the world works. You and I realize, when looking upon a chunk of wood, that our hand can smack into it—hard. However, when we see a puddle of water, we know our hand can splash through it and that the hand will be wet as a result. Our little guys don't know that yet, and no matter how many books we read to them, they'll never understand unless they experience it. They need to learn it by trying it for themselves. This is the beauty and importance of sensory exploration: it's both artistic *and* scientific in nature.

Through testing out different materials, our children develop awareness not only for how these materials behave but also for what they can expect from their own bodies. They naturally develop fine and gross motor skills—such as pincer grasping a bead or lifting a bottle of paint—as they stretch their physical abilities to match their desires to explore.

Calming Sensory Play

Such explorations are not only creatively, scientifically, and sensorially satisfying but they also have the capacity to be calming and relaxing. When's the last time you painted? Played in the sand or kneaded some Play-Doh? It's hard to stop, isn't it? That's because sensory play is great for soothing our anxieties and frustrations and regaining a sense of control and presence with what we're currently focused on. There is even evidence to suggest that sensory play supports language development, cognitive, social, and emotional skills, and even enhances our memory.

SENSORY VOCABULARY

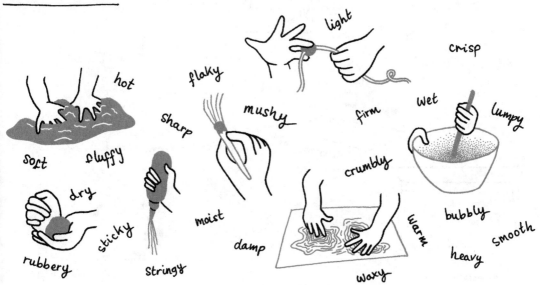

How to Set Up a Messy Zone

Look around your home and identify a spot where you could offer your child the chance to get messy. Ideally, find a place that has no carpet (save yourself some heartache) and is close to a faucet (for washing off grubby hands or filling water for paint). If you can, dedicate a worktable—as small or large as fits your space—to messy play. You'll want a storage unit of some kind, a caddy, a shelf within a cupboard, or some boxes on a shelf system. I would advise against storing your art supplies in an open and accessible fashion at your children's' height until they are mature enough to keep such a display orderly.

If space is tight, your messy zone could consist of just a large plastic tray that you whip out from under the couch, place on the kitchen table, and—*voila!* Add a box of supplies and—*presto!*—a

MESSY ZONE SOLUTIONS

a material cart

an easel

the bathtub

the kitchen sink

a plastic table cloth

a sensory table

a baking tray

an under washing machine tray

messy zone has appeared. Another option is to use an easel or large paper roll, with a caddie for supplies that you can easily fold and store away when not in use. If you're worried about the mess, contain it. I love to use a large floor tray *under* our small sensory table to catch the debris of my toddler's sand play. A large nylon sheet taped to the ground works wonders as well and doubles as a pleasing paint canvas.

Recycled Materials

You'll be amazed how many wonderful materials you probably have lying around the house or passing through it on a regular basis. Old cartons, cans, jars, and of course, the fan favorite, cardboard boxes, make for *wonderful* items to cut up, paint on or glue together. Plus, no harm, no foul.

Art Supplies

Of course, in your messy zone, you can incorporate all of the usual suspects: glue, scissors, paint, markers, crayons, stamps, watercolors, tape of all kinds. As our kids grow, we offer more complex or "dangerous" materials such as staplers and glue guns. You can also add in some razzle-dazzle by way of beads, sequins, stickers, pipe cleaners, ribbon, fabric, magazine scraps, and buttons.

Sensory Tables and Tubs

In addition to "art materials," I would look for anything that can be enjoyed as a sensory exploration—food items often work best, especially for young toddlers who will be eating what we offer them anyhow. Still, be mindful of choking hazards and watch little ones who are prone to mouthing small items. That said, dried rice, beans, lentils, and pasta make for mesmerizing play for little and big ones alike. Serve with measuring cups, spoons, and bowls.

Another way of getting that same pouring and sifting experience is with pom-poms, balls, or perhaps sand. If you do brave a sand sensory bin in your home, opt for kinetic sand, which is far easier to keep contained (check the internet for homemade recipes) and less likely to be found between your toddler's toes. Although, brace yourself; it will happen.

Water provides the ultimate sensory play and can be offered in a bin (such as a storage box), in the bath or sink, or in a water table. Paired with some funnels, pipettes, or simple cups, you can't go wrong. For older kids, liven it up with some plastic water animals, water beads, or dye capsules.

Maker's Space

My most prized childhood memories are made of hot glue and recycled junk. When I was a child, we used to visit Jerusalem often. Even though we lived in London until I was eight, Israel felt like our second home and eventually became our real home. The Israel Museum was my all-time favorite place to visit. It had an award-winning children's wing, and buried in a corner was the renowned Recycling Room.

As an adult, I realize there was nothing truly magical about this room—a few child-size tables, a row of hot glue guns, some plastic bins with odd bits of recycled trash—discarded CDs, toilet-paper rolls, egg cartons. To a child, it was pure wizardry. My sister and I would sit for hours, tongues sticking out in concentration as we fashioned our cardboard-buttons-and-wire masterpieces.

As your children grow, their interests in messy play may expand beyond Play-Doh, lentils, and water. They may be ready for tinkering and *making*. With very little fanfare, you can transform a corner of your home into a maker's space that allows your child to become the mad scientist, the visionary entrepreneur, the slick fashion designer. All you need is a table—or a tray if no table space is available—and a box of tinkering items—think odd bits and pieces, hole-less keys, pipes, etc.

Handling Mess with Grace and Boundaries

In a recent survey I ran, 36 percent of parents said they "couldn't handle" messy play. So, if crayons on your reclaimed wood farm table has you breaking out in hives, know that you're not alone. Given that tactile play is essential to childhood development and that your sanity may depend on moments in which your children are absorbed in creative play, here are some useful tips to "handle" the mess:

- Buy washable everything. Washable crayons, markers and paints are available, which means they easily come off clothes, carpets, and walls.
- Use protection. Use a nylon tablecloth or dedicate an old bedsheet for floor coverage when your little Jackson Pollack is at work. Aprons or dedicated overalls may be a wise choice too.

HOW TO AVOID MESSY
ZONE DISASTERS

Let's take it outside today and keep our house clean.

Yes, sweetie, you can do the clay. But-here-first please sweep up these beans.

Not today, honey. Sorry- I can't face the clean up...

Keep messy materials out of reach until. children are mature enough for full access

- Take it outside. If you have access to the outdoors, why not set up sand, water, paint, or tinkering on a spot in the shade? You get a double whammy: art *and* nature time, all at once.
- Take it to the tub. When I couldn't face the cleanup, I used to put my kids in the (empty) tub with some shaving cream, food coloring, watercolors, or even markers. (This one might require supervision in case they turn on the tap.)
- Dedicate a wall. We have painted one of the walls in our home with chalkboard paint, and whenever a child takes a marker to the wall, which happens about every Tuesday, we redirect them: "If you want to draw on the wall, go use the chalkboard wall." It *kinda* works. We still have crayon marks everywhere.
- Be discerning. Don't put out all your art materials at once. And choose materials wisely and in attunement to your child's age, stage, and temperament. If your *threenager* likes to distribute glitter everywhere but the tray she's working on, opt for other materials that won't make quite as much of a mess.
- Create boundaries. Teach your kids how to treat the messy zone. Don't leave this lesson up to chance; they won't respect the space if you don't teach them to. And don't wait until it's too late—that is, after they've wreaked havoc and your fuse is spent. Respecting materials, putting one thing away before starting the next thing, and cleaning up afterward—those are habits that need to be reinforced daily, throughout childhood.
- Say no. Before you embrace your inner mud goddess and open the floodgates of creativity for your child, remember that a happy parent is more important than any messy play. If you're going to "lose it" if they make a little mess, save it for a time when you have a little more patience. We can't always handle things that make us anxious, so if you're having "one of those days," offer yourself compassion and set a limit with your child in order to protect your relationship (better to say no to painting now than lose it with them later).

- Most important of all, address your mindset. Even though you should teach your children to respect the space, and even though you are allowed to say no, you can still work on loosening up a bit. Breathing deeply and asking yourself: What story am I telling myself about mess? Where did I learn that mess was so bad? Self-awareness is the first step to letting go of our hang-ups and moving into a more fluid and flowing energy with our kids.

Strategies for Displaying, Storing, Cataloging, and Decluttering Artwork

"Look at my unicorn!" My eldest grabbed my husband's elegant hand with his chubby, grubby fingers and yanked him toward our messy zone. He'd painstakingly created a unicorn out of sculpting clay, and it had just come out of the oven, hardened to a satisfying plastic-like consistency. He had made his own toy.

The unicorn was proudly placed on our "exhibition" shelf along with other recent creations: a wolf mask, a small wooden car, a self-portrait. There isn't an artist alive, to my knowledge, who doesn't want their creations seen and admired. Given that all children are artists, perhaps this applies to all children.

Still, when I see children's art *plastered* all over the walls or draped on the fridge, the designer in me gets a migraine and goes to sleep. In my efforts to advocate for minimalistic, beautiful environments, I think the best answer is to create a display area. A shelf for the 3-D items, a corkboard, magnetic board or a hanging-line for the 2-D.

Set yourself a goal to rotate these pieces of art in and out every month or so. And what will you do with your offspring's masterpieces, then, you ask? My own preference is to take digital photos of the special ones and include them in an album for each child's birthday. But you could create digital albums or simply have them in your photos. Then, I save the very favorite pieces in a storage container and recycle the rest.

I know it can be hard to let go of your child's artwork, but it's usually necessary to declutter at least a majority of it, to keep our homes manageable.

Remember that despite its name, this zone is by no means messy in and of itself. Rather, it invites messy, sensory, tactile play—the type of play where your hands are touching and manipulating various materials, where you can immerse yourself in projects and creativity. In fact, keeping it clean, well-organized, and well-stocked is a key to success. I find I need to organize the zone (sharpen pencils, replenish paper, clean surfaces, and sweep) about two or three times per week.

Action Steps

- Set up your Messy Zone. This is the space in your home where your child is allowed to play with art supplies and sensory materials that can get messy.

- Use a dedicated table, a large tray, an easel, or a huge sheet of plastic taped to the floor. Or if you're tight for space, use the bathtub or shower.

- Create a storage system that allows your child to reach only the materials they can currently be trusted with. Put the rest of the materials out of reach and take them out only when you can supervise.

- Keep the messy zone tidy! Use containers that work for you and your kids to keep the materials neat and fresh. In general, it works best to allow only one project out at a time.

- Recycle. Keep a big recycling bag in this space so there are always some cartons or boxes for your kids to paint or build with (the end results generally find their way into the recycling bin anyway).

- Only allow projects that you can handle. Does playing with water give you goosebumps? Does the idea of cleaning up a paint mess make you itch? Forget it, not worth it. Your kids need a relaxed parent more than they need to paint.

- Take care of your materials: frequently sharpen the pencils, throw out the dry markers, refill the paints. If you keep this zone well-stocked and inviting, it will be used regularly. If it becomes too hard to find an eraser or blank sheet of paper, watch as it becomes neglected.

- Display. Have a wall or shelf designated as your gallery so that your children can really enjoy and take pride in the fruits of their labor.

Movement Zone

Chapter

11

Watching a child makes it obvious that the development of his mind comes through his movements. **Maria Montessori, The Absorbent Mind**

I'm not telling you anything new when I say that children need to move, and today's children need to move more. If you're not living under a rock, you know that obesity is the number-one threat to many children today, and you know that obesity is linked to both nutrition and to an increasingly sedentary lifestyle.

Unfortunately, this sedentary lifestyle is starting earlier and earlier, with babies being confined to bouncers, strollers, car seats and highchairs for much of their day. As Richard Louv writes in *Last Child in the Woods*, "One U.S. researcher suggests that a generation of children is not only being raised indoors but is being confined to even smaller spaces. Jane Clark, a University of Maryland professor of kinesiology (the study of human movement), calls them "containerized kids"—they spend more and more time in car seats, high chairs, and even baby seats for watching TV. When small children do go outside, they're often placed in containers—strollers—and pushed by walking or jogging parents."

Louv makes a compelling case for getting kids outdoors and enjoying nature in free, unstructured, and unsupervised play. I couldn't agree more. Creating a movement zone does *not* replace getting into nature as much as possible. Still, we all need to spend considerable time at home, doing life.

The fact is that children were designed to move. Watch any other mammal cub and you'll notice your eyeballs darting around in your sockets as you try to keep up with them. Playing physically—touching, rolling, climbing, sliding, swinging, pulling, pushing, grabbing, stomping, squeezing, spinning, running, jumping, hopping, skipping, twirling— are all expressions of a healthy, learning child. Humans have not evolved to sit quietly. We have not been shaped—neither ergonomically nor mentally—to stay at a desk twiddling our thumbs, or to sit "crisscross applesauce" in a circle for any length of time. One of the main challenges (indeed, projects) of schools is to train children to *stay still.*

It's become apparent that we need to reexamine the value of this goal: Do we *want* people to sit still? Why? Just as we distract children with busy work and scheduled activities only to struggle as adults to learn to meditate and "do nothing," so too we train children to "sit still" for their entire childhoods only to struggle to "work out" and get moving as adults.

Instead, we should preserve children's natural tendency to move and offer approval and support for their bouncy, high energy ways, even dedicating a zone for it.

Ultimately, what we can provide indoors will never rival what Mother Nature can offer, but it can supplement it for those sick days, those times when Mama is cooking or those moments of high energy. Put it this way: If your kids are climbing the walls *anyway*, why not give them something to climb?

Movement Is Learning

You know that brain fog and restlessness that set in when you've been slouched in your seat for a while? Yeah, kids get that too. Only worse, because they're literally designed to be moving . . . a lot. Conversely, you know that sharp, laser-focused energy you sometimes get after an invigorating workout? That's what happens when our bodies move: we achieve better focus, faster cognitive processing, and more successful memory retention. When the body is active, we increase blood flow to the brain, improve neurological health, and experience mental clarity. In short, movement is crucial to learning.

Kids have the natural urge to move&Space missing. Ever watched a child playing in the park? You've likely seen the level of physical workout they are capable of — they break a sweat, pant, and *keep going.*

I believe it's our role as parents to preserve, protect, and serve our children's innate desire to move their bodies and honor their bodies' need to move—to lift heavy things, to push, to pull, to jump, run, throw, roll, squat, twirl. But the fact that this sensory experience is actually how kids metabolize information is vitally important. Climbing steps as we count "One, two, three . . ." provides a building block of kinesthetic learning that serves their deep grasp of these concepts. Feeling the thrust as a child propels forward on a swing and the draw as they fly back makes the concepts of "forward" and "back" real to them. Experiencing the static friction and the slippery pull of gravity on a slide makes the ideas of "up" and "down" have meaning and weight.

Movement isn't just to clear the brain fog, it's to integrate knowledge into our systems through our bodies.

Setting Up Your Movement Zone

A movement zone can be as simple and minimalistic as a foldable gymnastics mat you bring out from time to time, and as elaborate as a full ninja-warrior run in your basement. Like all the zones, it depends on your budget and space allowances. And, like all the zones, it's more about a mindset and intention than it is about a physical space. The mindset that movement is healthy will inform how "preciously" you decorate your home, how stressed you are over the state of your walls and how lavishly you invest in your furniture.

Your movement zone needn't be a dedicated spot: it can move around. Especially if you're tight for space, simply leave some floor room *somewhere* that you can easily dedicate for rolling around. Watch for sharp corners on coffee tables, or nearby stairs.

If you have a little more room, piece together a few options— an indoor swing, a gym mat, and a balance board or wagon, for example. Got even more space? Add a climbing dome or rock-climbing wall.

Rather than the items in it, it's your mindset and how you encourage movement that makes a movement zone.

Reclaim Play

Kid-Friendly Now, Pristine Later

Personally, my couch *is* for jumping on. Don't get me wrong, I am a designer by trade and I care a *lot* about the visual experience of my home. However, I have come to appreciate the freedom my kids earn and the chill I reclaim when I invest less and care less about our home while my kids are still young. There will be plenty of time for pristine decor in a few years. For now, I'm prioritizing opportunities for my kids to roll, run, and jump, even indoors. I can still choose items that I like, just not those I'm likely to want to protect.

Indoor Swings

My absolute favorite piece for any home with kids has to be an indoor swing. The possibilities that open up with a single ceiling hook (professionally installed, if you're not über handy, please!) are endless. We have a plethora of amazing sensory swings, varying from the high end to the ultra-simple, and we rotate them regularly. Every few days my children find a new swing (brought in from rotation) hanging in the living room or in their bedroom.

A single swivel-hook swing allows 360 degrees of spinning, so a child can twirl around on the spot. And the various swings that you can rotate in and out offer different physical challenges and movement opportunities. A trapeze swing allows hanging upside down or buddying up with a sibling on the bottom while one climbs to the top. A cocoon swing provides a cozy, dark hammock where you can envelop yourself into a tight ball and experience sensory pressures that many children need. A surfboard swing lets your children stand on a large board and ride invisible waves.

Of course, as with any movement, swings can be a little risky. But therein lies the fun. Not to mention the valuable body awareness, vestibular sensation, and balance stimulation that's core to the swinging motion.

Proprioception, or body awareness, refers to the feedback our brains receive from pressure receptors in joints and stretch receptors in our muscles, which enable us to gain a sense of where our bodies are in space and where our limbs are in relation to our core. This spatial awareness is a crucial part of healthy development. It allows us to perform simple tasks such as buttoning our shirt or bouncing a ball without looking and planning each step. Healthy proprioception can be supported through movement, such as swinging, hanging upside down, and twirling.

The stimulation of the vestibular system, including the inner ear, (as well as the brain, the eyes and the soles of the feet), keeps our inner ear fluid more supple and tells us our body's position in relation to gravity. It's how we balance our head on our spines, how our heads remain upright even when we sway our bodies back and forth. When children are spinning, rolling, and twirling, they're naturally developing their balance. It's our job to support that development with their environment.

It's true that swings require a little bit of space in a home—although we have always had ours smack-dab in the middle of the action in our living room. There are plenty of creative ways to install swings, even in tight spaces, such as doorway swings. Even in our two-bedroom rental in New York, we installed a swing for our three kids. I've had indoor swings in more than four different homes and dealt with many a ceiling and landlord in the process. They've always been worth their weight in independent play.

When indoor swings come up, so do disgruntled partners. So many Reclaim Play students share their trials and tribulations in partner-convincing around hanging a swing in the house. But I enjoy messages every day from happy parents who have happy (albeit upside-down) children.

Having a swing in the home allows a child to go and move their body, hang upside down, swivel, twist, and feel the wind on their face, all without leaving home. And while I strongly

encourage you to *leave home* and go outside, this is a great gap filler for those days and times when you're stuck indoors and your children would otherwise be climbing the walls.

DIY Obstacle Courses

"Floor is lava!" screams five-year-old Jess as she catapults her little body from one pillow to another. An easy way to introduce more movement in your home is to set up simple obstacle courses using pillows and blankets. Dot some pillows around the living room or bedroom and proclaim, "The rug is the sea!" Allow your children to rearrange couch pillows, blankets, yoga mats, rugs, chairs, tables, and stools in ways that challenge them. Once they've mastered an obstacle course as it is, make it harder by increasing the space between the pillows or adding a challenge such as doing it with one hand behind the back, hopping on one leg, or doubling the speed. The idea isn't for you to be consistently entertaining your child and setting challenges for them but rather to make it an acceptable and encouraged mode of play and allowing them to create their own ninja runs in and out of the house.

Moving Furniture Around

Often simply moving the furniture in their bedroom or the living room will spark movement. Pushing a table to one side and making some space or lining some chairs up together to form a balance beam-cum-bench can spark little ones' big imaginations and offer a new DIY Gymboree experience. If you can make a new area they're allowed to jump from, roll from, or climb up on . . . score!

DIY Ball Pit

I have invested in a collection of plastic ball-pit-balls that fill two garbage bags. I bought clear-colored balls because I personally don't enjoy the primary colors usually found in ball pits but love the bubble-like quality of the clear ones. I have a large, round

189

pack and play, but you could make a ball-pit work with any pack and play or even an under-bed linen drawer or the bathtub. Fill whichever container you have with the balls and allow your kids to enjoy it. Sometimes I'll strew out additional baskets, bowls, buckets, and a wagon so they can dig into some dumping, containing, and transporting schemas while they're at it. Speaking of wagons...

Wheels

Wheels are usually reserved for the outdoors, but sometimes we can get away with allowing wheels in the house. A compact ride on a toy, perhaps a wheeled wagon, or even a small scooter board can provide ample opportunity for movement, particularly when lugging friends or siblings around. Of course, as with any movement-zone activity, you know your child best, and you know which activities are too risky. However, remember that some risk is always present as children grow and develop. Babies fall down multiple times on their journey to gaining their balance. It's all part of a healthy childhood.

Forts and Pillows

Simple, old fashioned fort-building with a pile of bed linen or picnic blankets and some pillows to hold them in place as they're draped over the sofa usually offers hours of fun climbing in and out, crawling through and rolling up in rugs and blankets. Help your child see what's possible by building their first forts with them, and then sit back and enjoy as their imagination, skills, and architectural prowess develop and express themselves.

Climbing Walls, Pikler Triangles, Rockers, and Domes

There is a wide range of products designed to provide ample movement opportunities for little ones, from baby Pikler climbing triangles and planks all the way up to full ninja-warrior runs. Climbing domes are a great middle-of-the-road option as they serve both younger and older children, can (potentially) be put away (with effort), and cost less than a more fitted climbing structure. You could think about installing a climbing wall using rock-climbing grips (we have gray, natural-looking rocks so that it doesn't feel "childish" or loud). The options abound. While I don't think the expensive equipment is necessary, if you have the space and the budget, some of these can be solid choices that last for years and offer real independent play value.

Get Creative

There are endless ways to promote movement. Grab some painters' tape and draw a balance beam on the floor. Or a hopscotch. Play old-fashioned movement games like jump rope and Twister. Give your kids a series of challenges like going from room to room slithering on their belly like a snake or hopping on one foot. Or blindfold them and ask them to try to move about the house without the use of their sight. Movement games, prompts, and ideas are all around us all of the time. Following are some tried-and-true options.

Wrestling Matches

"I hate you!" he shouted. "You're the worst mom ever! You ruin my life!" Just this week, my eight-year-old was struggling with some overwhelming emotions. His anger was raging as he spewed unkind words at me and his siblings. I took him to his room to calm down and to protect him and others. There I sat, keeping myself calm and open, waiting for his rage to pass. He looked at me through slitted eyes and gritted teeth. Conjuring up my alter ego, peaceful ninja, I remained as loving toward him as I could, opening my arms to invite him for a long, soothing hug.

After several minutes of hugging, his big eight-year-old body on mine, I began to push him off playfully. He shoved me back, eyes now twinkling, flashing his big eight-year-old gapped-teeth smile at me. Challenge accepted.

191

What ensued was a wrestling battle of epic proportions. A solid thirty minutes of rolling around on our green floor mats as we made big proclamations ("Ha, you wanna piece of *this*?"), pinned each other to the ground and struggled and giggled, giggled, and struggled. We ended our legendary match with matching grins and a restored sense of connection. He's asked me for a rematch every day since.

As our children grow up, we touch them less. We naturally hold babies a lot, snuggle with them, massage them, and roll around playfully with them. As children grow older, they still need this type of primal, visceral bonding, but it becomes more challenging to receive and give it. Making the space for movement in the home is one way of putting playful touch back on your priority list. Whether it's a game of Twister, a dance-off, or a game of "steal Daddy's socks," moving around with our children gets our blood flowing and the emotions stirring.

The movement zone is exactly the place where the more wild playing is invited: wrestling, tickle fights (if your children enjoy being tickled; mine do), dance, and gymnastics can happen. For any of these activities, really, all you need is a piece of the carpet or a mat. Perhaps even allowing this type of play on your bed would work, if you have a floor bed. We enjoy having three foam gym mats that we can spread out in order to form a "dojo" of sorts, or a martial-arts corner. I love this because they fold up and can be put away when not in use. Thus, bringing them out serves as a form of strewing (setting out invitations for play)—my children suddenly remember how they love to do judo rolls or ballet spins when they see the mats are spread out.

Yoga

I've been practicing Yoga since I was fourteen. I credit Yoga with 85 percent of my mental and physical health today. There's really no reason to delay introducing our children to the types of physical (and spiritual) practices that serve us so well as adults.

Children can benefit enormously from yoga practice. Setting up some Yoga mats in your living room and propping up a laptop with some Kids Yoga videos and Namaste. Yoga enhances flexibility, strength, coordination, focus, concentration, and calm.

My children do *not* have a regular Yoga practice, and some of them even roll their eyes at me when I suggest it. However, when I pull out the mats and put on the Kids Yoga videos and start doing it myself, they're drawn to join in. Something to consider in promoting movement at home for both the kids and you.

Dance Parties

Crank up the music, put out some tutus, and shake your booty. Dance is not only a great way of staying physically healthy, but its therapeutic powers of self-expression offer children an emotional outlet. I'm hoping to raise my kids into adults who are comfortable in their bodies, love their bodies, and feel they can express themselves through movement.

To me, there is no surer way to elevate our energy at home, get out of a funk, and reconnect than a kitchen dance party for the family. But offering up dance can be an independent play prompt like any other. You provide the music; they'll do the rest. One fun prop to encourage little performers is a mirror; a nonbreakable acrylic mirror is safest. For kids who love to exhibit their talents, performing for themselves in front of a mirror could take up an entire afternoon.

Action Steps

- Set up your movement zone. Remember that movement is a natural urge. Rather than training children to abide by a sedentary lifestyle, cater to their natural tendency to move. If they're climbing the walls anyway, give them something to climb!

- Keep it as simple as pulling out a foldable gym mat and proclaiming it a wrestling ring or a dance stage. Or if you have more space, set up more elaborate climbing structures. The most crucial piece of the zone is floor space to move.

- Opt for durable, inexpensive, and kid-friendly furniture (albeit to your taste) to ensure that you don't prioritize the pristine couches over our kids' need to jump on them.

- Indoor swings (professionally installed) with a 360-degree swivel hook are the number-one choice for indoor movement. They answer all of the movement needs including spinning, hanging upside down, and climbing and can be helpful for children who are sensory seeking (a high interest in movement, lights, colors, sounds, smells, or tastes that excite them).

- Create endless Movement Zone offerings by setting up DIY obstacle courses ("Floor is lava!"), moving your furniture around, prompting fort building, pouring balls into a pack and play, adding wheels to the mix, or investing in climbing domes, walls, triangles, or slides.

- Get creative. Wrestling matches, yoga sessions and dance parties make quick options for indoor movement for you and your children.

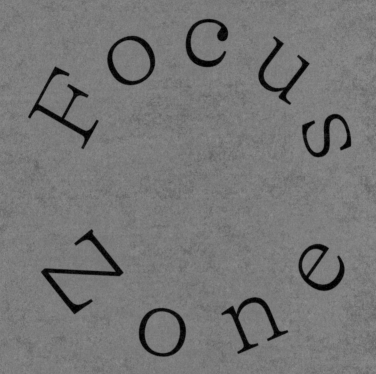

Focus Zone

Chapter

12

*When you teach a child something you take away forever
his chance of discovering it for himself.* Jean Piaget

A Crisis of Attention

Apparently, we now measure our attention spans against that of goldfish, and they're besting us. Goldfish. We're told that the modern human attention span has dwindled to a measly nine seconds (less than our finned friends) over the past few decades. Whether or not that's true, I think we all sense that our focus and attention are collectively slipping away with the rise in addictive technology and a culture of instant gratification. As I tried to write that sentence, I couldn't help but check Instagram twice, answer a text message from my husband, and reach for three sips of peppermint tea. The struggle is real.

And it seems I'm not alone. In just the United States, ADHD diagnoses in children between the ages of four and seventeen increased from 6.1 percent in 1997-98 to 10.2 percent in 2015-16, and the number of cases continues to increase; Between 2003 and 2017 there was a 42 percent increase in diagnoses. In 2016 6.1 million children between the ages of two and seventeen had been diagnosed with ADHD.

Our culture is concerned with the diagnosis of disorders and our children's abilities to focus for long stretches. While there are many potential reasons for and interpretations of this rise—and much debate about the meaning of these labels—they illustrate a (perceived or real?) crisis in childhood attention.

Attention and focus are incredibly important skills. Being able to stay with a task long enough to complete it is a prerequisite for success. You can't understand the teachings of the science experiment unless you follow it through to the end. Your article will never be finished and submitted if you're unable to follow through on the writing and editing process. Your puzzle can't get done unless you sit down and, well, get it done.

In order to make meaningful progress in any domain, we need to hone the skill of tuning out the unimportant and tuning in to the important. The ability to focus is a gift our children must cultivate, and we must support them in doing so. We'll need to teach children the internal processes that are necessary to stay focused.

But how? It will come as no surprise that I think design and play can be useful here. When we designate a space for focused play and treat it as sacred, we're helping our children to build that muscle every time they visit this space and abide by its expectations of them.

Childhood: the Time to Preserve Attention

Even though there seems to be a crisis in childhood attention, I believe that all children are born with a phenomenal ability to focus. We are not born scatterbrained and distractible; our environments make us so. The thousands of messages flooding our system every day from adverts to TV to phones to billboards . . . our fast-paced modern life, the rush, the never-ending stream of entertainment and conversation . . . All this trains our brains to seek novelty at every turn.

Rather than *teaching* our children to be more focused, let's approach this issue assuming that we can preserve and protect what they likely already have. Rather than *fixing* what is likely not broken, let's create a space and a culture at home that honors their inborn ability to give their full attention, their embodied presence, to the task at hand.

Why a Focus Zone?

Just as the messy zone allows our children to get their fingers dirty and the movement zone encourage our children to get their wiggles out, the focus zone is there to capture our children's sustained attention for specific projects. Remember that all these zones might take place in the exact same room; however, we mark them with a desk, a beanbag chair, a play surface, or a storage system, and treat them differently. The focus zone expects our children to

- Put away one project before moving on to the next
- Treat their materials and projects with respect
- Keep items orderly
- Take care of small pieces and delicate materials
- Be aware of what they're doing with their bodies and the volume of their voices
- Stay with a task until it's completed

In short, the focus zone is a space where children can work on projects, games and experiments that demand attention and need completion. This workspace is most helpful once your children are five or six years old or older and are starting to engage in projects that might require adult help and need to be done "correctly." Such projects might include

- Scientific experiments
- Puzzles

- Homework assignments
- Homeschool projects and classes
- Computers and tablets
- Board games
- Montessori manipulatives
- Any project that requires adult help

Think of the focus zone as the place for the more serious, mature "work" of childhood activities that demand to be done in a *particular* way. This is also the place for schoolwork, studying, or using tech. In the focus zone, children are invited to sink into tasks that challenge them, teach them, and demand their unwavering attention, even if it comes in fits and bursts.

How to Set Up Your Focus Zone

To set up this zone, look for a quiet spot in the home. The ability to close a door may be crucial if there are siblings or pets that may disturb this focused work. It may be impossible to expect success with math problems at the dinner table, when there's a hubbub of cooking noises and smells, doorbells ringing, and babies crawling in and out. The focus zone needs to be treated like the child's "study" or "office." It can be a corner of an adult office, a bedroom, or even a dedicated room, if available.

The main needs of the zone are a sturdy and comfortable workspace and an orderly and accessible storage system, mainly for you, the adult, to categorize and display the materials offered, such as puzzles, manipulatives—toys specifically designed to help children master particular skills such as the pincer grip or categorizing objects by size—and special tools such as microscopes or sewing machines. Higher shelving or closed cupboards are recommended too, especially for those materials that you don't want your child to be able to reach without you. I don't keep any sensitive, delicate, or expensive materials and toys within arm's reach of my children until they're mature enough to

Looks like you've got the wiggles - let's move our bodies and try again

fatty brain food

great sleep!

Benign minimalism

handle these respectfully. This saves a lot of frustration at losses, breakages, spills, and messes.

When you've set up your focus zone, it's time to help your child sink into a focused state. They may be constructing a Pokémon character with Perler beads, completing a Lord of the Rings puzzle, or constructing an electrical circuit with snap circuits. Whatever they're doing, it's our job to help them stay focused for a period of time. The actual duration is entirely personal and depends on the context of your unique child, the activity at hand, and the particular needs of the moment.

The Montessori Respect for Materials

In Montessori classrooms one can find low, open shelves lined with beautiful, simple "work" for children to choose from. Young preschoolers learn to take a tray with the manipulatives (such as a block tower of ascending size) they'd like to work on, to place it in the proper place on the floor, and to use the materials "correctly." It's impressive to see entire classrooms hum contentedly as the children go about their work, respecting the puzzles, blocks, and various activities set up for them by putting them away when they're done.

In our own homes we can instill these same values, teaching our children to keep materials together, to put things back in their boxes and place those back in their proper place. I know, it's easier said than done; my children are still far from diligent about respecting the games and toys I've curated, but it's a daily practice. Making an effort to care for our space and being a good steward of the educational materials in our possession helps us to convey their significance and lends weight to the energy brought to using them. Putting one away before bring out another helps to make our focused efforts possible and eliminates the frustration of losing pieces.

"I know it's hard. You can do it – let's look at it together?"

Helping Your Child Stay Focused

Don't tie yourself to predetermined expectations of how long your child "should" stay on task. Instead, focus on *helping them* develop this skill. There are large variations in attention span and temperament that can be attributed to the diversity of the human experience. We can view this as a strength rather than a disorder. There are myriad natural design-based ways that foster focus; use them. The ability to focus for long stretches of time can serve us and is worth supporting, whether you have a toddler or a teenager. What follows are some of the most effective ways to increase focus naturally.

"You're almost done! It will feel so good to complete this – let's keep going."

Setting Reasonable Expectations

When working in the focus zone, keep in mind your individual child, his temperament, what's going on in her life, *and* the task at hand. Is she tired? Super active? Does he need to move? Is she going through a tough time with friends or big life transitions? Does the task at hand fascinate him or bore her? Do your best to stay present in the moment, with whatever comes up, without comparing your child to others, to yourself, or to your fantasy of what he "should" be able to do. Instead, tune in to the reality of this person and her specific experience.

"You kept going, even when it got challenging. You must feel so proud!"

Following Your Child's Interests

Most children can find phenomenal focus when they're drawn to the project or playing a game they love. But like the rest of us, they lose interest quickly when they're being forced to do something that is out of their zone of interest. If your child is in a school where they must complete certain tasks that they find mind numbing (a topic for a whole other book), they're going to need much more support in order to complete it.

Ideally, the focus zone is a place for your child to sink into projects that absolutely light them up! A place where they sail through any doubts and curb their own fidgeting, because they're intrinsically motivated to do this thing. Remember that children are born with an insatiable need to learn, but rarely is that need satisfied with textbooks. Many kids will sink into a trance-like focus when they're piecing together a puzzle, playing video games, working through math questions, composing a poem, or creating electric circuits, so much so that we may have trouble "waking them up" from their flow in order to join us for dinner!

In her seminal book, *The Brave Learner*, Julie Bogart teaches us that one can learn everything through anything. She shares that we can access these areas of "adult approved" learning through the particular obsession that's filling your child's head these days. If you want them to learn a language, improve their reading and writing skills, master long division, or fall in love with chemistry, their current *interests* are the keys to the kingdom. Children who are obsessed with Harry Potter will devour a chemistry lesson when it relates to "potions" and "defense against the dark arts." Kids who are into Pokémon will likely love to write when it involves creating their own Pokémon cards. And those who love all things animal kingdom may be happy to learn the names of those animals in Spanish too.

Beyond entering through their interests, the focus zone is also a place to honor their unique learning style.

Honoring Their Learning Style

Because the focus zone is where traditional instruction and learning take place, it's worthwhile to detour through various learning styles and to consider ways to cater to each child's modus operandi. It behooves us to be wary of labeling people in neat categories, as it is unlikely your child falls neatly into only one of these styles, and we must always give ourselves permission, creativity, and freedom to move between and utilize them all throughout the day. However, if we're to support our children's focused play and learning, these are handy reminders:

- **Visual** *(spatial):* If you have a visual learner, she may learn best by viewing pictures, images, videos, and spatial representations of a subject. For example, a visual learner would learn the concept of 6 minus 3 best if they saw six blocks and you took away three.
- **Aural** *(auditory-musical):* if your child is a predominantly auditory learner, he may learn best through listening. Singing a song about six apples minus three apples equals three apples might help this type of learner solidify that information.
- **Verbal** *(linguistic):* for linguistic learners, it's best to talk through a concept using words, writing them down, and reading them. So you might be writing out the math problem using words: six take away three leaves us with ... ?
- **Physical** *(kinesthetic):* for kinesthetic learners, it's important to use movement, their body, and their sense of touch. They would respond best to being handed six pebbles, being asked to return three pebbles to you and discovering how many are left.
- **Logical** *(mathematical):* for logical thinkers, a mental riddle is a treat: Can you figure out the reasoning and systematic way to solve this problem? I had six, three were taken, how many do I have now?
- **Social** *(interpersonal):* these learners do best when other people are talking through the topic at hand with them; they like learning in a group setting or with you.
- **Solitary** *(intrapersonal):* Some learners do best when left alone with the material to explore it without being interrupted.

Consider which of these types sounds most like your little guys. Don't worry if it's unclear to you at first. As I mentioned, children (all of us in fact) usually blend various styles depending on anything from the subject matter to our mood. But ask yourself: Does my child focus best when moving? When interacting with

games

kits

tools

experiments

school stuff

manipulatives

puzzles

electronics

tech

others? Do they need to be asking questions? Do they focus when they're creating art or making music? Think about the modalities that support these interests and make decisions that honor them.

Bringing Attention Back to the Task

Elinore, thirty-nine, is trying to help Sammy, six, with a coding game he's received for Christmas. He loves the game and is excited to play it, but it's taking a long time to learn how to use the pieces correctly and he's confused. He's getting fidgety. Elinore asks him if he needs a potty break. He does, and once he's relieved himself, he comes bounding back into their family office room where his own desk is set up for his focused work, away from the prying hands of Charlie, his two-year-old brother.

Elinore recognizes that this is one of those times when Sammy is becoming distracted, not because he's hungry or tired, and not because he's bored, but rather because he's on the threshold of a challenge he needs to overcome in order to really enjoy his work and play. He can't master this coding game—and get creative with it—until he pays out some attention currency and learns the rules.

She decides to lead him through this challenging patch by demonstrating her own focused interest in the game. She has a million other things she'd rather be doing. *The whole point of this game was to keep him busy, not me*, she thinks. But she reminds herself that it's worth pushing through the initiation phase so that he can learn this coding skill and enjoy this focused work. She sets aside her to-do list for five more minutes and brings her energy to rereading the instructions.

In this way, Elinore is providing for Sammy what Vygotsky dubbed scaffolding: "builders do need support to reach a goal, students . . . may need support in their learning process . . . This scaffold must be clearly structured so that the students can benefit from it. But as for the builders working at a building, the scaffold must be secondary and the building of the learning primary.". Following the metaphor, the scaffold needs to be erected in the child's zone of proximal development (ZDP), a strategic "place" where their previously acquired knowledge and skills are nearing their limits, so that more input can be constructed while anchored on these solid bases. Finally, as new learning has been achieved, the scaffold (the teacher or parent's support) can be withdrawn and the child can be left to his own devices to master the challenges ahead. By following this strategy, Sammy is witnessing Elinore's focus and is being carried by it. She's holding his lack of attention with her own focused attention and bringing him back to the task at hand. She's fighting her own urge to check her phone or go and finish dinner so that she can spend a few moments increasing his stamina for focused work.

We will often need to be the container for our children's dissipating attention, gently and firmly guiding it back. This should feel like a light-touch guidance, never heavy-handed force. If our children are done, they're done, and we'd be wise to keep these focus-rich sessions short.

Short Sessions for Longer Attention

Most of us hope to help our children train their focus and we want to help them hold their attention on a task. However this can very quickly spiral into a counterproductive approach if we're pulling our children to focus when they've hit their peak. When there's a task or lesson to get through, even the motivated and interested child is likely to begin dawdling sooner rather than later. The same is true for most adults. There is no empirical evidence for how long an adult attention span typically is; however, common estimates are roughly between ten to twenty minutes.

Charlotte Mason, a classical English educator at the turn of the twentieth century, is an inspiration to homeschoolers around the world, myself included. One of her teachings is that adults should keep lessons very short. It is interesting that she suggested they should never be more than twenty minutes for children eight and younger. She reckoned that it's better to have concentrated bursts of focus—where the whole child is truly present—rather than a long, drawn-out lesson full of stalling and silliness.

"You want the child to remember? Then secure his whole attention". Her definition of attention is summarized as "the whole mental force is applied to the subject in hand. This act, of bringing the whole mind to bear, may be trained into a habit at the will of the parent or teacher, who attracts and holds the child's attention by means of a sufficient motive".

Whether or not we are homeschooling, it is relevant to pay attention to our children's attention. To invest in elongating their focus and stretching out their attention span but letting go as soon as they are showing signs of losing steam. As Julie Bogart says, "Tears mean the lesson's done." Mason put it like this: "Never let the child dawdle over a copy-book [penmanship] or sum, sit dreaming with his book before him. When a child grows stupid over a lesson, it is time to put it away. Let him do another lesson as unlike the last as possible, and then go back with freshened wits to his unfinished task . . . the lesson must be done, of course, but must be made bright and pleasant to the child".

Perhaps then, it's the consistent frequency of any one activity that will build proficiency and mastery over time, not the length

of an individual session. For example, if your child wants to learn to play the piano, it's the regularity of practicing that moves the needle, rather than how long they practice. If your child spends a short amount of time every day reading, pretty soon they'll have finished the book and established a good reading habit.

Encouraging and Reflecting Persistence

Understanding the importance of focus, attention, persistence, and an ability to work through challenges as they arise, we can pay special mind to modeling for our children how to come back to a task and re-engage when we've had to take a break. In her groundbreaking book, *Grit: The Power of Passion and Perseverance*, Angela Duckworth teaches us the importance of persistence and coming back to a task again and again. She encourages her children to quit those classes or hobbies that don't interest them, but not those that challenge them. The rule is you can quit, but not on a hard day. You can quit, but you can't quit until the season is over, the tuition payment is up, or some other "natural" stopping point has arrived. You must, at least for the interval to which you've committed, finish whatever you begin.

Similarly, I would suggest that within these short, less-than-twenty-minute sessions of focused work and play, we work through frustrations with our children, not letting them give up simply because of a challenge, but rather disengaging in the activity when there's a natural pause, such as finishing a level or completing the page or some part of the assignment. That way we don't learn to surrender to distraction simply because it's easier. Building grit means working *through* obstacles. It means handling our frustrations and finding ways to cope with them and still *stay the course*. What gentler, more gradual and supported way is there to learn these skills than through play? When could be a better time to lay these foundational life skills than in the safe, risk-free early years with our loving parents as our guides?

Modeling Focus and Perseverance

Any important task in adult life demands persistence, from building a business to writing a book to buying a car to making our marriages last. So do mundane tasks such as stitching up a seam, finding a missing library book, or keeping the minivan clean.

To help our children with their own attention spans, we must strengthen our own. Are we scrolling mindlessly on our phones or snacking mindlessly on chocolate? Are we distracting ourselves with phone calls and to-do lists rather than bringing our presence to the task at hand? I know I am often caught in a whirlwind of agitation and interruptions to my very thoughts.

We can use deep modeling to peel back the curtains hiding what it takes to "adult" successfully by sharing with our children when we've been knocked off life's horse and showing them our plan for getting back on. It could incorporate simple things, like using the moment when my baking isn't working out the way I want it to as an opportunity to coach myself—and hence my child—on staying the course and working through problems and figuring out the next step. Or big things, like using the moment when our business is struggling to show our children how much commitment and persistence it takes to bring our desires to life. "If you want to bring forth grit in your child, first ask how much passion and perseverance you have for your own life goals. Then ask yourself how likely it is that your approach to parenting encourages your child to emulate you".

Action Steps

- Set up your focus zone, a space where children can work on the type of projects and play that demand focused attention, a special respect for the materials, and adult supervision at times.

- The focus zone is simply a desk to work at and a storage area for materials. Putting delicate items out of reach can assuage power struggles.

- Borrow from the Montessori tradition and place special emphasis on teaching your children to respect the materials in this zone (and all the zones). Finishing one activity at a time and putting away materials before moving on helps them to treat their work with respect.

- Look to follow your child's interests and provide them with rich and novel invitations for focused play and exploration, such as puzzles, electronic kits, video games, workbooks they enjoy, manipulatives, and scientific materials.

- Honor your child's learning style; take note of how they best learn: visually, auditorily, kinesthetically, or perhaps through words, logic, or movement. Do they learn better with you there or alone? Remember that these learning styles can ebb and flow depending on the day and subject.

- Bring them back to task; build the attention muscle. It's our role as our children's guides and facilitators to help bring their attention back when they begin to lose focus.

- Remember that although there is a crisis of attention in our world today for adults and children alike, attention is a critically important skill in accomplishing almost anything we want in life. Childhood is the perfect time to preserve and protect our children's natural capacity for prolonged, deep attention.

- Keep Lessons or focused sessions short—no more than twenty minutes—in order to prioritize the quality of the attention over the quantity of time spent on the task.

- Model focus and perseverance in your own life as a way of helping your children to develop their own focus, attention, grit, and resilience.

Quiet Zone

Chapter

13

But a half hour or an hour of quiet, restful solitary time during the day is restorative at any age, and a habit worth cultivating. **Kim John Payne and Lisa M. Ross,** *Simplicity Parenting*

When you were a child, did you ever curl up under your quilt with a flashlight? Ever sneak in under a tablecloth and tickle your grown-ups' feet? How about creating a fort with blankets and pillows, and camping out with some biscuits? Children are notoriously drawn to small, cozy spaces.

Many of us have fond memories of those times when we were left alone to our thoughts, safe and happy. No rush, no fuss.

Quiet time, down time, rest . . . childhood is a call for us to bring back the slow pace, the nap time . . . the siesta.

Overstimulation

It is estimated that kids are exposed to upwards of three thousand ads per day on TV, the internet, billboards, and in print. By the time they're two years old, they'll have been exposed to more screen time, more advertisements, and more faces than any generation prior. Our children are *not* growing up in the same type of world or at the same pace that we or our parents or grandparents did. In fact, today's youngsters are five to eight times more likely to be anxious and depressed than kids who lived at the height of the Great Depression, says clinical neuropsychologist William Stixrud: "In the last six years, there's been this tremendous spike in anxiety disorders, depression, chemical use in young people, and all of these are stress-related disorders."

Our kids are so stressed for a number of reasons beyond the overstimulation of fast-paced media. Both adults and children are sleeping less than they did thirty years ago, which is shortening fuses considerably. There's a fierce sense of competition throughout childhood, especially in the United States, where the race to college begins before kindergarten (and sometimes in utero). And there's substantially less downtime for kids today.

Kids in the 1980s spent 8.2 hours outdoors each day. This average has dwindled to 12.6 minutes, with children remaining motionless around 10.6 hours each day. In the 1980s and 1990s, you could expect kids to clock an average of 2 hours of TV a day; for contemporary children this amount has skyrocketed: "In just five years, media use has increased from 6.5 to nearly 7.5 hours a day in children between the ages of eight and eighteen". Homework load has more than tripled in the last two decades to a whopping two hours a day for an elementary school kid. A generation or two ago, we could expect one or two extracurricular activities, which has now ballooned, as "42 percent of school-aged children are involved in sports, 30 percent are involved in lessons, and 28 percent are involved in clubs. Nine percent of children participate in all three extracurricular activities.".

Studies have shown that "compared to 1981, children in 1997 spent less time in play and had less free time. They spent 18 percent more time at school, 145 percent more time doing school work, and 168 percent more time shopping with parents. The researchers found that, including computer play, children in 1997 spent only about eleven hours per week at play". If you add up the adult-directed activities kids are subjected to daily—school, extracurricular, and homework—it adds up to more than a 60.6-hour work week. Show me the adult who works 60.6 hours a week and isn't anxious and stressed.

Cramming more and more into little brains is taking a serious toll on our kids, hence Stixrud suggests that parents introduce radical downtime: "Radical downtime is daydreaming or mind-wandering, meditation and sleep . . . When we have some time just to let our mind wander, we tend to solve problems better, we tend to be more creative, and when we meditate, virtually everything gets better because our brains work better."

215

As an adult, I spend significant time, energy, and money trying to establish my own meditation practice. I have to labor at unwinding, calming my nervous system, taking naps, and relaxing with a book. And I'm not alone. In the United States, 14.2 percent of the adult population are seeking daily meditation to reduce their stress and reconnect to their inner worlds, while 40 percent are doing so at least once a week. Why wait until the damage is done, and then try to rewire ourselves for success in adulthood?

It is important to note that if kids need to be awakened by an alarm clock, they are not getting enough sleep. People used to think that sleep was a waste of time. Some people still use the mantra "I'll sleep in the grave," thinking that productivity and sleep are mutually exclusive. But with the advancement of neuroscientific research, we now know that sleep is a crucial part of health, wellness, and happiness. We know that the brain *needs* sleep in order to enhance memory and executive function and to replenish cells. Fighting cancer, slowing the aging process, and improving metabolic health are all products of healthy sleep. So sleeping is not really a waste of time, as it turns out.

Similarly, "doing nothing" has typically not been an acceptable pastime in many households. When our kid daydreams, stares into space, rolls around on the floor or flicks mindlessly through a book, we might swoop in to "give them something to do." When our children say they're bored, many of us feel the rush to entertain, pacify, or get them some "busy work." We've collectively bought into the idea that time spent doing (what we perceive as) "nothing" is time wasted.

But downtime is incredibly important. I think about it similarly to our digestive system; there's a time for eating, and a time for digesting. If we never stopped eating, we would never give our system time to metabolize what we ingested; we would be in overdrive and suffer the consequences—discomfort, poor energy, and a myriad of weight-related diseases.

When we're consuming information and experiences *all day without pause,* we have no time to *process* what we've experienced, and our minds become bloated and stuffed. But when we take the time to simply be, our brain replays important experiences and catalogues the big takeaways. It processes the acquired information to make sense of it and keeps what's applicable to our lives. It's deleting the useless bits and emptying out the trash, so we have space to take in new ideas in the future.

Knowing what we know about the importance of downtime, of decompressing and processing what we've learned and integrating it fully into our brains, it stands to reason that we should design space in both our schedules and our homes for this exact purpose.

A Haven from Stress

Given that our kids are inevitably going to experience stress, one of the proactive ways to help them manage it is by creating a stress-free space.

Stress comes in all shapes and forms and looks different for each child. It could be caused by being shuttled between two homes, handling the hustle and bustle of a big city, or being rushed to get out of the door every morning. Take a moment to note what type of stress your child handles regularly:

- Are they regularly experiencing conflict (perhaps between you and your partner, or between them and a sibling)?
- Are they hearing the news? Are they aware of political debates (hearing intense conversations or highly charged newsreels)?
- Are they noticing financial worries at home (or just feeling your own stress around finances)?
- Do they need to hurry or do they regularly experience a rush (do mornings involve yelling or a lot of repetition and frustration)?

- Do they find their daily environment challenging (social or academic pressures at school)?
- Does someone in the family struggle with chronic health issues (are they in pain, discomfort or worried about someone they love)?

Before you beat yourself up about any of your answers to these questions, know this: if you're human, your child probably experiences stress regularly. And that is *not* a bad thing.

Not all stress is bad. In fact, a mild-to-moderate amount of stress is part of healthy childhood development. It's how children become resilient. Just like you cannot build muscle without lifting some weights, you cannot build resilience without handling some stress.

People *need* some stress, they need the challenge in order to build their grit, adaptability, and self-confidence. If people have no stress at all, their resilience atrophies and they won't be able to handle *any* of the curveballs life will inevitably throw their way. Of course, too much stress collapses the system too—just as we can get injured when lifting weights that are too heavy without proper training.

When our children are exposed to a healthy level of stress and are challenged to rise to the occasion, they also need a healthy level of downtime in order to recover. We can help them do that in *many* small ways throughout the day. But our quiet zone is the sacred space that is designated specifically for de-stressing.

So, as you look to set up your own quiet zone, ask yourself: Where does my child seem most relaxed? Where can they simply unwind, daydream, talk to themselves, and do *nothing?*

Emotional Regulation

Babies are born as entirely *reactive* beings. They function on reflexes and instinct: crying when hungry, uncomfortable, or tired. They cannot "calm themselves down," "wait patiently,"

HOW TO HANDLE A TANTRUM IN THREE STEPS

Take your child to the quiet zone

stay as zen as you can while your child releases their big emotions

When they're finally calm reconnect and snuggle

or "use their words" as we adults (sometimes) do. Our goal, throughout childhood, is for them to grow into beings who *can* overcome their immediate emotions and find socially acceptable ways to communicate their preferences and complaints.

Thus begins our childhood-long quest to master self-regulation: the ability to notice an emotion rising within us and to direct ourselves toward productive and respectful ways of expressing our needs and getting them met. We gradually coach our children through the process, and as their brains grow and develop, they gain the ability to master their emotional highs and lows.

One of the core tenets of self-regulation is the ability to pause between the event and our response. It's the difference between an automatic reaction and a thoughtful reaction. So, if my sister whacks me in the face, I can learn to pause before I clobber her back, and instead seek a parent for help, or talk to my sister to express my disdain for her behavior.

This is *not* something most kids find easy or natural—heck, most adults I know, myself included, find this to be a very elusive skill. That is why it's all the more important to dedicate time and space for learning to self-regulate.

A quiet zone can be that space. When a child begins to melt down, have an epic tantrum, or behave in prickly ways to other people, it's a sign that it's time to retreat to a quiet, private place and *calm down.*

I like to think of these emotional outbursts or behavioral antics as *poop.* If our child needs to poop (as hopefully they regularly do) we take them to the bathroom so that they can eliminate in a healthy, hygienic, and private way. We let them sit there as long as they need to, we help them clean up when they're done, and we don't spend *any energy* on wishing they *didn't* poop. We realize that this is simply part of a healthy digestive system, and we're grateful we have modern plumbing to make it that much easier.

Imagine seeing emotional needs the same way. Without frustration, anger, fear, or shaming, we simply notice that our kids have some feelings that need to come out right now. If it's just a little "burp" of a feeling, then there's no need to go to the "bathroom" for that. But if it's a full on "number two," then we're going to need to stop what we're doing and take them somewhere appropriate. It may not be how we most want to spend our time, it might get a bit messy, it might even stink a little, but that's okay.

Having a quiet zone means that when our children are upset, frightened, or furious, we can retreat to a physically comforting place. It assures us that there's a space to do exactly this: to talk about your feelings, to cry, to let the anger out. I think it teaches children that just as we don't poop wherever we are, we can't let our fury out at any old place and time, either, but we can absolutely go to our "quiet zone" and help ourselves to regulate and feel better afterward.

Connection

I know that you want to connect to your child. We all do. But perhaps, you sometimes find that even though you've spent your entire day with them, you feel like you haven't seen them all day. Probably because you weren't fully present.

It's those darn little miraculous screens in our pockets, it's the pull of the to-do list, it's the Velcro baby needing to nurse nonstop. At the end of the day we may not have looked our kids in the eyes even once.

Having a quiet zone invites us to sit together, to snuggle, cuddle and connect. It invites us to read—book after book— to chat, share, and giggle. Sometimes it takes this dedicated space to remind us that we *want* to spend time doing those things every day.

When I walk into my kids' room in the evening and see our poufy beanbag chair and pillows, I remember that I want to share that space with my little ones every day. I want them to squeeze in with me as they grab my cheeks in their hands, waiting impatiently for *their* turn to tell me their knock-knock joke or ask me in how many weeks their birthday is. Of course, we're connecting and talking this way all day, but in that spot, I'm reminded of my commitment to be present with them. To put my phone away. To muster up the patience to say yes to one more book. To invite my kids—even the bigger, lankier ones—to sit on my lap.

My hope is that this repetitive time spent together—even if only ten minutes a day—will embed a sense of fusion as a family, of closeness and intimacy and availability as a parent. Having the space that *calls* to that purpose helps me fulfill on this promise.

Setting Up Your Quiet Zone

A quiet zone could simply be your bed or couch. But I urge you to "anoint" it with quiet-zoneness, somehow—perhaps by adding a bed canopy, some extra pillows, a fluffy blanket, or a basket of your treasured stuffed animals. What visual items could signify that this is where we unwind, de-stress and connect?

Choosing beautiful family photos might remind you of your intention to connect and be present. Signs or posters or pillows that use words such as "Presence," "It doesn't get better than this," or "Breathe" might help you to pause and get grounded here. Or perhaps artwork, paintings, or a color palette that speaks to your soul will offer the inspiration you need to meditate, sink into a reading marathon, or enjoy a long, long cuddle.

Think of diffusing a particularly soothing scent here, such as lavender. Lighting a candle, if possible. Getting low, warm lighting such as a Himalayan salt lamp. Playing soothing music.

You can add some baskets of quiet-friendly items. Books are a perfect companion to the quiet zone. Audiobooks might work well too. Some dolls, figures, or puppets might be helpful for your child when discussing emotional issues. You could introduce play-based ways of processing these feelings or of explaining your point of view on their behavior. Anything that makes this spot feel cozy and calm is a win.

How to Use the Quiet Zone

There's no right way to use the quiet zone, but I would advise against ever framing it as a punishment. This is the opposite of a "naughty chair" or a "time-out corner." It's a healthy, happy, place to go to calm down, relax, and unwind—not a punishment. We don't "send" children to the quiet zone, but rather invite them there. We don't "force" a child to stay there, but rather join them in calming down and in easing their anxiety or frustrations.

When wondering how to use it, imagine yourself in a stressful situation, when you're *not* behaving your best. Say, for example, there's a hurricane-grade mess in your kitchen, the dog just pooped on the floor, your boss just sent *scathing* criticism on your latest article, and there's a delivery guy at your door, dropping off the *wrong* thing. As you let fly at this poor fellow, your partner comes over and notices you're in a downward spiral. Your partner gently places a firm but loving hand on your shoulder and says: "Honey, I got this. I've drawn you a bath upstairs, go and take a soak. We'll sort this out later."

Still buzzed on anger, you want to stay and *engage in all the mishaps*, but your partner steers you in the direction of the bath. And suddenly you're in a different zone. There's some gentle music, there's a candle. There's a bubble bath. Your mind is still racing through all the things that are going wrong, but you're taking a few moments to just let it race. Right now, you're going to focus on relaxing, on unwinding. As you sit in the tub, you can feel your shoulders melting away from your ears. You can feel yourself unwind. Finally your partner comes and joins you, and asks how you're doing. It's enough to bring all of the feelings flooding back, but this time you're less mad and more sad—helpless even. You burst out crying. Through the sobs you share your hurt at your boss's unfair criticism and your sense of dissatisfaction with your work overall. You share how you feel when you can't give your kids a square meal: like a failure. And how you feel guilty and embarrassed at the way you spoke to that poor delivery person, but how annoyed you were that nothing was going right.

Your partner listens attentively and says, "Hey babe, I get it, all of that is a lot to handle. It was a hard day. I can see you're really doing the best you can." This immediately calms you down.

Reset

Regulate

Relax

Rest

Read

Reconnect

You feel the empathic presence of someone who gets it, someone who sees the good in you and understands your struggle, someone who isn't overwhelmed themselves, someone who isn't disappointed or shocked at your behavior, someone who gives you the feeling that this will pass and you can handle it—someone who's in your corner.

The lavender scent and the sound of the water serenading you are working their magic at winding down your system, and your prefrontal cortex is coming back online.

It's okay, you realize, *I'm okay and it's okay. I can handle this. It's not an emergency. I've got what I need to figure this out.*

THAT is what we want our kids to experience when they are going through a tough time. We want them to know that someone who cares will help them take some time and space to calm down and feel better.

In time, we can learn to do this for ourselves. Eventually we learn to notice the signs of our brains getting frantic and unreasonable, and we learn to go and draw ourselves our own (figurative or literal) bath.

Eventually we'll want our kids to know how to retreat and calm down without our guidance. But at first we may need to be the firm, loving hand on their shoulder that guides them— sometimes even against their will—to calm down.

A Note about Spirited Children

Full disclosure here, I have at least one child who needs this type of calming down more than most and resists it more than anyone. When he is riled up and angry and ready to burst, he does not want to go and calm down. I've had to physically pick him up many times to take him to a place where he could calm down in order to stop him from hurting himself and others.

And I've had to shut the door and stay in there with him, as he screams and thrashes, for upwards of fourty five minutes at a time.

Some kids have particularly sensitive stomachs. They have more indigestion and need more bathroom duties from their parents than others. Some kids have particularly intense emotional digestive tracks too. They need a little (or a lot) extra when it comes to helping them learn to calm themselves down and to regulate.

I will not say it's easy to help such a child. But as someone who was particularly explosive, angry, and intense as a kid myself, I know that it is entirely possible to help spirited children to self-regulate and productively channel their fire. It takes immense patience, trust, and stamina on the part of their parents, but it is entirely possible. Take heart.

Ultimately creating and using a quiet zone is our way of saying to our kids, *In this home it's okay to get sad or angry. It's okay to need privacy or quiet. It's okay to daydream or do nothing. In this home we prioritize connecting, listening, and taking time together to simply be. Here's a dedicated space, designed especially for that.*

Action Steps

- Set up your quiet zone. The quiet zone should be a cozy corner with a beanbag, couch, or chair, low lights, a tent or canopy, some books or dolls, and pleasant scents and sounds.

- Use a quiet nook or corner of the house, or the child's own bed. Make this a safe little haven and an inviting place to retreat to from the stress of the outside world.

- Remember to use this zone for comfort: children today experience a lot of stress, anxiety, and depression. Some stress is vital for building resilience, but we all need recovery time. Radical downtime is important for children, as is a place where they can go to escape the pressures of life.

- A quiet zone is a designated place for children to have this downtime, let their mind wander, and do "nothing," which is incredibly important for combating, managing, and processing the inevitable stress that they'll experience.

- This is also the spot for emotional regulation—the ability to handle our emotional reactions to any given situation in a socially acceptable way. Children develop this ability throughout childhood. When emotions get very intense, we need to be able to go and calm down somewhere until our "thinking brain" comes back online.

- Use this space for time-ins. Unlike a time-out, offering children a quiet zone as a place to calm themselves is supportive of their need for guidance when emotions become too much and behavior becomes overwhelming.

- Connect with your child here. A quiet zone is the perfect place to intentionally spend time with our children and read, snuggle, chat, or play quiet games. It's a place to offer emotional processing after a difficult experience or emotional preparation for a transition to come.

Curation
Diva

Chapter

14

As parents we also define ourselves by what we bring our attention and presence to. This is easy to forget when daily life feels more like triage. By eliminating some of the clutter in our lives we can concentrate on what we really value, not just what we're buried under, or deluged with. **Kim John Payne and Lisa M. Ross,** *Simplicity Parenting*

The Default Reality: Unconscious Consumption

As I tentatively reached the final steps leading down to their sprawling basement, my breath caught in my chest at the room that appeared before me. Or more accurately: the room that didn't appear before me. I literally could not see the floor, and the white cube shelves that lined the walls were so laden with toys that I could hardly see the walls either. Welcome to Lisa's home.

Similar to my client Jenny, before her, Lisa was an unwitting victim of the unconscious consumption that plagues so many cultures today. She had fallen for it, hook, line, and Amazon prime.

The fact is that unless we turn our attention to what enters our home—and stand guard to protect our space from massive materialistic infiltration—our homes will quickly turn into dumping grounds that rival minefields. I'm not exaggerating with the above depiction of Lisa's home; in fact you can watch me help her tackle the mountains of unused, broken, and excessive toys on the book bonuses at ReclaimPlay.com. But sadly, Lisa is not unusual; her situation is more common than you might imagine.

Personally, I strive for my own version of simplicity and minimalism in the way that works for my family, and yet, the gravitational pull of consumerism has a greater hold on us than I care to admit: the casual trickling of "stuff" into my home happens more often than I care to notice.

If you, too, have found yourself buried in stuff, tripping over the mountains of manufactured bits and bobs that have somehow become "yours," you're not alone and you're not to blame. It takes a vigilant awareness and dogged commitment to guard our spaces to ward off this accumulation. As we have covered in the Declutter Boss chapter, decluttering is a crucial step for independent play. However—the other side of the decluttering coin is curation—being mindful of what we *do* consume—how, when, and why we consume it—is what we'll tackle in this chapter.

Guilt-Free Consumption

Rather than bemoaning our cultural norms or sinking into guilt and victimization, we might look to create a right relationship with our consumption patterns. I think of it like a healthy approach to eating. Some people go through feast-and-famine cycles, teetering between one extreme fad diet after another and binge consumption, never finding a loving, sustainable way to nourish their bodies, enjoy their food, and find optimum health and peace of mind. But when we detach eating from emotions and treat our bodies like temples, becoming aware of what we're eating and why we're eating it, we can begin to enjoy our food and develop a balanced relationship with it. This demands a commitment to attunement, awareness, self-compassion, flexibility, and a consistent honoring of what our bodies truly need at any given moment. Can we create a similar evolution in our relationship to "stuff?" Eventually reaching a place where we can enjoy buying things that serve us, and let go of those things that don't?

Becoming the Curator of Your Home

Museums are good examples of places that are the opposite of the haphazard, reactive, unconscious consumption that I found in Lisa's basement. A team consisting of curators is tasked with ensuring that every item in the room supports the experience they're aiming to create. There's a *goal* to the exhibit, namely, to elicit certain feelings, provoke thought, educate viewers in a particular way or inspire them. If an exhibit is there to teach children about the life cycle of bugs, but someone has left a giant Winnie-the-Pooh stuffy on one of the podiums, children would be confused and distracted. If an exhibit is showcasing the Impressionist era and we find a row of Coca-Cola bottles, we become disoriented or comment on the disjointed collection of items.

Putting on your museum curator's hat can help embody that level of intentionality—and creativity—as you choose the items to include in your home. Your home isn't a catchall for anything anyone can throw at you (read: *gift you*). It isn't a dumping ground where toys go to die. After all, even the most expensive Picassos wouldn't appear in an early-Renaissance landscapes exhibit. They just wouldn't fit.

You know that some things don't fit in *your home. Your palace!* And some absolutely enhance it and create an amazing, interesting, intriguing, connective experience for you and your family. Just as the museum curator is deciding what *not to include*, they are simultaneously pinpointing what *does* serve the exhibit.

Kitting out your home with things that reflect the "you" that you want to be can be a dynamic, ongoing, creative process. Not the frazzled, guilty, confused experience it becomes for so many of my clients and community members. And with birthdays, holidays, and numerous other occasions that are traditionally marked with buying "things," there are many natural times for you to put on your curation diva hat and consider where you'd like to "take" your people next. It's a privilege to get to choose what we own. Let's stay grateful rather than anxious about what we buy and keep. With this lighthearted approach in mind, let's look at some ways to be a successful curation diva for your own home.

What to Look for in a Toy

When looking to buy a toy, game, book, or materials, one can easily become paralyzed by the sheer volume of options out there. You know that overwhelming feeling intimately, right?

One of the reasons for this is the explosion of branded merchandise onto the toy scene. Toys are no longer purely in the domain of toy companies anymore, because now there's a merging of toys and every other area of a child's life, particularly entertainment. Every movie comes complete with action figures, plush dolls, puzzles, singing books, dress-up clothes and every other branded item you can imagine. It's no longer about getting a doll for your child, it's about getting an *Elsa doll* . . . until the next fad hits, at which point there's the expectation we get *that doll too.*

If TV and film merchandise have exploded our toy boxes, so have "educational toys" that are rarely educational and can hardly even be considered toys—a bright green laptop that reads to you; a phone that sings the ABCs; a weird-looking table that has a plastic book glued to it. The buzzword "educational toy" is literally devoid of meaning and designed to manipulate parental insecurities. Many of the well-known brands that made their mark as "educational" (see Baby Einstein) have never proven to advance children's learning, and in fact seem to impede it. As you'll see in this chapter, toys do not teach children anything. It's what we do with them that teaches.

A simple set of guiding principles helps me navigate these pseudo-educational land mines and fad-crazed rushes, and instead make choices I know I'll feel good about.

Open-Ended Toys

Open-ended toys are toys that can be used in many different ways. They're toys that offer the child a wide range of ways to play and leave lots of room for the imagination. On the far end of the spectrum, materials like Play-Doh or toys like blocks are as open-ended as it gets; there is literally no limit to the ways you can play with them. But even such detailed and specific toys as Playmobil figures or baby dolls offer a lot of openness to the child's interpretation and imagination. But generally, the more detailed and specific a toy, the less open-ended. Consider the difference between an ultra-realistic, highly detailed military helicopter versus a simplified general aircraft: Which one could be imagined as a helicopter, harvest plane, passenger Dreamliner or anything in between? A general rule of thumb, especially for the younger ages, is this: the more open and vaguer, the better.

Passive Toys

While I'm laxer about open-ended toys (we love our Schleich animal collection, for example), I firmly advocate passive toys. Passive toys are toys that don't animate themselves, don't dance, sing, play music, entertain you, don't pee in their diapers or sing you lullabies. Active toys, toys that "do" things are stepping in and filling those creative spaces where the child actually gets to "do" the things. If the soldier shouts "Fire, soldier!," when does the child get to decide what's happening in the battle? If the baby cries, when does the child get to direct the show and choose whether the baby is happy or sad? Even the most detailed but passive toy—such as a realistic action figure—leave heaps to the imagination, provided it doesn't do all the playing *for* the child too. "Passive toys lead to active children".

Well-Made Toys

Well, this one just about eliminates the remaining 85 percent of the toy aisle, I'm afraid! Unfortunately, ever since planned obsolescence became the way we create products, our toys have suffered from a severe decline in their life expectancy. Sift through our land mines and tell me I'm wrong. About 97 percent of the random toys that people gift my children break within days, if not hours, of receiving them. Meanwhile, my childhood collection of LEGO and our 1980s Fisher-Price dollhouse still stands proud and serves a generation of grandchildren *and great grandchildren* in my parents' home. Toy manufacturing, for the most part, isn't what it used to be.

SHOULD I BUY THE TOY?

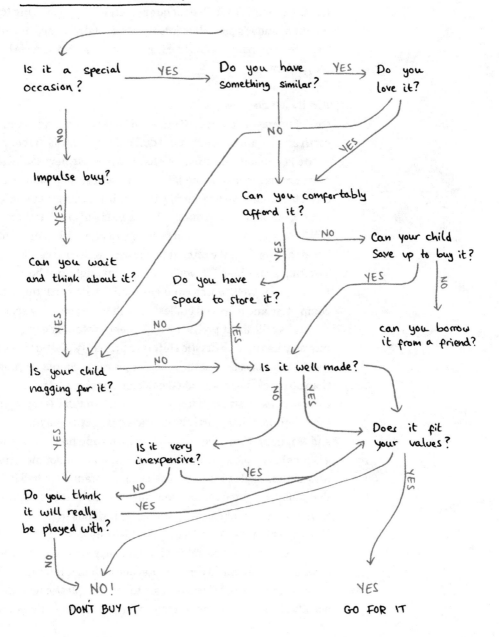

Curation Diva

But buying cheap, breakable toys is pretty awful for all of the usual reasons: it's terrible for our planet, it's disappointing for our children, and it's poor stewardship of our budget. Choosing toys that are well made means looking for toys that can survive being played *hard*.

Kindly Made Toys

One of my favorite ways to "buy kind" is by being kind to the earth and buying secondhand. I don't always do this, but our entire Playmobil collection, our Barbies (yes, we have Barbies! More on that soon) and our bikes are bought secondhand. We often find items we love on free local online swap groups and get most of our books from our local library. It's likely that there are families near you who would be happy to part with some gently loved toys for free. We often find our best items on the sidewalk awaiting a new home. If you're lucky, you might just have a local toy library as well, which would minimize your earth impact completely and offer you endless refreshers of your play space.

Let's talk about plastic for a moment as well. The toy industry has made a drastic shift into primarily plastic toys over the past few decades. At the moment plastic accounts for more than 90 percent of toys and takes a considerable ecological toll each year, as plastic toys find their way to landfills. Our playroom most definitely has plastic in it—including LEGO, Playmobil and Magnetic Tiles—we cherish those toys and hope to have our grandchildren play with them. However, many if not most plastic toys are not made to last. They're cheap, vibrantly colored items that kids get excited . . . for a few minutes. Then they break and turn into underfoot clutter, joining their friends in the waste stream, where they will decompose basically never.

Even without researching how the toys are made, by whom, or what their chemical composition does when it interacts with our children's skin, I think it's safe to say that plastic toys aren't usually the friendliest option to people or the planet. However, in some ways they've become almost unavoidable. One key to buying plastic in a way that lessens its impact is to buy toys secondhand, which keeps toys in rotation and out of landfills for longer. And to revisit an earlier point: buy plastic toys that are going to stand the test of time.

Toys that Support Your Values and Goals

A wonderful opportunity within being a curation diva is the chance to pepper your child's early experiences with items that are symbolic of your values and tastes. A simple example is the toy kitchen I mentioned. I hope my children value preparing nourishing food, and playing with a toy kitchen lines up well with that. I hope my children value caring for the young, and so a baby doll is a great fit for our home.

Similarly, if you're trying to teach your children a certain skill set, the items you buy could support your endeavor. It's an obvious example, but if you'd like your children to learn to ride a bike, you'll buy them a bike, right? And what if you'd like your children to be physically strong? You might buy them a push-up bar or a trapeze swing. What if you'd like to support your child's fine motor skills? Well LEGO, threading beads, or pegboards might be just the thing.

Perhaps you're bilingual and want to help your child maintain their second language. How about a set of the language alphabet, a language game, or a series of books in that language? If you want to encourage your child to enjoy your religion, you might find some toys that represent the special holy days or origin stories such as a nativity set for Christmas or a plush Lulav and Etrog for Succot.

Considering these purchases as opportunities to express yourself and communicate your values, heritage, and culture infuses these purchases with meaning and helps guide your hand.

Following Your Child's Interests

My children have barbies and guns. There, I said it! In all seriousness, I'd like to unpack this a little, because in contrast to my earlier point that toys are symbolic of our values, Barbies and guns are not necessarily symbolic of mine, and yet I happily own them. Why?

As you already know, play is a complex thing, offering a cozy creative space where our kids get to develop and learn in all manner of ways: emotionally, physically, academically, socially . . . Some types of play can be gently guided by our curation and ushered into reflecting our cultural, religious, spiritual belief systems. Other types of play need to be the domain of the child's own self-expression and curiosity. Enter Barbies. And even guns.

I played with Barbies until I was twelve years old! I loved playing with them, engaging them in social dramas and outfit changes. Yet when my little girl began asking me for Barbies, I wasn't enthused. In my years of growing up I had become critical toward the (in)famous dolls. To me, they symbolized a negative body image and would be a negative role model for my daughter to measure her own real-life womanly curves against. Plus, I worried that they reinforced a societal stereotype that I simply don't condone.

Yet, she persisted. My daughter wanted Barbies and would fawn over them whenever she played with them at someone else's home. So, I did a little research and quickly found that Mattel had heard our parental concerns and addressed them. Barbies now came in three additional shapes—petite, tall, and curvy (admittedly not all that curvy really, but at least they look healthy)—and in *many* skin tones and even levels of ability (some Barbies have wheelchairs). And unlike the Barbie of my childhood, Barbie has graduated to become a doctor or astronaut and represents powerful historic figures such as Frida Kahlo and Rosa Parks. When I found these, I was much more sympathetic to my daughter's cause. Finding these dolls secondhand on eBay tipped the scales in my daughter's favor. She's now the proud owner of a collection of lovely Barbies from around the world, and we both enjoy playing with them. Furthermore, they help spark great conversations about beauty, health, and women's roles.

My point here is that I would move away from a "forbidden fruit" model when it comes to toys you're not comfortable with and move into a "working together" model, where you look for ways to make your child's favored type of play palatable to you.

Guns. Another example that often comes with a trigger warning. When I think of the number of parents who have written to me worried about gun play, I'm reminded of my older brother and sister-in-law and their attempts at curbing gun play in their own home. No sooner had they forbidden toy guns than their son had turned a screwdriver, a stick or his own fingers into his gun. "Bang, bang!" he'd yell, and they could hardly set a limit on *that*.

Guns, like Barbies, could invite great conversations, learning opportunities, and ways of working together to meet all of our needs. Many kids are drawn to play fighting, but this does not make them violent or mean that they'll grow up to be serial killers. In fact, play is a place to explore the exact areas of life that are complex, intriguing, and sometimes scary. As we explored in chapter 2, play is designed to let our children pretend they're in challenging situations so that they can develop the muscles and skills to rise to those challenges.

Many Peaceful Parenting experts discourage toys with violent themes, such as guns, handcuffs, or military action figures. Playing out war themes with ninjas, soldiers, and cowboys is just fine. In fact, even the adults in our home—or visiting uncles—enjoy our laser tag and nerf guns and will often get into a dramatic game of "steal the flag" or "cops and robbers". Acknowledging violent themes is necessary and healthy in children's (and, most often, boys') play. The key is to focus on the consensual, mutual and fun of the game itself. Even if the violent theme—war, battles, hostages, arrests—is acceptable—

actual violence or destructive behavior is not. If it is a fun, mutually enjoyed fighting game then it is highly productive play. Remember that ultimately, it's the cruel or unkind behavior that needs to be addressed, because just removing the toy likely won't change it.

"Research further demonstrates that playful aggressive behaviour is a neglected, yet important element of socio-dramatic play, especially for young boys. Children who engage in play fighting are simply pretending to be aggressive as they develop a fighting theme that commonly involves symbolic weapons or war toys. . . However, educators must be cognizant of supervision, a key component for supporting play fighting. . . . Young children need the establishment of clear guidelines and reinforcement or redirection from educators to ensure their safety is assured within developmentally appropriate play." **(Hart and Tannock 2013)**

Heather Shumaker, author of *It's OK Not to Share* and *It's OK to Go Up the Slide*, is an advocate for uncensored play. She believes parents must trust their children's play and allow them to act out whatever themes intrigue them, including violent play: "Good guy/bad guy play is about morality. War play is sometimes called 'mythic play.' Whether it's monsters, cops and robbers, Star Wars or Harry Potter, kids are playing out age-old themes of good and evil, life and death, power and protection. Exploring what's right and wrong, good and bad, is fundamental to developing morality. That's something we want to encourage."

Shumaker wrote her article for *Huffington Post* titled "Why Gun Play is Still OK" in response to the chilling mass shooting that occurred inside a movie theater in Aurora, Colorado, on July 20, 2012. An outspoken voice in favor of gun play, Shumaker responds to the tragedy by deepening her argument that gun play should not be associated and does not lead to real-life violence, explaining that "weapon play is often about saving people with kids in the position of being the hero, the rescuer. 'I'll save you!' they shout. Whether the game is firefighter, knight or space bomber, kids are often trying on the role of hero."

Further, she teaches that empathy emerges in curious ways, often by trying on different roles, including those of the bad guys. When children pretend to be a pirate, we don't worry they'll grow up to be a thieving, murdering pirate. In fact, Shumaker argues, playing scary and violent themes can help kids to combat their own fears and feel safer and more empowered in the face of their own demons.

If they don't have toy guns, kids will use a stick or a banana to wield. It's not the toys that lead to the violent play; toys are simply props in the type of play the child needs. In truth, what matters is how children behave in real life. "Are kids having fun? Treating other kids well? Do they stop and become concerned when someone gets hurt? Actual behavior counts. Tell kids 'people are not for hurting' and set limits to enforce it." According to Shumaker, there's no need to take away the guns.

Allowing kids to have toy guns makes this kind of play acceptable and offers us the opportunity to talk through the importance of safety, respect, and concern. As a family, we've established some helpful rules that make gun play pure fun to us—and each family gets to decide on their own comfort level and rules. For example, we only ever buy guns that look like bright, colorful toys; that way there's never any confusion between a toy gun and a real one, which could be potentially dangerous. We only ever play guns with people who *want* to play, and even then, we *never* aim at someone's face. Playing guns is (usually) only allowed outside. And we craft a safety word so if someone doesn't want to play anymore, we stop immediately. "Stop!" isn't a great option as that's often shouted as part of the game. "Potato!" or "Shoelaces!" works better.

Thus, gun play becomes rich in learning and devoid of shame. It's okay to enjoy the rush of a "risky" game, so long as there's no true violence or disrespect to people or property. And isn't that a healthy lesson for life?

Buying toys that excite our children is another way of showing them that we honor their interests and believe in them. And if there are items you simply do not want to buy right now or ever, offer your children support in finding ways to come up with the money themselves.

Gendered or Gender Neutral?

Many parents offer their boys toys like trucks, cars, blocks, and soldiers, and their girls toys like dolls, dress-up, and kitchen play. On the other hand, some parents find this practice outdated and consciously encourage their boys to play with dolls and pink, glittery toys, and their girls to play with engineering toys or tractors. It's important to note that both approaches have some truth to them: gender norms are real and rooted in biology, and this is reflected in our children's play. At the same time, play can be a place where we expand our children's interests and support them in being exposed to new types of play they may not naturally be drawn to.

Enter our heroes, a group of 34 curious and playful rhesus monkeys, who were studied to see what types of toys they preferred. Yep, there are sex differences in response to children's toys in nonhuman primates. This research was carried out to see if there were any similarities between the toy preferences of monkeys and human children. And, as it turns out, there were some pretty wild similarities!

The research found that male monkeys, just like boys, consistently showed a strong preference for wheeled toys, like cars and trucks. Meanwhile, female monkeys, similar to girls, showed more variability in their toy preferences and seemed to be drawn to plush toys, like dolls and stuffed animals. This means that even without any gendered socialization, the monkeys still showed a preference for toys that are typically associated with their own gender.

So, what does this all mean for us as parents? Well, to start with, it's completely fine to let your kids play with toys that fit into stereotypical gender categories. These are the toys they seem to prefer naturally and are often in line with evolutionary biological patterns. That's why girls tend to train themselves from an early age to care for and nurture their young, while boys are more drawn to productive and protective play.

And what about the idea that toy preferences are shaped by socialization? Well, the researchers behind this study have a hypothesis that these preferences may actually reflect hormonal biases that are influenced by social processes. This means that, while socialization plays a role in shaping our preferences, there may also be some deeper biological factors at work. On average, girls are more interested in relationships, while boys are more interested in things. However, even though these are the norms and averages, it's still important to follow your unique child's interests and not to adhere to gender stereotypes at the expense of their natural interests. If your boy wants to play with a vacuum toy, let him! In fact, it's important to expose your kids to a wide range of play styles, as this can help them develop diverse interests and perspectives.

It's true that there really is no such thing as gendered toys— all toys are for all people. But it's also true that on average, boys and girls are drawn to different types of play. That's not bad or wrong but it's also not some ideal we must uphold. Let's not disapprove of our sons because they're interested in war play, and let's not tease or berate them if they are interested in dolls. Let's not dislike our daughter's interest in make up and tutus, and let's equally encourage her love of science or trains. Leave it up to the child to decide. The next time you see your son playing with a truck or your daughter cuddling a plush toy, remember that these

241

preferences may be rooted in biology and shaped by socialization. Most importantly, let them play and have fun!

Non-Toys = Best Toys

For his eighth birthday my nephew asked for, and received, a power hose. How awesome is that? He loves machinery, tools, power, and . . . helping people. And with his birthday gift, he's cleaned the houses and cars of his grateful friends and neighbors.

In a recent video that made the social media rounds, a baby—no more than nine months old—is propped up in a high chair. Her mom experiments with placing a toy and a non-toy item on her tray. A pair of keys vs a rattle. A remote-control vs a ball. A kitchen whisk vs a plush doll. In each and every case the baby grabs the non-toy item and ignores the toy. Every single time.

Given the amount of money we spend on them, it's jarring to realize how little children are interested in toys and how unnecessary they really are. Despite my well-stocked playroom,

WAYS TO SAY "NO"
TO MORE TOYS

Say "Yes" to the wish, but "No" to the reality. "Oh, wow! That _is_ cool! We're not going to buy it today but I can see why you really want it!"

Share authentically why it is you don't want to buy more:
"I'm not looking to spend more money on toys right now."
"I feel we have enough toys."
"That toy looks poorly made, I think it will break quickly."

Give your child a way to work towards it:
"Well, I'm not buying anything new until your birthday but let's find a way for you to earn enough $ to buy it for yourself. How about dogsitting?"

242   **Reclaim Play**

I know full well that my kids don't need *any of that stuff, even the beautiful, open-ended, well-made, wooden ones.* Kids make their own games and find their own imagination in rocks, sand, and leaves—toys are unnecessary. And often, as with the baby in the high chair, it's the tools and household items we take for granted that would interest them the most.

Let's use this to our advantage as we curate our home. Let's put at least an equal emphasis on offering our children access to non-toy (but kid-safe) items to explore. In Montessori environments, you'll find that children use real, metal tools, glass pitchers of water and real flower arrangements. It's these non-toy activities that offer a wider and richer range of materials, textures, and weights and most accurately answer children's needs to master adult skills.

We have a vintage typewriter at home, a set of (real metal) tools, a tape measure, some random keys and a broken laptop, all of which get equal play to our magnetic tiles or dolls. Home Depot stores, your local vintage thrift store, or hardware stores often make the best toy stores, and kitchen cabinets often make the best toy chests.

When to Buy

If you're wondering about a good time to buy toys, I think it's best to utilize the typical times that people gift within your culture, which often is special holidays and birthdays. We aim to buy no more than one item per child per birthday, and the same goes for holidays. However, I'm not beholden to that schedule. If one of my children needs a bike, or I find a game they're really into, I'm happy to treat us to these just any old time. Just as with *what* to buy (or borrow or ask for), so too with *when* to buy (or borrow or ask for), establish some guiding principles but allow yourself some flexibility.

I recommend that you don't establish a rigid expectation for more toys every holiday and birthday. Expand your children's

243

definition of what a great gift means so that when you find your playroom overflowing, you don't feel the pressure to buy yet more toys simply "because" it's his or her birthday. Instead include non-toy gifts, such as experiences, tickets, or memberships in your birthday/holiday gift repertoire.

Gifts You Don't Want

What about items that you have less control over, such as prizes handed to your child at the dentist or gifts your generous family members bring? Those are the times in my life when I "let it go." I focus on the gratitude I have for the abundance and the generosity of those around me and I use it as an opportunity to help my children with social etiquette, proper thanking (we usually make short thank-you video messages in our family). Remember all the techniques you learned as a declutter boss in chapter 7.

If you're particularly close to a family member who repeatedly buys toys you really don't want—and you feel that you can communicate with them about this—here's a script that might help, once you make it your own:

"Hey Alice, I wanted to thank you so much for all the generous gifts you buy the kids. They're always so excited about them and it's so kind of you to think of them. I'm really trying to be more aware of our carbon footprint and of the plastic in our home and wondered if you might consider bringing them books or art materials instead. Only if this works for you, of course, I know they really love Play-Doh, and we can never have enough paint in our house. Does that make any sense?"

Or perhaps something along these lines:
"Hey Martin, you know the kids are still playing with that Winnie the Pooh plushie you gave them last year. It was such a hit, thanks again. I wanted to mention that we read some interesting research, and we're doing a bit of an experiment in our home and trying out how having less toys affects our kids

play, so we've decided to minimize incoming toys. If you're planning to get them anything this year, and we totally don't expect you to, but if you are, they're really into Audio books and could use some credits. Or they would absolutely love a special outing with you to the museum!"

Sometimes you can make this kind of honest request of well-meaning family members. But often that would put too much of a strain on the relationship and it's better to focus on your own buying habits. Those toys that are poor quality, annoying or ugly can be played with for a while and get decluttered when your child loses interest.

Children Are Buying it For Themselves

Finally, your children themselves may receive an allowance in which case they may have some autonomy over how they spend their own money. So how should you handle helping them in their curation efforts?

Here's another area where you'll establish some boundaries and offer some guidance. Boundaries might be those things that, as the parent, you don't allow them to spend their money on. Yes, as the parent you are the leader and you do get a say even in how they spend their own money, especially in the early years. As they mature into tweens and teens they can gradually earn more autonomy. The fact that you are legally and morally responsible for your child means that they can't simply spend their money *however* they choose. You wouldn't allow them to buy porn, the state wouldn't allow them to buy weapons, and the store wouldn't allow them to buy medication. Similarly, I do not allow them to buy candy or any of the toys that are disruptive to our home, such as loud or obnoxious toys.

As long as what they want to buy isn't in direct opposition with our family's needs (for relative peace at home) or values, they're free to spend their money as they choose (at the time of this writing, primarily on Pokémon cards). However, I offer them extensive guidance when they're making their choices. We have them ask questions such as: Will I really use it? How does it impact the earth? How long am I likely to enjoy it? How does it compare to other successful or unsuccessful purchases I've made? Do I like the company that stands behind this product? Do I feel that it benefits me and my friends when we play with this?

Guiding questions such as these aim to lay the foundation of conscious consumption and they don't end when the purchase is made. They continue as reflective questions that usually come up next time they want to buy something. Was I happy with my previous purchase? I was so excited and anxious to get it *before*, but did I still feel as happy with my choice after a few days of using it? Why or why not? Do I need *more* of this item? Why? How much of this would enhance my experience and what might actually overwhelm me, making it hard to keep track of my things? How does this impact the other people around me, those that made it, those that are going to use it, those that will help me clean it up? Is it worth it? What else could I spend this money on?

Remember that often making poor choices is the best way to learn. My kids have often opted to spend their money on cheap plastic and have learned that these toys don't hold up and are usually not worth their hard-saved money. I encourage these "mistakes" because I know that as long as I gently reflect on them with my kids, they'll learn what feels like a good, healthy choice and what doesn't. It will take years and perhaps many mistakes, but these lessons will reach far deeper than yet another lecture from me.

Action Steps

- Become a curation diva. Our default reality may be that we are inundated with too many toys that don't serve us. Launch a counterattack to that unconscious consumption and give yourself a chance to be intentional about the toys and items you choose to line your home with.

- Opt for open-ended toys that can be imagined into lots of different things, such as general vehicles, blocks, or simple dolls that can be used in myriad different ways.

- Choose passive toys that don't entertain, don't sing, dance, or flash lights, and invite the child to operate them as the puppet master and director of the show.

- Elect well-made toys that stand the test of time and are thus a better investment of our money and the earth's energy.

- Find kindly made toys that use materials and processes that are earth, animal and people-friendly. Additional ways of "buying kind" include buying secondhand, receiving hand-me-downs, or borrowing from libraries.

- Don't adhere too strictly to gender-stereotypical toys, as all toys are for all people. Toys are one way we can break down unhelpful stereotypes and offer all the different types of empowering play to all children, from nurturing baby dolls to feats of engineering. With that said, it's perfectly normal, healthy and rooted in nature and biology that children prefer stereotypical gendered play.

- Use your curation powers to support the values, culture, and skills you're aiming to distill by choosing items that ignite further interest and development in those things that are important to you.

- Remember that often the best toys are non-toys—i.e., items such as tools, household objects or vintage finds can be the best gifts for children and can earn the most play value in your home.

- Curating the items in your home can happen at any time. The main challenge will be curbing the items incoming from others. However, you could rely on the typical birthdays and holidays as times to add an additional item to your repertoire.

- Incoming gifts you don't want might throw a wrench in your carefully curated toy collection. That's okay! Ignore any perfectionistic urges and focus on gratitude and social etiquette, only making gentle requests of family members you feel will take such requests well.

- As your child grows and has their own spending money, set boundaries around items that are off-limits, guide them to make their own curating choices with coaching questions, and allow them to make and learn from their mistakes.

Strew Pro

The teacher's task is not to talk, but to prepare and arrange a series of motives for a cultural activity in a special environment made for the child. **Maria Montessori, The Absorbent Mind**

We're about to get into one of the easiest and most effective ways to ignite play for our children (bonus: it's free!) but before we do, I want to frame up the two main problems that the technique of strewing—setting out materials you entice your kids to play with—solves for us.

Been There, Done That

"I'm bored," announces Leslie—she's five—as she stares listlessly at her pile of untouched toys. Margret, her mother, sighs in exasperation. "How is it that I've spent thousands of dollars on the top-of-the-line toys for her, and yet all she says is how bored she is?"

There are so many reasons that children complain of boredom, and it's a wonderful, wonderful thing to be bored, in my opinion. However, in Margret's case, there was an easy fix. And there might be one in yours too.

You might identify with the teenager who looks at a closet full of clothes and announces, "I have nothing to wear!" When we become overfamiliarized with something, it can become invisible to us. We don't notice the beauty of the artwork on our own walls because we see it every day. We don't marvel at the pattern on a leaf as we did when we were children. It's all become so familiar and obvious that we tend to take it for granted. As the saying goes, you don't know what you've got till it's gone.

When kids are used to their toys, the toys become invisible, uninviting, and boring. Strewing solves this problem by creating novelty and intrigue where before there was none. But before we go further with strewing, what's that second problem it solves?

I'm In Charge of Me

My husband is a doctor, and for years he was telling me about the importance of calorie restriction and intermittent fasting for health and longevity purposes. But I didn't really want to hear and wasn't really interested. It felt too hard and too extreme. "Go for it, my love," I would say, "but I don't like skipping breakfast." Until, one day, I met Melissa, a fellow mom and health practitioner at the playground, and we hit it off immediately, becoming close friends. "Actually, I'm on day five of a fast right now," she told me. My jaw dropped. "Tell me more," I insisted, and she did. Something about the fact that *I* was asking her for the information suddenly got me ready and curious to hear it, and it hit home. It triggered a wave of Googling and podcast listening, and I've been hooked on intermittent fasting ever since. Of course, my husband felt a little miffed. "I've been telling you about this for years," he griped, "now along comes Melissa and you're all 'wow—intermittent fasting!' Why didn't you believe me when I told you?"

The truth is, I needed to discover fasting on my own (or in this case, from someone else). And this is as true for me as it is for everyone else. We all cherish and believe in the things we discover on our own terms. Have you ever had an experience at school where *you* figured something out? *You* discovered it? Contrast that to the passive experience of being told, being shown, or even being lectured at.

Strewing solves this problem too, because rather than ushering our children into play, showing them *how* to play, or directing them to "go play," strewing creates an opportunity for them to discover something on their own terms. It cuts out the middleman (us!) and preserves the child's independent discoveries intact.

What Is Strewing?

If you've never heard the term *strewing* before, don't worry. It just means setting up casual play prompts. Picture an adult positioning some toys in an inviting manner for a child to discover on their own—bingo! It's similar to Reggio Emilia's notion of "invitations" or "provocations" or "explorations". The general idea is to purposefully set out items that might spark play for your child. It could be books, household items, sensory materials, or imaginative toys . . . It could be complex and fancy, or extremely simple and quick. There are no rules other than that you don't take it personally if your child doesn't "bite." Try again another day, another way.

Strewing is just one more back-pocket "tool" to spark and inspire independent play, not a dogmatic dictate that you should now add to your to-do list. If the fancy strikes, go for it. If not, get yourself a margarita and watch *Friends* reruns. No biggie.

Toy Rotation

If strewing is the act of taking toys (or other items) and setting them out for play, rotation is the act of putting some toys away for a while, only to bring them out again at a later date. Rotation means we don't always have all the toys we own available. Some are put away for a time. Just as it can be exciting to rediscover your favorite summer sandals after winter has passed, children get excited about toys they haven't seen for a time.

Just like a house that sits too long on the market, toys that are constantly available "go stale." Take a leaf out of the best realtor's book: take them off the market before you try to "sell" them again.

How to Set up Your Rotation System?

My favorite rotation system is transparent storage boxes stacked on top of one another in a neat column that can be easily stored in a garage, closet, or—if you have no storage space like me in that

New York City apartment—in the corner of your child's bedroom. Before you put the toys into the box, consider using pillowcases, tote bags, or Ziploc bags to keep pieces together and to conceal the contents of each box from little ones.

The key to a great rotation system is to make sure it's one you're going to actually use. This is not a graveyard where toys go to die. It's an energetic toy "charging station," so to speak, where they go to rest before they come back out to do the hard work of play again.

Toys can stay in rotation for as little as a week or as long as six months. Deciding it's time to put them away depends on when they go stale. Often rotating in toys out of the storage slumber is a Christmas-morning moment of excitement, so use it on those mornings when you really need a lie-down or extra time to work at your computer.

Anatomy of a Good Strew

A good strew consists of setting something up in a way that is pleasing, appealing, interesting, funny, strange, different, weird, or magical. Its purpose is to lure the child, for the child to *notice* it and to be powerless to say no. Okay, that might be taking it a bit far, often you'll set up an earnest strew—solid as they come—but your child won't give it so much as a passing look.

There are some ways to spruce strews up that can help you on this creative journey. Consider the element of surprise. You could consider placing toys in a surprising place such as dinosaurs eating out of the children's breakfast bowls. Or try surprising combinations of materials such as a set of little cars served up with shaving cream.

You could also elaborate on a strew, going for a full-fledged teddy-bear picnic scene in your living room. Or spending time building the castle of your dreams with magnet tiles. Students of Reclaim Play have been known to get a little too much pleasure out of playing with their children's toys while their children

a book for inspiration

toys that relate to the theme

sensory materials

DIGGERS

Place the strew in an interesting spot (the floor? the table?)

a tray to hold it all together

some whimsy

sleep, none the wiser. It sounds silly but it can be therapeutic, fun, and an act of love toward our kids: creating fun experiences for them to discover with the things we already have at home.

How Often to Strew

I'm always asked how often I strew and how many strews per child. My answer is: it depends (shocker). There's no magic number. You can strew on the go, setting up another invitation while your child is busy with the first. You can do it when they're asleep at night. (I'm always a little exhausted but this is my favorite time to set out those morning "surprises" for them. Plus I get to take it easier in the morning, when they're happily engaged, usually.)

I tend to pick up strewing again when things start to feel heavy, slow, or just uninspired. I do not do this every day. But I challenge you to give it a try on a regular basis. Establish a new habit and experiment a little with your own creativity, with what works and what doesn't, for your child, right now.

Or, if you're more of a rule-follower and enjoy structure and order to your days, make strewing a daily or weekly habit that you anchor to another time-sensitive event, such as bedtime.

To get your creative juices flowing on strewing, I'll share some categories of strews that have taken our community by storm and have yielded real results in terms of deep play for our children. Take what works for you, try it on, and keep rolling on to the next idea when one doesn't "stick."

Kitchen-Items Strews
Age range: 6 months to 2 years

Your kitchen probably holds the perfect items for this age range to play with. In fact, so many parents report that their babies and toddlers prefer household items to colorful plastic store-bought toys every day of the week. Offer your baby the following easy go-tos to play with, from teething to practicing their stacking:

- Wooden spoons
- Tupperware containers
- Measuring cups
- Silicon spoons
- Stacking bowls

Little-World Strews
Age range: 3+

Little worlds to take charge of can be really enticing to preschoolers. But sometimes the act of "setting it all up" actually stops them from sinking into the play. Sometimes "setting it up" is the play itself. Consider train tracks, for example. If a child is interested in construction, planning, engineering, and the "connection" schema, they'll delight in building the tracks themselves. But if they're currently more interested in being the director of the show and working through conflict, problem solving and dramatic play, they'll be more drawn to a track that's all built and has trains ready to go. Experiment with both!

- Setting up the furniture and dolls in a dollhouse
- Building an elaborate (or not) train track
- Creating a little farm, zoo, safari, ocean by putting animals into an environment of pebbles, blocks, or sand
- Building a castle or fort with blocks or boxes and adding figures

Plastic sheet

old cloth

egg carton

bowls

ice tray

cups

tray

organic objects

found boxes
+ packages

a jar or bucket

a piece of paper

divided trays

cutting boards

Pots & Pans

baking trays

serving trays

with compartments

Art Strews

Age range: 3+

When setting out a craft or artistic exploration, try to remember that true creativity has no predetermined outcome. Don't expect or direct your child to make a carbon copy of what you (or the box) had in mind for these materials. They may and probably will surprise you with their own interpretation. You can set out some kind of inspiration such as a book on a particular topic of interest, instructions for a particular craft, or postcards, newspaper clippings and magazines with artwork or photography.

As we already discussed in previous chapters, a word to the wise: Please, please, please don't offer art or sensory strews if you aren't comfortable with the potential mess. If your children aren't mature enough to use materials only where they're allowed to be used, you'll need to watch them to ensure the beans stay in the bin or the shaving cream doesn't end up under the couch. No amount of independent play is worth exploding at your kids because they just rubbed slime all over your heirloom curtains. Protect you and your children and only invite them to play with the materials you can handle right now. (Hint: no kinetic sand when you're at the end of your rope.)

- Painting: with fingers, sponges, leaves, feet, acorns, twigs
- Playdough (store-bought, guilt-free, or homemade)
- Gluing loose parts (such as sequins, buttons, or pom-poms)
- Cutting snippets
- Clay
- And the "riskier" tools for older ones, such as sewing, punching holes, stapler, hot glue gun

Loose Parts Strews

Age range: 3+

The theory of loose parts was developed by architect Simon Nicholson in 1972. Materials that can be moved around, tinkered with, put together and taken apart, grouped and ungrouped, designed and redesigned offer infinitely more creative options than static materials. Children are drawn to loose parts and to putting them together in new ways, and this undoubtedly maintains and develops their natural creativity and curiosity. It can happen with anything:

- Empty cardboard toilet-paper rolls
- Electronics that no longer work (please take batteries out for safety)
- Cardboard boxes (punch in some holes and add silk scarves for a great tissue-box effect)
- Real tools, screws, and a cardboard box. My kids (when they were three and five) would spend a long time pretending to be builders, hammering blunt nails into a cardboard box.
- A tinker box: set aside a box where you keep old keys with no locks, locks with no keys, electronic parts that have no use, broken laptops, strange cables and unusable headphones. The idea is to offer children their own "tinker" box where they can screw things, take them apart, see their inner machinery, bang, stretch, hammer, and smash to their heart's content.

Music Strews
Age range: 1+

Exploring sound in all its forms is a wonderful provocation for play, just not on the day you have a migraine. Leave out musical instruments or "pots and pans" types of drums, and play some favorite playlists in the background.

Just like any other toy, though, mind that musical instruments go stale also. You can rotate them away for a few weeks and then strew them out to great effect.

- Rattles, tambourines, drums, rainmakers
- Keyboard, piano, xylophone
- Guitars, ukelele
- Flutes and whistles, kazoos

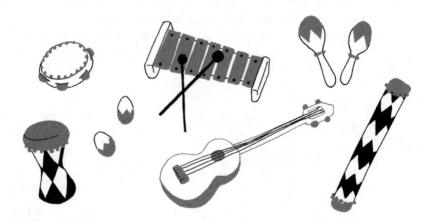

Real World Strews

Age range: 1+

One of the magical things about play is that it can serve as a practice ground for real-life scenarios. As your children watch you prepare dinner, do a load of laundry, or feed the baby, you'll often catch them repeating these actions with their dolls. Remember, play is also often a place where children go to process events after the fact.

Case in point: Has your child ever obsessively played "doctor" after a particularly notable doctor's visit? Often the children themselves want to be the doctor, to play the role of the powerful and authoritative figure and balance out the experience that may have left them feeling vulnerable, small, or confused. Give them the tools to mimic you or to process their relevant life events by strewing out the toys or items that support that play.

- Housework items such as those for cleaning and cooking
- Toys that reenact errands and activities such as picking vegetables at the market or going to the grocery store
- Tools for life events such as moving to a new house, going to the doctor, or welcoming a new sibling

Learning-Inspired Strews

Age range: 5+

For children a little bit older who are able to read and follow instructions, strewing out any kits and projects encourages getting them "into" it. You can make your own little challenges: if you have an electronics kit or a big puzzle, just having these on the shelf doesn't inspire anyone to take action, but once they're laid out in an inviting way, children naturally drift into flow with the project.

Word to the wise: Don't suggest that your child take a look or try it. Practice staying silent and simply let the invitation do its work, so that your child has a sense of free choice. When we tell children to do something, especially children who are used to being told what to do in school all day, they're likely to feel some resistance. Almost as though it couldn't be fun if we were "making them" do it. When they're ready, they know where to go for help.

- Science kits
- Experiments
- Counting, threading, color matching
- Montessori manipulatives
- Puzzles
- Board games
- Globes
- Counting toys, math manipulatives

Nature/Outdoor Strews

Age range: 1+

Many strews can work just as well outside, if not better. Don't hesitate to take your artwork, floor games, little worlds, and sensory play outside. Get the added benefit of vitamin D and fresh air while you play. Outside you can also strew some pretty magical play provocations that would probably not be welcome inside:

- Bubble play
- Sprinkler play
- Digging: shovels, mud, and a truck or two can work wonders
- Car wash: take some of your vehicle toys, rub them in the mud, and provide a soapy bucket and sponge.
- Sidewalk chalk
- Ball play

Strewing really is a never-ending creative process. Sometimes months will go by and you'll forget all about the power of strewing, only to rediscover it. Sometimes your child will "bite" and play for hours with a simple or even accidental strew; other times they'll completely ignore an elaborate strew. Sometimes you'll rotate toys in and out religiously, other times you'll allow everything to be dumped out all at once. Life with children is nothing if not ever changing. But try strewing: it can be magical.

If you fall off the strewing bandwagon, no worries. Hop right back on with a late-night strew when you know you'll be tired in the morning and you'll want your child to be busy for a while so you can have a lie-down. Or consider a "doctor's office" strew to help prepare for an upcoming appointment. Use strewing in a way that serves you.

Strewing For Flow

Strewing is not just for kids. I use strewing to make my adult tasks run smoother and to encourage myself to do things I might not be motivated to do. For example if you want to work out in the morning but have a hard time getting started, strew out your gym clothes and shoes the night before. This is a way of caring for your future self. If you know it's about to be bathtime and you'll have your hands full, prepare the toothbrushes with toothpaste and set out the pajamas, the bottle or any other bedtime props you'll need—in advance. In many ways strewing is simply putting intentional forethought to what we might need in our lives.

Action Steps

- Try becoming a strew pro by setting out prompts and invitations for play that your child will find alluring and intriguing.

- Experiment with different materials, setups, locations. Place items on a tray and see what happens.

- Strew on the go while your child is busy with one thing—to line up an activity that might entice them next.

- Strew with more intention while your child is out or asleep, to prepare for a smoother morning or an easier transition into bedtime or bath time.

- Don't take it personally if your child isn't interested—see it as a curious experiment and get creative with trying something else.

- Use strewing for yourself and other adults—putting out your clothes for the morning or setting up the things you'll need to cook later is also strewing and can help you stay on task.

Play
Guru

Accepting our children in their as-is state requires us to surrender our ideas of who they "should" be . . . For this to happen, all we need do is yield to the ever-shifting adventure of parenthood. Our children will lead the way. **Dr. Shefali Tsabary, *The Conscious Parent***

Chances are you've been to a Yoga class before, but in case you haven't, take everything you know about Yoga and imagine with me, if you will, the ideal Yoga teacher. Before we go any further, we need to note that there is no *one* ideal Yoga teacher. Yoga has many styles, notably Ashtanga, Vinyasa, Yin, or Bikram, and every studio has a different setting, décor, and even price point. Still, there are common threads that typically make teachers "good" in the eyes of their students. Analyzing these traits will give us a useful metaphor to what it is to be a play guru.

Meet Them Where They Are

"Oh my God, your hamstrings are über tight. Is this your first time doing Yoga? You look really clumsy. You're doing everything wrong," said no amazing yoga teacher ever. Why? Because in Yoga there's a clear reverence for each individual and his or her path; a complete and utter surrender to how this moment, person, and situation shows up. A total suspension of judgment. If you walk into a Yoga studio for the first time, a complete newbie, tight in all the wrong places and confused about which way to face, a skilled Yoga teacher puts you at ease, reminding you that you're exactly where you need to be and when you need to be there. Reminding you not to compare your downward dog to anyone else's, and instead to stay on your own—literal and proverbial— mat. She gently sends you messages of self-love and acceptance and guides you to be present with this moment, this body, this posture, this breath, as it is.

As play gurus, we want to be a confidence-boosting guide as well, suspending any judgment of our children as "good" or "bad" at playing. When parents come to me complaining that their kid is too "clingy" or *never* able to entertain themselves, I remind them of the concept of meeting their children at their "level." Rather than criticizing their character, wishing away their temperament, or comparing them unfavorably to siblings, friends, or fantasy children, skilled play gurus meet their children at their level, in the moment.

We remind ourselves that everyone has their own unique and brilliant composition of genes, personality, nature, and nurture, and that everything in nature is ever changing in each and every moment. Thus, we don't label our children as "good" or "bad" at playing. We don't categorize them as "this" or "that" *type* of kid. We realize that, just like Yogis, everyone comes to the mat different each day: some are adept at single-handed headstands, while others struggle with cobra. However, Yoga doesn't care. Play doesn't care either. Play doesn't care how long your child plays or in what modality—be it LEGO, Barbies, Play-Doh, or Minecraft. Play is a space where our children can go, a safe haven, a creative land they *get* to visit.

When we roll our eyes at our children, get exasperated at their clinginess, or complain about them having short attention spans, we're not meeting them at their level. This doesn't mean pandering to them, coddling them, or overprotecting them. It doesn't mean succumbing to their every whim or humoring their whines, in fact, doing so can create an unhealthy codependency and enable their helpless mindset. "Meeting them where they are" simply means shifting our mindset from measuring, judging, and commenting on how they showed up to the day. In the wise words of Dr. Shefali Tsabary:

"While we may not endorse a particular behavior, we must always unequivocally and wholeheartedly endorse our children's right to be who they are in their core state. Accepting our children enables us to raise them without judgment, dealing with them from a neutral state. Responding to them as they need to be responded to, instead of in a manner reflective of our own past conditioning, requires unequivocal surrender to the wisdom of who they are, who they are yet to become, and what they can teach us about ourselves in the process."

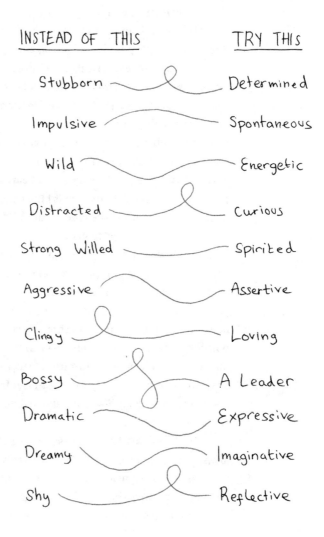

INSTEAD OF THIS — TRY THIS

Stubborn — Determined
Impulsive — Spontaneous
Wild — Energetic
Distracted — Curious
Strong Willed — Spirited
Aggressive — Assertive
Clingy — Loving
Bossy — A Leader
Dramatic — Expressive
Dreamy — Imaginative
Shy — Reflective

Preparing the Environment

If you show up to Yoga class and there is a pile of smelly shoes in the room, bags and coats all over the place, mats in total disarray, and bright, fluorescent lights on ... you might do an about-turn. In fact, no matter how *brilliant* and mesmerizing the teacher was, she would have a bear of a time overcoming the many and decidedly un-Yogic messages of the chaotic room.

There is a reason why Yoga teachers take such pride in ensuring we don't enter the space with shoes on our feet, that we line up our mats in neat rows, and carefully return our blocks and straps to their correct shelves at the end of the class. There's a reason they diffuse essential oils, light candles, and play music. They know what Maria Montessori, Rudolf Steiner and Marie Kondo all know: the environment is our partner.

Your home environment is your best partner in parenting. It's there to support you, if you let it. Just as a Yoga teacher prepares her environment for all the Yogis to come in and *experience something,* so too does a skilled play guru take pride in the consistent upkeep of a play-full home—a home that collaborates with you in providing play opportunities and invitations for your little ones, guiding them to use this space like *this,* and that space like *that.*

We've already waxed poetic about becoming a declutter boss, a strew pro, a curation diva, and a play architect, and so I won't linger here. Suffice it to say a play guru does not "go it alone," but rather harnesses the incredible power of the environment to set the stage for play success.

Before you use this as a black cloud to hang over your guilt-ridden head, catch yourself. Meet *yourself* where you are and take baby steps to begin to take charge over your environment. Rome wasn't built in a day.

Supporting and Adjusting

When our children are climbing the walls, directionless, flitting about from activity to activity, and showing a general disinterest in everything, it's our time to be igniters of play, and to support them and adjust them when they're taking the wrong path ("Sharpening pencils into stubs is wasteful, my love, let's find something else to do with your time.").

In the early years—babies and toddlers—we might call this "redirection." Remember back to our schemas—the urges that drive our children to explore certain actions like throwing or twisting or mixing. As play gurus we redirect those energies into safe, manageable, and acceptable avenues. As kids grow, we can continue this redirection practice, gently guiding them to a way they can explore their interests without causing any damage. Thus, if your eight-year-old wants to build a ninja-warrior run with your vintage cigar-box collection, you can redirect them to using the couch pillows instead. If your five-year-old wants to go on a fossil hunt in your yard, you might help them to dedicate a patch of soil where they're allowed to dig. If your six-year-old wants to play hairdresser and cut all their dolls' hair, you might unravel a spool of thread and tape some "hair" onto a basketball for her to cut.

The point is that we see ourselves as a facilitator, there to spot their proverbial headstand, in case they should need us to fall back on. We're not the directors and dictators, but rather humble assistants to help troubleshoot, find solutions, and bounce ideas off.

Support might look like setting out a new strew for them quietly and seeing if it "takes." Or we might use language in supporting our older children, with guiding questions such as, "We have an hour before dinner. Would you like me to help you get out the animals and blocks to make a jungle? Or if you like I could set up the paints for you. Let me know how I can help."

TOTAL TURNOFFS
FOR PLAY INDEPENDANT

over powering
over directing
over involvement

making it an
unpleasent chore

interupting
constantly

narrating
constantly

too many distractions

over correcting +
Constant teaching

bribing

praising

Attention to Ignite Play

Yoga instructors may walk around the room, speaking their choreography to the class. But if they suggest we should all meet in a dragon fly, and the Yogis look around, confused, you'd better bet the teacher is going to spring into the shape herself. If we don't know how to do a certain pose, we need to see it done so that we can emulate it successfully. Next time, perhaps we'll get there on our own.

Our children, too, may need this type of leadership to ignite their own flow of play. If you've set up a strew and you're giddy with excitement to see your child explore it, but they don't bite, try sitting down to play yourself. Watching their adults is the main way children have learned throughout millennia of evolution. Kids are primed to observe us and imitate our every move. It's how they learn to walk, talk, and run a business. So, if our kids aren't sinking into play, the very best way we can light a spark in them is to sink into the play ourselves.

Sit down and fiddle with blocks for a while, start cooking something up in that pretend kitchen, or rock a doll to sleep on your shoulder. Watch as your child's eyes widen and the "me too!" gene kicks in. Monkey see, monkey do.

However, be mindful not to overpower your child's play with your own direction. Some adults can get so "into it", so carried away that they become the directors. Playing in this way is only supposed to be the ignition of your children's creativity, not meant to drive the show. So, spark the interest and gently pull away—just like the Yoga teacher who shows the pose and then pulls back to let the class do their own.

Not a Babysitter

Yoga teachers are *teachers* and they are there to help us to learn and grow in our practice. But ultimately, it's *our practice.* And they are the first to say: if something doesn't feel right to you, don't do it. You can always come back to child's pose, if you need a rest.

model being
playful in your
own life

play briefly with
your child's toys to
spark an interest

Strew a redirect
when kids are "bored"

Similarly, when our kids are having a hard time sinking into play, we can try to support them, but we need to remember, this is for *them.*

I'm the first proponent of the powers of independent play in shaping a child's life and in easing a parent's burden, but I'm also the first to say that independent play is *not* a babysitter. As powerful and transformative as independent play is in a family's life, it cannot be relied upon when a parent needs to get work done or take a break. Sometimes the more we *need* our children to play, the more attached and disinterested they become. They sense our neediness and often interpret it as rejection, and cling to us even harder. If we actually need some reliably kid-free time, we're going to need another pair of hands and eyes—a mother's helper, a babysitter, grandparent, or your partner. It's true that Independent play can often allow parents long hours of productive work at home. It's how I've written this book and run my business. But sometimes it doesn't, and we cannot put that type of pressure on our children's play practice.

Inspiring through Modeling

To be an excellent play guru, you need to prioritize play in your own life too. Children need to see that we are not just pushing *them* to play but rather that play is an inextricable part of our family's identity and culture. In other words, they need to know that everyone in our family sinks into regular bouts of flow while focusing on creative and meaningful projects.

They may not get to see your most meaningful "play." Maybe for you it's your weekly run, your meditation practice, or your quiet evening journaling. Maybe play happens for you at work (I hope it does!), where you get to express yourself and create new and amazing things. Maybe play for you is expressed through your hot-and-heavy date nights with your partner. Or maybe it's how you curate your Instagram account. It doesn't matter; just the fact that you summon inner playfulness throughout the day means that you're living and breathing playful energy, and children feel that in the air.

However, there are some very tangible and visible ways to show our children that we value play and playfulness. Rather than them seeing us glued to our phones or constantly cleaning, let's make sure our kids catch us sinking into a good book for a few minutes, having a dance party as we clean up breakfast, or pulling out our knitting project as we sit beside them on the floor. We want our kids to see that a zest for life, an energy of creativity, a submergence into flow and focus isn't just child's play.

Here, too, the mirror neurons are going to kick in. Our children will be building a mental model of adult life as including, indeed being built upon, a foundation of playful energy.

Giving It Time

Often parents come to me requesting a measurements chart: How long should a two-year-old be playing? How much will my child's attention increase if I create zones? What's considered a "good' amount of play for a six-year-old? I hate to disappoint, but as the beloved Magda Gerber would say, it all "depends."

In our culture we've really developed graphs and charts, on measuring our children from every point of view, as a crutch. While there's a time and place for this, mostly I think of it as a tool of anxiety and torture for parents and urge us all to live an unquantifiable life with our children. A life where the value of things can't be expressed in numbers.

Rather than expecting a predetermined number of minutes of independent play from your child, I would recommend developing a trust in and a love for the process. See it less like lifting weights in the gym (where we might keep track of the number of pounds lifted) and more like a flower blossoming (where we appreciate the beauty and are in awe of the unfolding of each step).

STAYS ON HER OWN MAT

REFRAINS FROM HARSH JUDGEMENT

SHOWS UP WITH CONSISTENCY

SHE "SHOWS" MORE THAN SHE "TELLS"

Remember that a Yoga teacher doesn't expect you to come into your first class as a master Yogi. She's not busy measuring your downward dog, keeping track of your pigeon pose or comparing your humble warrior to that of the rest of your age group. Instead, she's there to support you to practice in a way that serves you best, today.

If a child is struggling in school, handling a major life transition such as a new sibling, or being shaken up by a new developmental stage such as teething or learning to read, they may simply be exhausted or have no mojo left to play. That's okay. If a child hasn't fully connected with you recently, feels they need to elbow their way past siblings to get some love from you, or is going through some frustration with their peers, they're probably going to feel out of sorts and unable to really sink into a state of flow.

There's a general expectation of children to show up fully to whatever they're doing, all of the time. But kids are just people, very young and still developing people, who have "good" and "bad" days and go through phases just like the rest of us, only more so. So rather than labeling, measuring, and analyzing their play, let's cultivate it as a place for them to feel safe, express themselves, and unwind.

Rather than telling them to "go play!" (subtext: "get out of my hair!"), let's create an inviting, beautiful practice for them to join, as they are, in a way that serves them best. Perhaps painting today with some classical music in the background? Perhaps a vigorous rough and tumble today? Maybe a full-blown enactment of a bank robbery?

And just because your child isn't sinking into play today doesn't mean they won't tomorrow.

Consistency

A play guru shows up consistently for their little players. Just as the inspiring Yoga teacher rarely misses a lesson, comes on

BELIEVES IN HER STUDENTS

SHE MODELS
WHAT SHE WANTS TO SEE

KNOWS IT'S A LIFELONG PRACTICE

HAS EMPATHY FOR HER
"OFF" DAYS

time, and gives her all to the practice, so too must we be there as reliable, unwavering play gurus for our children.

A play guru doesn't "give up," doesn't "let it go." It takes stamina to raise children, I know! It's a day in, day out practice. But like anything worth doing, it demands a consistent effort, over many years. Think back to that blossoming flower: Does it need one burst of sunshine and a bucketful of water, followed by days of dry and dark? No! It needs a little bit of sunshine and a little bit of water, drip, drip, dripping over time. Similarly, if you go to *one* Yoga class, can you expect to see results? Increase in strength and flexibility? Decrease in stress? Not really. It takes many practices over a long time to see the external changes that are the result of the process.

When it comes to independent play, we need to support it day by day, little by little, again and again. We mustn't fall prey to the fast-food culture that thinks that one major decluttering and a few expensive wooden toys are what make children play. When we buy into that kind of thinking, we quickly become demoralized by children who want more screens or complain of boredom and think "it doesn't work." But viewing just *one* day of the flower blossoming, we might think it hadn't changed at all.

All of this is particularly important if you're making a change later in your parenting journey and your children are already used to being entirely dependent on you, a screen, a class, or entertainment to busy themselves. Slowly breaking that dependency, reclaiming play for your children, and offering more free-form time to play will take immense consistency and commitment on your part. But the results are well worth the effort.

Action Steps

- Become a play guru by becoming the master of the energy in the home, just like an enlightening Yoga teacher shifts the energy in the room and brings her Yogis into flow.

- Meet your children where they are and avoid labeling, judging, and scolding them for not playing "more" or "better."

- Your environment is your greatest partner in inviting your children into deep, satisfying play. Use the environment and prepare it in ways that invite play.

- When your children are aimless, bored or lack focus, bring them back by supporting them in finding the right activity.

- Another way to spark that interest in play is to give the project, toys, or book your own attention. Start playing yourself, and watch as your children are drawn to the activity.

- Remember that independent play is not a babysitter, don't put that kind of pressure on your children's play. Keeping play as something they "get" to do, rather something they "have" to do actually increases the likelihood of them engaging deeply. When you absolutely need child-free time, you'd be wise to find another pair of hands to help with your children.

- Inspire playfulness by prioritizing it in your own life. Let your children witness you sinking into a book, dancing in the kitchen or modeling clay too. Even when they can't actually see you in your flow, they'll feel it if you regularly get creative and playful yourself. And they'll feel it if you don't.

- Developing into deeply immersed independent players takes time. Like the blossoming of a flower, it can't be rushed and needn't be measured. It's wise for you to focus on the gradual unfolding and not worry about how "long" they play.

- Be consistent: being a play guru takes consistency, like a good Yoga teacher showing up for her class every day. It's not a one-and-done type of thing. It's a lifelong lifestyle of repeatedly creating and curating play opportunities for our families.

Part Four: Reclaim Play and Special Situations

Chapters 17—20

Chapter

17

Only Children

Only children are often described as being lonely,
selfish ,unwilling to share and lacking in patience, but
these characteristics are typical of toddlers in general
and a lot of adults, whether they had siblings or not.
Denise Duval Tsioles, *PhD, quoted in Kagan Whelan, "Only Child Syndrome"*

"Levi's not letting me be a superhero! It's not fair!" bawls five-year-old Asher as he tugs on his mother's pinky finger. "You have to come and tell him! I get to be a superhero if I want to, he's not the boss of me!"

Siblings are a double-edged sword when it comes to independent play. On the one hand, siblings provide built-in playmates. They can play—independently of adult intervention—*together!* It's a wonderful thing to have a friend who lives at home. To have someone to play the daddy to your mommy when you play house, or to help you balance the blocks as you attempt to build the Tallest Tower Ever. All too often I hear of the fears in the hearts of parents of an only child: that she's lonely; that he has no one to play with. And they're often at the receiving end of such judgments from concerned strangers: An only child? Hurry up and give them a sibling or they'll be socially deprived.

Not so fast, though, because there's the other edge that siblings provide: *plenty of friction.* Just as they can be wonderful playmates, so too are they the ones who won't share their toys, hit you when you don't share yours, hog all the good toys, boss you around, and interrupt your focus. As the youngest of six and the mother of five—not to mention auntie to twenty-eight—I've had my fair share of sibling friction over the years.

Now this isn't a book about whether or not siblings are a good idea—what matters is what works for your family. But I do want to provide some real-life solutions to the challenges that come up with only and with multiple children. Only children might be kids without siblings, or they might be kids who are home when their siblings are in school or elsewhere. And "multiple children" might relate to siblings, or to friends, cousins, or children gathering together for a playgroup or in a preschool setting. What I'll focus on is how the play itself is influenced by the presence or absence of other children.

Only Children and Independent Play

"Ever since he was born, my three-year-old son has wanted to be with people whenever possible and has never shown much interest in independent play. It's a great theory to say that all children benefit from independent play, but is that really true? Are there kids who just aren't into it? Is this another expectation we're forcing on our kids?" This question from Zoe, sparked a deep conversation in our community and led me to refine some of my thoughts around independent play.

There are those children who are talkers, babblers, interactors, conversation seekers, who find it challenging or nearly *impossible* to entertain themselves and sink into their own world without someone else joining them there. There is a lull, a pull, a draw to the energy of others playing nearby that sometimes helps us settle into play ourselves.

To return to the comparison between play and sleep, there are many different temperaments and needs, including those who seek skin-on-skin contact and like to hear their loved one's breath throughout the night. And then there are those who want complete solitude. Many Reclaim Play students who are parents to only children have found a bigger challenge in supporting their children's independent play, especially if they see their children as extroverted social butterflies who crave conversation from morning until dusk.

Even though I have five children, when I am alone with one of them for a few hours—as happens quite often—I do find a complete shift in the focus and attention to their own play, and an increase in my child's need to interact with me, seek my approval or direction, or involve me in their games. There's no doubt that siblings play a big role in independent play. However, the benefits of independent play are yours for the taking, whether your child has siblings or not. Let's look at some solutions and reframe.

The Fallacy of the "Only Child Syndrome"

It's incredibly important not to get hung up on the idea that your child is more dependent or plays less "because" they are an only child. So many parents share their guilty feelings over not "giving" their child a sibling when they "need" one.

The simple fact is that your child would have the same qualities with or without a sibling. Siblings do *not* create independent players and are *not* the solution to behavioral or emotional challenges. Siblings might in fact exacerbate them. Plus, sinking into guilt over this does *nothing* to help your child enjoy the wonderful life they have with you. Your child and your family are complete and whole as you are, with or without more children. Please don't ever forget that. You deserve to enjoy this precious child you have without feeling like you deprived them of something (you didn't!) or like you're lacking in some way (you're not!). If siblings are in your child's future, great; if they're not, great.

Your child isn't clingy, needy, or attention seeking *because they're an only child.* All of the same challenges would exist if they had siblings, I assure you. Lindsay, one lovely student has shared: "I have two kids, they play beautifully together (as much as you can expect) and still my four-year-old begs me to play with her five hundred times an hour. No lie. When we go to playdates, she plays with friends but still prefers me. And asks me to play all the time. So, I say all this just to assuage your guilt or worry about him being an only child!"

Playing with Your Child

If the message you've received from this book is *not* to play with your child, I want to take a moment to remedy that. I believe it's absolutely wonderful, magical, meaningful, and emotionally healing for adults to play with their children *when they want to.* I am firmly against *forcing ourselves* to sit down and play begrudgingly simply because we "should." Just as I do not benefit from a "begrudging" lunch date with a girlfriend when she really doesn't have time or patience to listen to me, or a "begrudging" hug from my husband when he's really not in a warm and cuddly mood, so too, I believe, children won't benefit from an unwilling play partner. Children feel our vibe, our body language, and our *real* intentions.

However, if you have the energy and the heart space to play with your child, game on! This can absolutely "count" as independent play, so long as you remember to be the assistant, not the director. If you are there as a sounding board, as a second fiddle, as an audience, or as a collaborator, great. You are their willing, supportive playmate, and you're helping them to develop their inner worlds.

You may, in fact, notice that as you play with your child and they become engrossed in their building, painting, or dance routine, they need you less and less. You could be applying the "attention to ignite play" rule right there: easing a child into a playful flow and then extracting ourselves to go about our business when our capacity for play has worn thin.

Adjusting the Expectations, Not the Child

It's easy to look around and think, *Well, my child just can't.* Or, *He doesn't have the attention span.* Or, *She's just too chatty.* However, this type of mindset actually stops us from noticing that independent play is *already happening.* It's so easy not to "count" the play your child engages in, because it's "too short" or not the "right" kind of play. You probably have some image in your head of setting up an elaborate tea party, building a beautiful structure, or painting a realistic image, whereas tinkering with bits and bobs or jumping around the living room isn't classified in your mind as "play."

I invite you to reconsider. To put on some rose-tinted-glasses and look for evidence that your child is *already* playing, expressing themselves, and independently directing their own ideas—it just might look a little different from what you initially imagined. Adjust your expectations accordingly.

Play as an Invitation

It's important to remember that play is an invitation. We're not here to force it. It can't be forced. If you're demanding that your child "go play!" or feeling exasperated if they don't, the energy in the home may have become a little negative and the child is building up an "anti-play" theory in their heads: *Well, Mom gets really angry when I don't go and do this thing. It doesn't seem like much fun. I don't want to do it.*

Instead, maintain an approach that considers play as your child's birthright, as theirs for the taking, when the fancy strikes, and as theirs to decline. Just this mindset shift within ourselves will likely increase our child's interest in playing independently.

Experimenting with Strews

If you find your child isn't sinking into *any* kind of play, double down on experimenting to find their "thing." "My daughter," says Carrie, a Reclaim Play student and mother of one, "also" loves imaginary play with someone and I struggled to get her to play alone. We've found our way in through art. That's where she will engage for large amounts of time on her own. She still doesn't really technically "play" alone. Although, once I found art was her draw, she will drift into some of her own little imaginary scenarios more often." As Carrie's story illustrates, different children connect to different modes of play, but giving up too soon might mean you never discover that for *your* child right *now* it's all about balls, soldiers, or clay . . . This is an ongoing, lifelong investigative journey, don't give up too soon.

Creating Playdates

Playing with other children is still considered free, unstructured, independent play (because it's independent from adult direction, supervision, and measuring). Lindsay offered Zoe: "My suggestion would be to find a friend or two with kids of the same age and arrange frequent playdates. Playing with strangers at a park is hard for everyone. Playdates with good friends is my saving grace from being a constant playmate with my four-year-old."

Playdates sometimes get a bad rep for being too formal, but to me they simply mean having friends over or meeting friends to play. They do not need to be scheduled days in advance. If you're lucky enough to have neighborhood kids around, make every effort to open your home to them and get close to their parents too.

You may need to embrace "scrappy hosting," opening your doors even if your home isn't in mint condition and you have nothing but crackers to offer. That's okay, prioritize connection and friendship over unattainable, perfect hosting.

You may need to step out of your comfort zone and reach out to other parents at the playground, at a music class, at church, or by simply knocking on their door with a basket of muffins in tow. It's worth reaching out and making the connections that fulfill your child's social play needs.

You may strike gold and find that one kid who your child can play with peacefully for hours. It took us *years* to find the right "group" of friends for us—families where both the adults and the kids jibed. But when we finally did, they became as close as family and have answered a deep need in all of us.

Mother's Helper

Another wonderful yet overlooked opportunity is to hire a young mother's helper. This is an older child who can come and play with your child while you are home. They do not have to be responsible, capable, or know CPR. They are just there to play and

Likely to be
very inexpensive
(or even free)

Lots of patience,
love of little kids,
Eager to please

High energy.
Playfulness
& Being closer
to childhood

read books together while you rest, work on your computer, or do housework. We have a fourteen-year-old girl come to our house every Sunday morning to give my partner and I some time to spend one-on-one with each child or with each other. Tamara, my right-hand lady at Hi, Fam!, hires a homeschooled nine-year-old girl to come and play with Lucas, who is four. Tamara is in the next room, within earshot, getting work done, but Lucas, an extroverted, bubbly little socialite, couldn't be happier with his playmate.

Often children are actually more drawn to and play better with children who are older than they are. There is no sense of competition, and the older child can lead the younger child in more complex play or read them books they can't tackle alone. Plus, a mother's helper tends to be far cheaper than your average babysitter.

An additional way of finding playmates is looking for a volunteer grandparent. One student, Nicole, was wondering how she could find more help on a tight budget. Thinking creatively, she suddenly realized she was living in an apartment building full of senior residents. She hung up a hand-drawn "ad" in their communal laundry room, stating that Brendon, age three, was looking for a "volunteer grandparent" to read and play games with him once a week. Within a week, Brendon was booked in for two playdates with his new adoptive grandma. This deep service not only relieved Nicole of her never-ending play duties but also gave a retired resident a joy-filled connection with a small child. Win-win!

Steps

- If your child isn't playing much independently, don't blame it on them being an only child. Your family and your child are complete and whole as they are, with or without a sibling in the future. And your child's temperament and personality will not change just because of a sibling. Kids with siblings can be just as needy of attention and adult connection.

- Play with your child. Don't think that the focus on independent play means you can't or shouldn't be your child's playmate. Simply remember to do so when you feel happy to and not because you feel you have to. And when you do play, ensure you assume the assistant role, allowing the child to be the director.

- Adjust your expectations of what independent play looks like and how long it lasts. Maybe it's not a fancy dress-up game but a tinkering session, taking apart an old laptop. Follow your child's lead.

- Don't force independent play or get annoyed when it doesn't "take." It's an invitation and is supposed to be joyful.

- Experiment with different strews and find the ones that "catch" your child in their lure. Perhaps LEGO isn't the thing right now, but finger painting is. Be creative and keep at it.

- Create playdates with peers, neighbors, classmates . . . go out of your comfort zone to find other children who can become close and reliable friends for your child.

- Hire a mother's helper. Even a child as young as nine can be a great playmate for your young child, reading them books and playing with them with much more patience than you, and for a fraction of the price of a babysitter (if any price is asked at all). You may even find a volunteer grandparent for free!

Sibling Play

Chapter

18

Half the time when brothers wrestle, it's just an excuse to hug each other. **James Patterson**

So, we've established the ways that only children—or children who are home without their siblings—can claim independent play for themselves. Now, let's delve into the ways that children play *together,* whether with siblings or peers.

There are many books and bodies of research that help us raise siblings who are happy together. However, my focus in this chapter is helping siblings specifically with their *play.* First, let's take a look at the types of play children may or may not engage in together. Mildred Parten, sociologist and researcher at the University of Minnesota's Institute of Child Development, identified stages of play according to their level of engagement together. Simply knowing about these stages can help us be aware of how children engage and play together.

Types of Social Play

Solitary Play:
When young children are together, sometimes they don't relate to each other at all but simply play side by side. As they play alone, they are seemingly unaware of others in their vicinity. I like to think of this as a comfortable sharing of space without the need to interact.

Reclaim Play

Unoccupied Play:

Often we think that a baby or a child who is simply sitting and watching other children is not engaging with them. However, Parten classifies this as a stage of play in its own right: watching and observing others. This is important because often adults rush to coax more active engagement between children—yet simple observation is a stage of connection too.

Onlooker Play:

A child will sometimes watch others play with interest, pointing, laughing, talking about what the others are doing, even if he himself is not participating. In this type of play the child is clearly aware of and activated by what the others are doing.

Sibling Play

Parallel Play:

This is when children play side by side and are relating to each other, not quite interacting but perhaps mimicking, pointing, or taking some interest in each other's play.

Associative Play:

Here children are interested and interacting with each other, but without any agreement or plan. One might be out of sync or unrelated to the other's actions.

Reclaim Play

Cooperative Play:
This is when children organize a game or decide together on imaginative play such as dramatic play and playing *together*.

Say you've just begun a new job and are at an office party with a bunch of colleagues you don't really know yet. I imagine you'll feel and behave very differently from the way you show up to a family dinner. Sometimes we adults hold strange and rigid expectations that children should "play together," even when they've *just* met, even when they *don't yet know how,* even when they're in a bad mood or engrossed in something else. So, the first thing for us to understand is that there are endless ways that children relate to each other while playing. It behooves us adults not to rush to "engage" them with each other, not to scold them when they're simply sitting and observing, and not to wonder if there's something "wrong" with our children if they don't get along with others just yet. These are all part of what can be natural stages of development.

However, often children *are* playing together, and the challenge is the conflict that might come up. Let's take a look at the types of disruptions that can occur when children try to play together.

297   Sibling Play

Ownership: Sharing/Turn Taking/Fighting Over Toys

"Sharing is caring" Erin says sternly. Four-year-old Arielle hands her sister, Jade, the shovel she's using to build her castle. "But I *need* it, I'm in the middle!" Arielle protests, even after she's succumbed.

For whatever reason, "sharing" (I use quotation marks because it rarely involves actual sharing, but rather a child being forced to give up what he wants in favor of what someone else wants) has become a hyper focus of our culture. It's reached the point where parents can feel deep shame or humiliation (emotions usually reserved for nightmares about finding yourself naked at a board meeting) if their three-year-old kid grabs Thomas the Tank Engine instead of waiting "nicely." Can you tell I've been there?

The very nature of sharing—its true definition and the expectations that surround it—is misunderstood. It's become a behavioral box to tick. Or, as one three-year-old's mom once said to me, "We're doing sharing bootcamp this summer!"

Obsessed with the idea, we parents struggle with ways to meet this expectation. We force turn taking with our eye on the clock; we buy two identical toys so that everyone has one. We threaten punishment—"If you can't share, no one gets it!"—and we pull at our children's (very young) heartstrings: "But it makes Jamie so sad when you don't share with him."

But when we really drill down into what sharing is and what it isn't, and what it means to share, we might find ourselves misaligned, misinformed, or simply mistaken.

Sharing develops over time. Expecting two-, three-, and even four-year-olds to share is actually not in sync with what is developmentally appropriate for those ages. Think about the brain development that needs to take place in order to share: A child needs to recognize someone else as a separate individual from them, understand that someone else's wants and needs might be different from their own.

That is a whole lot to ask of someone who's only been on the planet a few short years. When you look, you will find incredible acts of cooperation (peekaboo, waving, smiling) in even very young children and babies. But we're fixated on sharing being the indicator of "prosocial" behaviors. This is a harsh and unrealistic way to judge a child's behavior.

Is sharing a reasonable request? Even if children have the capacity to share with some people some of the time, they may not always want to. And ask yourself, Isn't that fair enough? Children's toys and food are among the few things they actually have ownership of and control over in the world. Expecting them to automatically give them over to friends, siblings, and sometimes even complete strangers seems unreasonable. Not to mention, a clear double standard seeing as we, as adults, don't rush to share our shoes, cars, laptops or lipstick with any friend that happens to appear. One way to help kids with the demand that they share their toys is to ask them, pre-playdate, which toys they're not going to want to share today. Together you can store those toys out of sight so that they have some preemptive control.

Ask yourself what lesson you want to teach. When you think about it, the point isn't really whether or not your child gives up the goods. The lesson you really want to teach here is that being generous and kind makes people feel good and ultimately makes the world a better place. But when you demand of a child to share, you are missing out on all that. You are simply forcing the outcome, and probably making them defensive and self-pitying along the way. Ever been the recipient of begrudged kindness? It feels awful. Giving a child the space and autonomy to choose whether, what, and when to share means that when they do it, it will be a true act of giving.

Sometimes the conflict is the point. As adults we tend to see things in black and white terms. Sharing = good. Arguing = bad. Turn taking = good. Grabbing = bad. That's why we go out and buy two of the same toy, so everyone can have one. Or we force turn taking with our egg timer, so that each turn is mathematically accurate and fair. Our tactics fall on deaf ears, because we're missing the real point. In truth, humans are much messier than that, and children are interested in the social connection and exploration . . . What happens when I grab this toy? How can I engage this other child? He has it, it must be interesting! When we call children "terrible sharers," "selfish," or "greedy," we are missing the real motive behind their behavior and we are unfairly and unkindly labeling them.

Facilitate problem solving or stay silent. In fact, my favorite approach is to do nothing. To hold my tongue as I watch the children figure it out. It can be a real lesson in self-restraint. When we swoop in with our statements such as, "If you're fighting over it, then no one is getting it!" or, "You have it for one minute, then you have it for one minute!" or ,"You're the big boy so you should give it to him!" we rob our children of the opportunity to problem solve. We might not like the solutions they come up with, but my rule is that if they're happy, I'm happy. There are incredible lessons here: negotiation, compromise, give and take. When adults get too involved, we muddy the waters with our evaluations and judgments, seeing victims and aggressors where there are only children at play. I've watched my brother—a father of five and parenting role model to me—when one of his children runs up to him and tattles on another one. He looks at them with kindness, trust, and empathy and says, "Hmm, that does sound tough. I'm sure you'll figure it out." They almost always do, and if they don't, he's there to help.

In her book, *It's OK Not to Share*, Heather Shumaker explains that forced sharing teaches children to be wary and untrusting of others, knowing that they have to fight for what they want and protect it vigilantly. "Kids who are forced to share on demand will typically hog the ball and take extra-long turns when first given the opportunity to keep an object as long as they like. This makes sense. They simply don't trust the system." When children are forced to share it doesn't teach them to be kindhearted and generous, it teaches them to be bitter and resentful of the (usually little) siblings who get everything they want.

Ownership is a natural area of conflict. Just visit your local courthouse and see the list of open cases and their subject matter. We adults have not learned to share either.

One of the classic solutions parents come up with is to buy double *everything*. But supersizing your playroom doesn't really solve the problem, and it introduces a whole host of others such as a bleeding budget and double the stuff in your house. Sure, there are some items where everybody needs to get their own, but often the fights over ownership don't end simply because there are duplicates. In fact, in many ways this can accentuate the problem. The message is: it's impossible for you to take turns, so we need to double up on everything.

The best solution to the "sharing" problem is teaching children to negotiate terms and take turns. Together with you, they can agree on the parameters and length of each turn. Sure, they can use a timer if that's helpful. Or, it could be as simple as teaching them to say "You can have it when I'm done". Teach them to sweeten the deal by offering something else the other child can have, as in: "I'm not done with the shovel but would you like a turn with my bucket meanwhile?" Every child will feel resentful toward a child they've been forced to share with. However, if they are offered the chance to decide themselves how much time they need with a certain item, they're likely to be ready to give it over when they're done.

Protecting Younger Siblings' Play

Younger siblings are born into a family where there is already play happening. And older siblings often rush to initiate their baby sister or brother into the joy of play; it can be so sweet to witness them complaining about why their newborn sibling doesn't yet *build with LEGO* or *ride a bike*. It's worth helping our

Stagger their play
so the little one
can't reach.

Put the little one
in a play pen.

Put the big one
in a play pen!

older children to slow down and lower their expectations around the younger sib's development, finding other ways they can engage with and help take care of the baby.

As the baby grows, the urge for the older sibling to intervene, control, and "do things" for and to the baby grows as well. Often siblings who are close in age act out the dynamic of "Boss and Employee," where the older sibling is calling all the shots, shouting out all the answers, and owning all the "goods." It's helpful to be mindful of this dynamic and support younger children's independence, giving them a voice ("I just want to check, are you enjoying this game?") and turns to make choices for the family ("Okay, but where would *you* like to go today?"), so that they don't lose themselves to their older sibling's play.

Protecting Older Siblings' Play

Often we're skewed toward protecting younger (Cuter! More helpless!) siblings from their older siblings' harsh words or poking fingers. And that, evolutionarily, makes sense. However, often we lump our older children with needing to tolerate, make space for, and accommodate some very intrusive and disruptive behaviors from a very needy little sibling. And it's not surprising that this doesn't endear their little brothers or sisters to them very much.

Adam, four, is building an elaborate Magnet Tiles structure. Oliver, two, toddles over, excited to grab those shiny tiles from the top row of Adam's castle. Adam growls as fiercely as he can at Oliver, trying to scare him away. Oliver bursts into tears, and Lauren, their mom, comes rushing to his defense. Adam feels doubly hurt: first, his cute baby brother was trying to *demolish* his prize creation, and second, and perhaps worse, his mother was siding with Oliver. *How unfair!*

Rather than demanding that Adam let Oliver play *with* him, Lauren can protect Adam's game. She can:

- Help him to relocate his structure to a place that Oliver can't reach, such as on top of the dining-room table.
- Close the door and keep Oliver outside that room so that Adam can continue his work.
- Sit with them and keep Oliver busy with other games so that Adam's work is protected.

Let the older child play behind closed doors

This shows Adam that his play is important and worth protecting. And it teaches Oliver that he will need to respect Adam's space and possessions. This will go a long way in setting up the habits that each child's play is respected and in contributing to Adam's patience toward Oliver in the future, knowing that his mom is there for him.

Gate off an area for the older child

Disagreements on *Which* Games to Play, Assigning Roles and Rules

Often the disputes are not a fight over a toy (typical of the younger crew) but a fight over getting a *say*. Elementary-age schoolchildren are entering what Harville Hendrix calls the stage of concern, where their social standing and relationship to peers becomes paramount. They might argue over who gets to pick the game, who assigns the roles, and which rules to follow. They'll disagree one what's "fair" and have challenges around winning and losing.

Let the older child play up at the table.

It's an extremely healthy, crucial rite of passage for children to learn (firsthand) how to solve these types of social challenges. It's not easy to lose, as it requires us to eat humble pie and be faced with our shortcomings. Neither is it easy to be a graceful winner, which demands humbling oneself and extending empathy and sportsmanship. It takes negotiation skills to agree on rules when you each have a different version. You

303

need sensitivity to assign roles each child accepts, and you need flexibility to accept the role you've been assigned. These are all rich learning experiences.

Unfortunately, much of our culture is robbing children of these opportunities to learn. As recesses get shorter and school days longer, as homework loads get heavier and summer holidays more structured, so too goes the open-ended, long hours of group play where children learn to navigate sticky social challenges. Sometimes it's peers who best smooth out our rough edges and round out our sharp corners.

In general, if you have children who are disagreeing on rules and roles, you can empower them to solve these issues themselves. Children have an innate sense of fairness and are able to creatively solve such conundrums without adult intervention, if they're given ample opportunities to practice these skills. Healthy adult modeling contributes greatly to this as well, which is why I advocate for resolving differences you might have with your partner *in front of your children* as often as possible, although only if you both have the skills to do so with civility and respect.

There are those rarer cases with a pattern of one child exercising overt control over the other or others in a repetitive and eventually damaging way. I say *rarer* because I think as adults, we're erring on the side of being too quick to label one child as "bossy," and intervening on behalf of the "victim." However, sometimes there is a need for some guidance and balancing of the power.

When to Intervene

Dr. Laura Markham, an esteemed mentor and dear friend, has helped me and hundreds of thousands of other parents learn the tools of coaching siblings through their conflicts with her popular book *Peaceful Parent, Happy Siblings*. She contends that parents need to step in when conflict arises so that we can use the opportunity to teach them relationship skills for life. "So, while you can't control your children, you can control someone who has a tremendous influence on how your children relate to each other. You".

If you're raising siblings, then you probably already know that many different conflicts will arise: jealousy over who gets what, vying for your attention or a seat on your lap, telling each other's secrets, or teasing each other in a number of ways. All of these conflicts will benefit from skillful coaching and handholding from a loving adult.

WHAT TO THINK & SAY WHEN YOUR KIDS ARE FIGHTING

"I'm here to help you figure it out."

"Shall we use a timer?"

"I won't let you hit."

"It's sometimes hard to be a big sister."

"We need to be respectful. How can we solve this with a win-win solution?"

"Let's list out the rules we agree on."

"It's sometimes hard to be a little brother."

However, differentiate between these interventions and getting involved in children's play together. This is an area where we might be wise to tread more lightly.

It can be wonderful to coach our children through conflict, but sometimes our interventions make things worse. We might think that ushering a baby brother into the big girls' game is a good idea. We're teaching them to include him and giving him what he wants (to get in on the game). However, the residue resentment might lead to picking on him in the game or "punishing" him later. Sometimes it's best to simply empathize, validate, support, and reflect. Remember: "Even though we mean well, forcing kids to play together backfires. Often the child we are trying to help is not fully welcomed into the play, which can lead to greater social rejection. We unwittingly make the problem worse. Instead of trying to avoid rejection, view it as a new learning opportunity".

Other times getting involved is definitely the right thing to do, but we may not have the emotional resources to do that. If we're getting triggered, yelling, throwing out threats or grabbing kids' arms, we may be doing more damage than good. I personally fall into this trap often; however, my goal is to parent by the doctor's oath: First do no harm. So even if my children are at each other's throats, my goal is to try not to intervene—save actually stopping the violence— until I am in a good position to facilitate the conflict skillfully. I call this being a peaceful ninja. So how do I know if I'm ready to help? Ten indicators:

1.   I am calm and not triggered.
I have cooled myself down first. I am alert and present but relaxed. I know this because my shoulders, hands, face and jaws are relaxed.

2.   I can see both children with empathy.
No victims or aggressors, just children who need help.

3. I am here to help the children figure this out.

Not to "teach you a lesson." I am open to suggestions. I am curious about how I can be of service. I will not lecture.

4. I am ready and willing to keep each child safe.

I will use my leadership role to set boundaries in order to protect children. I will use my hands to keep them safe.

5. I am able to set boundaries.

I'll physically remove a child if they can't stop themselves from hurting others or destroying things.

6. I will follow through on my boundaries.

If a child is being unsafe, unkind, or destructive, I will follow through on our family approach by removing the child from the situation or giving them a way to calm down safely and make amends.

7. I am focused on the solution.

Not on blame, shame, guilt or punishments. I am looking for the best way to move forward now.

8. I trust my children and myself.

I recognize that conflicts are inevitable; they're not my fault or the children's fault. I know that we have what it takes to figure this out.

9. I can let go when I'm getting triggered.

I know there will be many more opportunities to coach children. I know this isn't an emergency. I will release control if I'm starting to become overly involved.

10. I believe in the power of repair.

I know that we all say or do "unacceptable" things in the heat of the moment. In that case there is always repair, apology, and reconnection. When I can't manage to do all of these, I quote my brother: "I'm sure you'll figure it out."

How to Intervene: Nonviolent Communication

Marshall Rosenberg, an American psychologist, mediator, author, and teacher developed a brilliant blueprint for nonviolent communication. Here's a four-step framework for coaching siblings through play conflicts, based on his approach:

1.   Observe the situation:
"I see there's a lot of grabbing at the same truck!" "I see hitting." "I see there's a problem happening with this puzzle." Tip: Don't use the children's names, as this spikes defensiveness ("It's not my fault!") even if that's not how it's intended. Instead state what you see as though the children weren't there.

2.   Label the feelings:
"Hitting hurts!" "Being left out feels bad." "It's frustrating to be disturbed." "It's annoying to be tickled." "It's uncomfortable to be squished." "It's infuriating when your work is ruined." "It can make us jealous when someone gets something we want."

3.   Express the needs:
"We need gentle touch." "We all need our work to be respected." "We need some personal space." "We need some quiet for our ears." "We need to feel safe." "We need to use words." "We need to get help."

4.   Make a request:
"Would you like to move over here to finish the puzzle?" "Would you like to tell Emily that you want a turn after her?" "Would you like a truck all to yourself?"

Setting a Physical Limit

Sometimes the above framework won't suffice, because when violent or destructive behaviors are involved (as there often are in my home), talking isn't enough. We need to physically follow through on keeping children, ourselves, and our property safe. In that case, I'll try to rely on the following framework, while gently but firmly blocking the child's hands from doing any further damage or picking the child up and removing them from the room.

1.   I see that ...
"I see that you can't stop screaming." "I see that you're hitting her." "I see that you won't let him build in here."

2.   I will help you by ...
"I will help you by holding your hands until you're ready to stop." "I will help you by taking you to your room until you're calm." "I will help you by sitting between you until you're ready to be gentle."

3.   Follow through:
On the limit you're setting (hold her hands, sit between them, take him to his room, etc.)

4.   When/then:
"When you calm down, then we can go back to playing." "When you stop screaming, then we can move on to have our snack." "When you use gentle hands, then I can release your arms."

All of the coaching and intervening must be done with as much warmth, kindness and connection that you can muster. Remind yourself that these are your precious, sweet children—who are having a hard time. Remember you are there to help them learn. Offer as many snuggles, hugs and cuddles as you can along the way. Often children who are lashing out at each other are actually crying out for connection with you.

Forced Apologies

When a conflict has erupted, repair is in order. For many of us, this means a quick "Say you're sorry!" and all is well. But the fact is, no one loves apologizing. It's hard to tolerate guilty feelings that can come with recognizing you've hurt someone else or done something wrong.

People usually justify themselves to defend themselves from these painful feelings. This is why apologizing—essentially admitting we're in the wrong—is incredibly difficult for most adults, let alone children.

I mean, seriously, how many adults do you know who are graceful and easy apologizers? Exactly. Forced apologies are as common as forced sharing in our culture. But apologies that are insincere are also ineffective. We are actually teaching our children inauthenticity when we force them to apologize.

When you force them, they may be apologizing through gritted teeth. They are learning that they should say what is expected of them regardless of their internal experience, something that doesn't develop a healthy sense of self.

On the other hand, knowing how to repair relationships, and being moved to make such repairs, is critical to developing meaningful friendships, which is something we all want for our children. So how do we encourage an honest, authentic apology?

I think there are two major components to this:
The first is modeling an apology. I talk to my children in ways that are unacceptable in a healthy relationship several times a day. I snap at them, bark orders, sometimes embarrass them by telling them off in front of others, and sometimes I totally lose my cool and yell. Any behaviors that I wouldn't tolerate in them warrants an apology from me. So, several times a day,

you can hear me saying things like:

"I'm sorry I raised my voice just now, that wasn't a kind way of speaking. Next time I will try to phrase my request more respectfully." "I apologize for rushing you. I know you were in the middle of your project. I'm late and I should have left more time."

When children are apologized to, they see that apologizing is a normal, healthy part of a relationship, nothing to be ashamed of and nothing to mumble about. In my personal and rather narrow experience, this creates a child who apologizes with relative ease and regularity.

When you model an apology, make sure you're modeling a good apology. It really is an art. Here are some insights I've learned along the way:

Always err on the side of taking the infraction more seriously than you might. Typically, our defense mechanism works overtime to convince us that it "wasn't so bad," while the person we've hurt is equally insistent that it was terrible. Horrible. Awful. There is nothing less effective when apologizing than making light of the situation in the eyes of the recipient.

Never use the word *if* or *but*. When you use these words, you're essentially canceling out all of your responsibility, and therefore rendering your apology void. When you say, "I'm sorry IF I hurt you," you're telling the person you're not truly convinced that you hurt them, but you're willing to go along with their fantasy play and satisfy their childish whims. When you say: "I'm sorry, BUT ..." you're negating your apology by saying that your actions were justified and, at the core, were basically asked for.

An apology should be a completely one-sided communication. An acknowledgement of guilt and regret on your side, asking nothing in return, including a response or forgiveness.

Take full responsibility. For your behavior or your reaction in the situation. Do not explain or blame the other person. There can be time later on to discuess their side in contributing to the series of events.

The second step is to encourage apology. This means that when your child does something unkind to someone else, or to you, you can kindly and gently mention that an apology might be in order. But doing so without any force, shame, or anger will make it much more likely to produce an authentic apology.

For example, saying, "It didn't feel good when you demanded your drink like that," or "It looks like Johnny's feelings are hurt," might leave an open-ended invitation for repair, which may or may not come in the form of apology. Whatever form the repair takes, celebrate it and accept it. Hugs, kind looks, and other thoughtful gestures are all forms of repair. It can also be appropriate to prompt: "I think Katie might feel more happy to play again after she hears that you're sorry". Or: "I'll be happy to forgive you when you're ready to take responsibility and apologize." Ultimately, children need to actually learn the skill of apologizing well and be encouraged to practice it.

When your child does apologize, take a moment to acknowledge the repair they made. Thank them so that they know that this is meaningful. Remember that people take different amounts of time to process events and feelings, and sometimes an apology might come a lot later than you wanted it—hours later or even days. That's okay; as siblings they will have a lifetime ahead of them to practice many an apology.

Action Steps

- Remember that there are many different types of social play, as Mildred Parten outlined: solitary, unoccupied, onlooking, parallel, associative, and cooperative. It's best not to judge a child for how they are engaging (or not engaging) with others, but to allow them to move through the stages of development naturally.

- Remind yourself conflict is normal. Siblings' fights over play tend to circle ownership and control. It's normal for children to fight over toys or over what the rules of the game are. It's okay for them not to share, as Heather Shumaker teaches us, and it's okay for them to learn to take turns and negotiate the rules on their own.

- Become a good coach. When arguments are getting out of hand and are unkind, violent, or recurring, adult coaching is helpful. According to Dr. Laura Markham, teaching children the skills of problem solving will set them up with relationship skills for life. However, if we're interfering too much or if we ourselves are triggered, we may not be in a position to help.

- When we *are* in a position to coach, like a peaceful ninja, we can use the nonviolent communication steps: observe the situation, label the feelings, express the needs, make a request .

- Set physical limits, where necessary, with the minimum required force. If there's violent or destructive behavior involved, we'll need to set a physical limit: say what you see, say how you'll help, follow through on the boundary, and explain what needs to happen in order to continue playing.

- Don't forget to infuse a lot of parental connection. Your children need that and sometimes act out this need on their siblings.

Screens

It's good to be curious about many things. **Mr. Fred Rogers**

Let's touch upon the conflicting schools of thought and ask ourselves: What are the core concerns around screens, when it comes to play? Do screens inhibit or enhance play? We'll differentiate active and passive screen usage and outline strategies for creating a healthy relationship with online games while still embracing real-life play. We'll discover the path of Aristotle's golden mean: the commitment to embrace the wonder of technology and harness its power for creativity and connection while still being aware of and setting boundaries around the more destructive and addictive qualities screens can induce. We'll move away from technophobia and demonizing of screens, but we will not succumb to screens eating away at the fabric of our family connection, our time in nature, and our need to move our bodies.

Confusion

Screens are easily the most confusing element of modern-day parenting. The leading thinkers and writers in the world of mindful parenting are split down the middle and represent dichotomously opposed views. On the one hand, we have leaders such as Dr. Laura Markham and Janet Lansbury, who advocate a screen-free childhood. And on the other, writers such as Dr. Peter Gray and Lenore Skenazy call for an embrace of limitless technology for our children.

I have felt and continue to feel the very real conflicts surrounding screens and parenting on my own skin. Modus operandi has always been to try to educate myself, expand my perspective, and gain deeper insights from the thought leaders of family health and wellness. And yet, here is a topic on which all of my heroes seem to be at odds with one another, arguing opposed stances, each convincing. On this topic I have felt like a Jekyll and Hyde mother, going from an unschooling approach (Screens for everyone! Zero limits! They'll self-regulate as necessary! Trust!) to a

screen-free childhood approach (No screens before teens!) and back
again, quicker than the next episode of *Daniel Tiger's Neighborhood*
can load on my toddler's iPad.

On the One Hand...

Leaders of Silicon Valley, such as the late Steve Jobs—the very
mavens who've shaped the use of screens as we know it—have
famously been portrayed as never allowing their own children
to use the very iPads they designed. This discovery created an
uproar complete with conspiracy theories over the effects these
machines have on children and how damaging they must be if the
people who make them—and know their effects best—won't allow
them at home.

But it's not just hype. Many researchers, thought leaders,
and research-based psychologists advocate for delayed screen
usage or a screen-free childhood. Dr. Laura Markham, author of
Peaceful Parent, Happy Kids and a close friend and mentor of mine
says: "The earlier we introduce screens, the more it affects the
child's brain development and the more likely they will have
trouble managing their addiction to screens and technology later
in life".

Magda Gerber, founder of Resources for Infant Educarers
(RIE) advised delaying any screen exposure until the age of six
and closely monitoring which shows our children are exposed to
thereafter. Janet Lansbury and Meghan Owen expand the idea
that the shows our children watch should be slow paced, such as
Sesame Street and *Mister Rogers' Neighborhood*, based on the findings
that fast-paced shows cause a reduced ability to stay on task.

Screens have been connected to a shorter attention span,
later bedtimes and less overall sleep, excessive weight gain and
childhood obesity, and an increase in aggressive behaviors.
Furthermore, some of the promises we parents hope to fulfill
with screens, such as teaching valuable lessons, often backfire as
children receive the opposite message to that intended: learning,

for example, to be fearful of differences rather than to embrace them, even if the opposite lesson was the expressed message of the show. When I see this research, it seems conclusive: delaying screen introduction (to the age of six or beyond) and providing as much of a screen-free childhood as possible, seems to be just what the doctors are ordering.

But on the Other Hand...

We have the unschoolers, led by Dr. Peter Gray, who advises strongly *against* limiting screen time. Gray says: "Why would we want to limit a kid's computer time? The computer is, without

LOVE SCREENS   HATE SCREENS

connect with people from far away   solitary
                                                      lowers focus
                    responsive   threshold?
educational?   learning   sensory
                                  overload
available!   online predators?
convenient!   Bullying?
fun!   Unrealistic &
                                                     Violent
                                                       imagery?

        Social?   negative content?
                  addictive
Gamification - learn cause & effect   at the expense of social play
         trial & error   sedentary   the expense of
         patience & persistence   comes   at social play
                                     outdoor, physical & social play

318   **Reclaim Play**

question, the single most important tool of modern society. Our limiting kids' computer time would be like hunter-gatherer adults limiting their kids' bow-and-arrow time. Children come into the world designed to look around and figure out what they need to know in order to make it in the culture into which they are born".

Many parents have found that the underbelly of the anti-screen research findings is that in limiting screens, we pay a price in our relationships: becoming controlling, labeling their interests as somehow "bad" and "unhealthy," or making screens into an alluring forbidden fruit that brings with it ongoing battles. They find themselves exhausted in the face of ongoing barricading of their children against the influx of screen culture. They find themselves wondering if they're overprotective, or even holding their children back somehow from a modern-day luxury, entertainment, and educational tool.

Even much of the research about the harmful effects of screens has been refuted and disputed. Dr. Alexandra Lamont from Keele University led a study to measure the effect of fast-paced shows on children, explaining: "There is a widely held belief that television watching in young children is responsible for behavioral problems, attention deficits, and developmental challenges, but there is little research that has addressed this to date for young audiences".

Furthermore, Dr. Gray assures that "whenever we prevent our kids from playing or exploring in the ways they prefer, we place another brick in a barrier between them and us. We are saying, in essence, 'I don't trust you to control your own life.' Children are suffering today not from too much computer play or too much screen time. They are suffering from too much adult control over their lives and not enough freedom". His adamant argument for choosing freedom over strict control makes me wonder. Which value is more important? Which is the riskier path? Risky freedom or protective control?

319

As Dr. Gray writes: "Why do we keep hearing warnings from "authorities"—including the American Academy of Pediatricians—that we must limit kids' computer play? Some of the fear-mongering comes, I think, from a general tendency on the part of us older folks to distrust any new media. Plato, in The Republic, argued that plays and poetry should be banned because of their harmful effects on the young. When writing came about and became technically easier, and was enthusiastically seized upon by the young, some of their elders warned that this would rot their minds; they would no longer have to exercise their memories. When printed novels became available to the masses, many warned that these would lead the young, especially girls and young women, to moral degeneracy. When televisions began to appear in people's homes, all sorts of dire warnings were sounded about the physical, psychological, and social damage they would cause."

When refusing to incorporate innovative technologies into our lives, perhaps we should be aware of our historical fear of the unknown and of what's new.

Permission to Find Your Voice

So, are screens a friend or foe? I won't give you the definitive answer, as it seems that there isn't one. It's up to you to find the truest answer for your unique family, in this present moment. Every child responds differently to screens, and every type of screen use is different in turn.

You probably already have a sense of what works for your family and within your culture. Often when there's a polarizing topic such as screens, the truth lies somewhere in the middle.

Loving the Times We Live In

One of the most beautiful thoughts to come out of *Simplicity Parenting* is the practice of loving the times we live in. As we look to simplify our lives and reclaim play, it's easy to wax nostalgic about an earlier time, some previous generation in which raising children was idyllic, safe, and earthy. However, one can argue that we live in the most fantastic time of human evolution, with the most advanced medicine, the safest cities, the lowest rates of poverty, and the longest lifespan. Even though it might not always seem so, war and disease are at an all-time low unimaginable by previous generations. Rather than hating screens, I want to embrace a love and acceptance of our lives as they are, including technology.

Not All Screens Were Created Equal

I wouldn't compare a Skype conversation with Grandma to a cinematic movie night with the family, or to six hours straight of *Fortnite*, taking an online course on coding, playing Minecraft with a friend, and so on. It seems vital that we stop putting all screen usage under the same umbrella, given the endless ways we can use our devices and the notable variety in the quality of those interactions.

The Radical Middle Approach

Fire is a good servant but a bad master. **Proverb (Anonymous)**

To establish a healthier relationship with technology, we need to understand how it can serve us, and when we, in turn, *are serving it*. Just as in the proverb above, fire is incredible energy: as a servant it keeps us warm, lights our space, and cooks our food. But as a master, it burns our house down. Similarly, we can find the ways that screens serve, teach, connect, enrich, and entertain us, but set up careful boundaries so that they don't "burn" us with addiction, consuming our social life or interrupting our opportunities to move and explore the great outdoors.

Perhaps you'll opt not to limit some screen usage for activities such as researching for a project, watching educational shows, video conferencing with friends and family, working on a creative activity such as an animation video, or writing a book. Whereas "vegging out" in front of cartoons or playing video games might be fun and worthwhile—for a while—you might opt to limit these usages to make time for other activities and ward off some of those ill effects of a sedentary lifestyle. You might decide that some content is off-limits altogether and some is free for all. You might decide that some days are "unlimited screen days," whereas other days are "screen free." You might decide that you are there to facilitate and moderate with your child as they explore the boundless worlds of the internet, or that you carefully utilize protective walls that block violent and sexual content. Hopefully, you'll develop an ongoing, open conversation about the themes, ideas, and lessons that come forth from the shows, movies, and games your family members interact with on the screen. What is the message the creators of the content under discussion trying to impart? Do we agree with that message? How do the characters behave? How are the scenes like—and unlike—real life? This is how we develop critical thinking and media literacy.

Honoring Computer Play as Play

I still hold definite stigmas around what makes up "true play," but I'm trying to dismantle those. The truth is that in many device-based activities children can find a deep sense of flow, just as they can in playing with physical toys or in pursuing sensory explorations. Remember that flow, as defined by Mihaly Csikszentmihalyi, is "being completely involved in an activity for its own sake. The ego falls away. Time flies". Watch a child play Minecraft, and this is surely what you'll witness.

The magic of gamification—which allows the challenge to be customized to our precise level of skill and continually increase as our skills increase—is in fact an essential part of flow. The fact that we engage in these activities simply for the pleasure of them (and don't need to be rewarded or punished to complete the tasks; they are self-rewarding) illustrates their intrinsic value to us as an experience. And the way that children (and adults) can play for hours without needing to come up for air is a testament to the deep state of flow they enter as they play video games. In addition, the immediate feedback loops help children know if they are successful or not, another strong element of flow.

Video games have a deep potential as educational tools. Through games children can learn patience and persistence as they work to master one level before the next, and creative problem-solving skills as they crack the next challenge. Many reluctant readers learn how to read as they're mastering a game. They can gain meaningful real-world skills, such as music appreciation, coding, CAD design, hand-eye coordination, spatial reasoning, strategy, logic, math, cartography, mental clarity, creative writing, and even receive a financial education as they balance a budget. Through games, children can be inspired to take more of an interest in history, art, and STEM subjects. Contrary to popular stigma, collaborative video games can even develop social skills. They can serve as stress relievers and offer a sense of control and mastery.

Playing video games with our children can actually help us develop a more powerful bond with them as we meet them in their worlds of interest and level the playing field between adult and child (or flip it in favor of the child, I know my son finds my Minecraft skills—or lack thereof—hilarious).

Setting Limits around Screens

With all that we know about both the pitfalls and benefits of embracing technology in our lives with children, how can we do so mindfully and set boundaries that will guard our attention, our family time, our time spent in nature and with friends? And more specifically, how can we ensure screens support—not compromise—our children's play?

The golden mean approach calls for embracing certain screen usage at certain times. It means we are discerning: we use our critical mind and our intuition to make customized plans and choices around screens (or anything else), cherry picking and experimenting with what works for our family. It means we evolve, adapt, and learn through trial and error.

We observe the ways that screens warm our children like a special campfire we gather around, cook with, and light our way with and, conversely, the ways that screens might be burning their bridges to others, to physical wellness, or to developing other aspects of their lives.

It might go without saying, but let's reiterate anyway: our own relationship with screens will be what dictates the vibe of our home. If we're modeling a healthy relationship with screens and their creative use, as well as spending time outdoors and on physical movement and having meaningful eye-contact-based relationships with others, we can be more confident in setting the same expectations and forging the same path for our children to follow.

We will all need to craft our own boundaries. Some of the boundaries in our family include a screen-free Sabbath every week for adults and children alike. Screen-free meals, screen-free bedtimes and no use of screens until our other commitments for our morning routines have been done, we've been outdoors, and we've connected with each other. We're relaxed about using screens to research, practice skills, or connect with family. We're more discerning about how long we spend on screens to simply veg out. And we do our best to introduce screens as late as possible to our little ones, something that becomes ever more challenging as older children use screens. We do our best to connect with our children over what they're watching, playing, and learning and to help them learn to protect themselves online, choose high quality content and games, and apply critical thinking to the ideas and scenes they observe.

We also try to model how we embrace technology and the ways in which we feel grateful for it. My entire career as a parenting coach and my husband's entire career as a neuro-radiologist both take place almost completely on screens. We do our banking, shop for groceries, and maintain our relationships with extended family abroad through screens. This is a huge blessing.

HOW TO SET LIMITS ON SCREEN USAGE

Pick a time of day or week when screens are allowed and stick to it.

Choose the types of devices, games and content you allow and follow through.

Keep screen usage in the family area - where you can see it and oversee it.

Coach your child on the dangers of the internet, online predators and bullying.

Set up parental controls and child proof internet

Model healthy screen usage yourself and talk about it openly

Value Screen's Contribution to Play

We value the place of screens in play, while still ensuring there are *many hours* of screen-free play per day, outdoors and with friends. In our home, most days are screen free days where no tv shows or video games are permitted. However if a child wants to watch a drawing tutorial, play an educational Osmo game or look up information for a school project—screens are a-okay. Playing Minecraft or video games, or learning Photoshop on a device absolutely counts as flow. It's just insufficient to cover children's need to use their hands and bodies, and to connect to nature and others. Just as a child who only engages in gymnastics for hours upon hours might need some balance to support other areas of development (social and academic for example), so do we need to ensure that the addictive qualities of screens don't consume our children's entire energy reserve and timetable. However, there seems to be no reason to demonize screens and every reason to embrace them as presenting real, valuable play and learning opportunities, within healthy boundaries and contexts.

Action Steps

- Treat yourself kindly: screens are by far the most confusing element of our modern-day parenting journey, with clear and compelling evidence both for screen limits and against them.

- You're right to be suspicious of screen usage: those who advocate for limiting screen time for children cite the research that shows that screens shorten attention span, interfere with focus on task completion, increase violence and aggression, decrease the quality and quantity of sleep, and contribute to the rise in childhood obesity.

- You're also right if you suspect that screen usage has some major benefits: those who promote unlimited screens for children see screens as a necessary modern tool. They argue that limiting screens makes them into a forbidden fruit and deprives children of the very learning tool they need in their generation. Limiting screens also creates family tension and recurring conflicts, labeling the child's interests as "bad," and generating guilt and frustration in the parents.

- Give yourself permission to find your own complex, contextual and personal approach to screens that takes what you know from the research and blends it with your personal experience.

- Consider the golden mean, which implies that we neither demonize screens nor succumb to screen addiction. We need to use screens to serve us, not allow them power over us.

- Remember that computer play has been shown to be meaningful play with all the qualities of a state of flow, such as losing oneself in an intrinsically rewarding activity for the sake of it, being sufficiently challenged, building skills, and losing a sense of time.

- Even with all the benefits of computer play, ensure your child is getting sufficient time outdoors, with friends, learning real-life skills, using their hands and bodies, and pursuing additional creative projects that don't take place on a screen.

- Take time to map out your current limits around screens. These might include a specific time of day, a specific day of the week, or after other chores and projects have been completed (such as schoolwork, outdoor time, time with friends, and contribution to the household). It could include discernment of which type of content can be consumed, when and where.

- As adults we'll have to set the tone of our family with our own behavior and relationship with technology. Are we being mindful to be screen free at meals and family times? Are we modeling and explaining what we're doing on our screens and why we're using them? Are we displaying an appreciation for technology while also setting boundaries for ourselves?

A
Play
Filled
Life

We don't stop playing because we grow old; we grow old because we stop playing. **George Bernard Shaw**

Sometimes, when people hear that I advocate for the reclamation of play, they worry about all the "real" things their children need to learn and achieve in order to "succeed" in their lives. Our society has entered the "readiness" rat race, in which every stage of our lives is there merely to prepare us for the next—as though the entire point of preschool—aptly named—is to prep you for . . . school, and the whole point of seventh grade is to get you ready for eighth, and on and on until you graduate college. At which point will you "arrive"? Perhaps we can step off the hamster wheel and choose to be in the present moment, accepting ourselves, and celebrating ourselves as we're showing up right now, and our children, for who they are in this moment, not who they could be in the next.

But there is a growing body of parents who realize that children and babies are whole people, right now. People who deserve freedoms, respect and to express their creative impulses in real time, not only when they are "baked" and considered legal adults. All parents wish to guide their children to grow into healthy, ethical, joyful, productive and self actualizing adults who pursue meaning and have fulfilling relationships. And still, these parents realize that *they* deserve to enjoy their children *now*. They wish to dampen the fears and anxieties about the "outcome" and "product" of childhood, instead sinking into the pleasure and value of the *process.*

The "readiness" obsession is also unrealistic—as if we really know what hard skills the global economy will ask of our children a decade from now. My own career—coaching parents—didn't even exist when I was in college. Perhaps many people would classify my career as not a "real job" because it's playful and creative, because it doesn't adhere to the industrial nine-to-five rules, because it has developed in a nonlinear way. But my career is but one example of a work life rooted in play that not only brings me great satisfaction and meaning but also financially sustains my team's families and mine.

So, does offering ample time and space to play hold children back from preparing for adult life? For the "real world?" To me, there is no better preparation for the "real world" than a play-full childhood that will hopefully lead to a play-full adulthood. Playful adults are able to pursue their creative endeavors, to solve their problems, and to *enjoy* their lives so much more. Personally, I hope my children *never* stop playing. While they must master resilience and grit, I hope they play their way through their "serious" endeavors and through their lives.

In 2012, psychologists Werner Greve, Tamara Thomsen, and Cornelia Dehio, from the University of Hildesheim, Germany, conducted a study of 134 participants, who, presented with a list of seven statements, reported the degree to which they aligned with their own childhood experiences from the time they were three-to-ten-year-olds. The statements included, "Looking back, I tried many things and experimented a lot by myself;" "From time to time, I set out on my own or with friends to discover the neighborhood;" and "My parents always were in fear that something could happen to me, so they did not let me do many things by myself." They also expressed their level of agreement or disagreement with ten statements designed to measure what the researchers dubbed as "social success." These included "Friends come to me for advice;" "My work is appreciated by others;" and "If something goes wrong, I have friends by my side that support me".

It was not surprising (to me, at least) that the researchers found a significant positive correlation between how much time they spent playing freely during their childhood and how socially successful they are and consider themselves to be as adults. The free time they enjoyed as kids was closely related with two key competencies for thriving adults: the flexibility to adjust one's goals and high self-confidence. Through this research they concluded that:

The more time we have to play and the greater the diversity of experiences we can make, the greater our accommodative flexibility throughout adulthood and, hence, the greater our developmental and social success over the lifespan. In contrast to strongly regulated playing (e.g., learning to play the piano), unguided playing (i.e., the possibility for trying out things) should be of particular use here. As a consequence, the extension of child play should predict not only more concrete preconditions of social success (e.g., self esteem, psychological health), but more generally the individual's adaptivity. The degree of the individual's flexibility (adaptivity) is claimed to be one important aspect of the relationship between child play on the one hand and evolutionary success on the other.

In other words, free play allows children to develop the flexibility needed to adapt to changing circumstances and environments—an ability that comes in handy when life becomes unpredictable as an adult.

So, I hope you feel incredibly confident in your choice to reclaim play. I hope that you see it not only as a preservation and protection of a precious childhood, but also as the most fertile, nutrient rich soil for their future play and creativity.

As we begin to implement everything we've discussed in this book, the inevitable ebb and flow of life will bring us challenges and wins along our parenting path. Whenever faced with such challenging times, we are invited to view it as a beckoning back to our basic values. As an opportunity to reclaim play in our lives.

Keep Your Creative Designer Hat On

Remember that we started this book by putting on our designer hats? By looking at our children's environment as something we get to shape through the choices we make? It's helpful to always remember to put that hat back on. Parenting is your artistic project. It's creative work. You get to craft, mold, shape, and contour it as it fits your unique vision and mission in life. Seeing raising children as a creative endeavor liberates us from dogmatic, one-size-fits-all thinking as we begin to tap into our more playful side.

One Reclaim Play student, Leah, whose daughter Annabelle was sensory seeking, looking for ways to experience sensory input in a stronger way than other children, hung up not one, but two indoor swings in her home, allowing Annabelle to squeeze into a cocoon swing or hang upside down from a trapeze. This relatively small action had massive ripple effects as Annabelle was able to find the sensory experience she needed without jumping on Leah herself or running out of the house. Heather, another student, commits to strewing every evening because she swears that this small effort on her part creates peaceful mornings for her family. She gets to nurse the baby peacefully as her four-year-old discovers some intriguing new play invitation. Considering she's using only what she has and puts in only two to three minutes per evening, that's a pretty magical result. It sure beats the frustration that happens when whiny four-year-olds want their mommies back from their baby brothers. For Alishia, another beloved student, "wearing the designer hat" meant taking a creative look at the way mainstream school was not serving her family and redesigning her child's educational path in a hybrid homeschool model.

Whenever you come up against challenges in your parenting—as you will daily, no doubt—use your designer hat and ask yourself, Can something in the environment be tweaked to serve us better? How can we creatively solve this problem? Rather than making *our child* (or ourselves!) the problem, making the problem a puzzle you get to solve.

Remember the three stages of design thinking that can help you tackle any parenting problem: empathizing, ideating, experimenting. This can apply to all manner of things.

Whether it's teaching our babies to sleep well or feeding them well at meals, a designer hat helps us stay in our creative, scrappy, innovative seat and wards off the helplessness that is synonymous with a victim mindset.

Perfect is the Enemy of Good

One of the cognitive fallacies that *really* tend to trip us parents up is perfection: the idea that there is one right way to do things, often reinforced by our time spent on social media, seeing picture-perfect representations of highly curated, edited moments and then comparing those to our messy life. It's disheartening. But it's also simply a deficient approach to life. Whenever you get demoralized on your playful journey, take a moment to self-diagnose your "comparisonitis." Are you measuring yourself unfavorably against your perception of others' "perfect" lives?

I know that if someone has a gorgeous picture on Instagram that awakens the green monster of envy within me, it's a great moment to notice that this is a "marker"—a signifier—of something I might desire too. It's a wonderful little "ping" that I'm receiving from the universe, helping me to sit up and notice what I'd like more of in my life, what I want to work toward. But it's also a moment of grace, gratitude, and self-compassion. Just because my life (my body, my bank account, my home, my diet, my lifestyle, my marriage, my kids . . . you name it) doesn't resemble the image that's reflected before me, it doesn't mean I am less. It just means there are endless ways of doing life with kids, and I can admire other people's choices without embracing them myself. *And* I can take inspiration from those parenting styles and approaches, from the toys, homes, and schedules that I *do* aspire to.

Which Type of Tomato Are You?

Recently I was listening to *Wow in the World* with my kids, an energizing podcast by NPR all about science for kids. In it they asked, "How many varieties of tomatoes do you think there are in the world? What would you guess?" I was thinking maybe . . . twenty? Thirty, if I'm generous? Turns out there are fifteen thousand types of tomatoes. Mind. Blown. To me this serves as a potent reminder that there is no one right way of being a human in the world. There isn't even one right way of being a tomato.

In my work I explore useful and universal tried and tested truths about building strong and resilient families, but it's important to remember that each family is unique and must discover their own way of creating a family life they love. Key guidelines for building close bonds, a sense of togetherness, teamwork, and a meaningful family culture can be helpful, but each family must intentionally design and experiment to find what works best for them. Building a family culture is like building a house—all homes need a blueprint, strong foundations, and interiors, but each home will be unique. Your family needs play, bonding, and rest, but how these aspects are expressed will be unique to you.

It's important to approach parenting advice and any other guidance with an open mind and take what works for you, while disregarding what doesn't fit your specific situation. Every family is unique, and what works for one may not work for another. It's a process of finding what works best for you through trial and error, and being flexible and adaptable as your family grows and evolves.

Play is Your Meditation

Dr. Shefali Tsabary, New York Times bestselling author of *The Awakened Family*, is a dear friend and esteemed mentor. She has taught me that parents to young children *do not need a spiritual practice.* This is because parenting *itself* can be used as our spiritual practice.

Every time your child is playing, this is an invitation to enter presence. Every time your child cries, this is a moment to overcome negative self-talk and emotionally regulate. Every time you watch your child sleep, the awe-filled emotions that overwhelm us can be a gateway to connect to something that's beyond our selves. Every time we stop, on our slow, dawdling walk down the road, to admire a crack, a worm, a blade of grass alongside our toddler who is *rapt* with fascination at the world's tiny wonders, we are slowing down our monkey minds to enter the present moment through the eyes of our child.

Resist the urge to quantify play. Refuse the cultural practice of valuing only that which we can measure. *Don't* write asking me, "How long should my two-year-old be able to play?" or "Does dressing-up play *count* as imaginative play or should they also be building with blocks?" Not because I wouldn't love to hear from you; I would. But because you don't need these types of permissions or charts or graphs to grade you and your child. Play is an organic, breathing, living journey. There aren't right and wrong answers, only what's right or wrong for you and your child *right now.*

Instead of fretting, assessing, and evaluating where your child "marks" on the play "scale," see play as more akin to the weather, or to prayer, or to music: it's something to be enjoyed, experienced and surrendered to, not analyzed *ad nauseam.* The most surefire way I know to "kill" our natural joy in play is to begin to quantify it and set fixed and rigid expectations about what it "should" and "shouldn't" look like.

Play Applies to Everything

Remember that play is not a separate, compartmentalized "activity" that our children have on their "to-do list" each day. Instead, it's more of a constant space that we occupy—the backdrop to our children's *entire day*—interspersed with some structured activities (lunch, homework, an outing) here and there. See play as the default, not the exception. See play as the given, obvious thing they'll be busy with all day, if we just get out of their way.

Be an astute observer of your child's play, notice how they sink into their own world, their own body, their own projects, and see if you can "borrow" that energy and apply it to other areas of their lives. If you notice your four-year-old loves to pretend to be a puppy—as mine does—perhaps when you're trying to usher her into the car, you could say "Here puppy, here!" If your six-year-old is really into drawing and coloring his own characters, you could make sure to bring along the markers and papers to a doctor's appointment so he'll have something to ease an anxious experience. See where you can build bridges between their worlds of play, imagination, creativity, and the mundane day-to-day chores and activities that need to get done.

Playful Parenting

The focus of this book has been to encourage our children's play. But as you begin to reclaim, support, and facilitate their play, don't let it stop there. A beautiful, powerful and potent aspect to having a play-full family is being playful ourselves, as adults. Playfulness is about being lighthearted, not taking ourselves or this parenting gig too seriously, and learning how to have *fun*.

The burdens and responsibilities of adulting sometimes have us grown-ups taking life with a heavy, frowny energy. Dr. Lawrence Cohen, the father of Playful Parenting and author of a book by the same name, says, "The fact is, we adults don't have much room in our lives for fun and games. Our days are filled with stress, obligations, and hard work. We may be stiff, tired, and easily bored when we try to get on the floor and play with children—especially when it means switching gears from a stressful day of work or household chores". But that's one of the gifts of having little kids around: they're fully embodied in the present moment, by definition. They respond well to making things into a game, doing them with an infusion of *joie de vivre* and a lightness of step.

Playful parenting is also an incredibly effective parenting tool. Toddlers reportedly hear *no* approximately four hundred times a day. And that's a problem, because as Dr. Dan Siegel, professor of psychiatry at the UCLA School of Medicine and author of *No Drama Discipline*, *The Whole Brain Child*, and *The Yes Brain* explains, there are actually two types of brain states your children might utilize: a "yes" brain state and a "no" brain state. The "yes" kids go through life with a positive outlook, while the "no" kids often shut down emotionally. In other words, a "yes" brain state will "approach life with all of these positive features versus a 'no brain' state, which is created when we feel threatened and we shut down." If your child hears *no* repeatedly, learning new things or being open to new experiences can prove more difficult than if they were encouraged via "yes" statements.

Rather than constantly giving our children commandments all day, we can fill our parenting toolbox with a myriad of colorful communication tools. One of the most effective? Playfulness. What does this look like? Here are ten ways to set limits with young kids (or even with teens) while being playful:

1.   Get into Character

When you say something in a different voice, with a new or funny accent, with a "costume" (read: *hat or glasses*) it turns *whatever* you're asking into a game. Rather than nagging our five-year-old *again* to get into the car we could put on a low, hushed whisper and say: "Special Agent Mama, reporting for action. Our mission: get into the car without being detected! Hop to it!"

2. Become Contrary

An absolute favorite with the younger crowd who *love* the sense of power in defying you! Because you say it in a clearly exaggerated tone, they know this is a game and you're not *teaching* them to be defiant. If they're a little confused, Dr. Lawrence Cohen teaches us that you could step out of character and whisper to them, "It's just a game, okay?" Say you wanted your three-year-old to get dressed, but they're dawdling. You might say: "I don't believe you can dress yourself! No way! Show me, I just can't *believe* that!" or for your four-year-old to wash her hands: "EEEWWW, please don't wash your hands with soap, that is so gross. Only very dirty germy people wash their *hands!* Eeeeewwwww!"

3. Be in Full Agreement

This is a great game when your kids are nagging you for *one more ice cream,* or *five more minutes*—and you're so "done" with not being heard. Instead, say: "Yes, of course we can stay at the park. Sure! We NEVER should go home! Let's sleep here! Let's stay forrr-ev-errr!"

4. Use Silly Language or Singing

If your child isn't hearing you anymore, can you sing it? Can you say it in a funny new way? Can you make it fun, ludicrous, outlandish, and bizarre? Rather than, "Get your shoes on, *now!*", how about: "bemenopepipo-SHOES-geegeerooroo-ON-shmegilan-feligan-FEET!"

5. Get Physical

Sometimes we adults just like to sit there and bark orders, don't we? But getting our bodies moving moves the energy and helps our children move right along with us. Need to bring your toddler up to the bath? Need to bring everyone to the dinner table? Or get everyone out of the house? Perhaps rather than saying it over and over, try getting up yourself and jumping, dancing, hopping, handstanding your way over there. Generally, moving our bodies with our kids makes a massive difference, as we've already explored in our Movement Zone. Always prioritize moving: getting outside, wrestling, and roughhousing.

6. Tell a Crazy Story

Stories are intrinsically mesmerizing and can be used instead of lecturing. Instead of, "Washing your hair is important to stay clean," you could make up a funny and outrageous story: "You will NEVER believe what happened to me when I was a little boy and I refused to wash my hair."

7. Switch Roles

In a game of perspective switch and role play, become the child yourself and watch your child giggle with glee: "I don't want to get dressed either! I want to stay in MY pajamas!" "I want you to make me ice cream for breakfast!"

8. Become Incompetent

This one has little kids falling over with laughter. Cohen shows how hilarious and empowering it is for kids if once in a while their adults become completely incompetent, mumbling, fumbling fools. "Hey, what is this? A toothbrush? How does it work?" "Oh no! I don't remember what our car looks like, can you tell me how to get there?"

9. Use Dolls (or Hands as Puppets)

Doll 1: "That mommy is getting so MAD that Lilly is pushing Sam." Doll 2: "Yes, I can see, she's about to blow!"

When the situation starts to get frustrating, step out of it and use your hands, or dolls, to act out in third person what's happening. This makes it less personal and sometimes *really* funny, helping both parent and child calm down.

10. Start Giggling

Sometimes we can use a dose of "laughter therapy"" —and it's a fake-it-till-you-make-it—simply burst into giggles with abandon and watch them turn into real belly laughs for all.

> "Using Playful Parenting, we can help children release all this emotion in ways that aren't hurtful to others. We do this by just spending lots of time giggling together, but also with some specific techniques. To help children with fears, for example, it often helps to play as if you are the one who is scared, and really exaggerate it. Make sure they don't feel mocked or humiliated. It helps if you don't imitate them exactly, but just take the general idea and exaggerate it."—Lawrence J. Cohen

Playing *with* Your Children

Making a case for independent play does not mean making a case *against* parents playing with their children. I think it's absolutely wonderful, meaningful, necessary time spent playing with our children. It's time where we get to bond over joint interests, to unwind and connect and to help them sort through big emotions and ideas. Play is children's love language. As Dr. Cohen says, "Children don't say, 'I had a hard day at school today; can I talk to you about it?' They say, 'Will you play with me?'"

That said, I think it's crucial that we give ourselves permission to play with our children only when we are truly emotionally available to be present and enjoy that time with them. In other words: only when we truly want to.

There seem to be a lot of guilt-inducing posts out there on social media that remind us that childhood is a limited, precious time. "How many summers do you have left until your children are grown?" "On your deathbed will you wish you worked more or played with your child more?" Or as this poem by Ruth Hulburt Hamilton ends:

"The cleaning and scrubbing can wait till tomorrow But children grow up as I've learned to my sorrow. So quiet down cobwebs; Dust go to sleep! I'm rocking my baby and babies don't keep."

It's Okay That You're Too Busy Sometimes

It seems the idea is that we should set all our "to-dos," housework, and even career work to one side, because childhood is to be savored and that means playing on the floor with our children. But the truth is that this sets unrealistic expectations. The truth is cleaning and scrubbing *can't wait* until tomorrow, at least not every day. The truth is that each of us has to stay sane, positive, well cared for and live in a home that feels pleasant and well run. We have to manage our finances, maintain other relationships, work our jobs and make dinner every day. And many of us have little time or patience for pretend play. All that's okay.

It's Okay That You Don't Enjoy That Type of Play

Some kids want to play chess, others want to play firefighters, and still others want to make clay sculptures. And maybe the type of play your kid is into just isn't something you can get excited about or even "into." That's *okay*. It's okay not to be fully invested in each of your child's interests; you are different people, after all. It's healthy for your child to learn that their interests and ideas of fun are not conditioned on *yours*. That you're authentic and real, and when you don't really feel like it, you'll say so. This allows them to trust you and believe in the integrity of your word, because when you *are* interested and having fun in a game, you'll say so too.

It's Okay for You to Play Only Rarely

Your child deserves to play with you when you can actually enjoy it—authentically. That might not be every day. They desire to see a parent who is having as much fun as they are. They want to connect with you, not have you "put up with them." When you force yourself to play because you'd feel guilty not to, you're not really there. You're distracted and even building resentment toward their demands. Such resentment will erupt on them at a later time. It's as though the child had signed an invisible contract: "Mommy will play with you now, although she doesn't want to, but she will be more irritable as a result. Sign on the dotted line." No child signs that contract. Instead, it's okay for you to play only every few days.

I have a standing LEGO date with my six-year-old every Saturday. He knows that the rest of the week I'm not available for playing and building with him—something I genuinely love to do—but on Saturdays I will sit on the floor and build enthusiastically for a couple of hours. It's not much, but it's real, it's fun, it's dependable, and there is no contention or frustration around it. I've set genuine expectations and I follow through on them, and I know he'll grow up with the sense that I really played with him.

It's okay not to want to play with your children very often and to keep it for every few days. It's okay not to say yes to every request. It's okay *not* to play games that don't light you up. Play is the *child's* work, the *child's* realm of control. In many ways adult involvement can overshadow their imagination, create a dependency on pleasing others and even teach them that they should accept begrudging company over their own solitude.

Adult Disruption of Play

It's really not our job to play with our children. It's an amazing opportunity, it's something we should make time and space for from time to time, but only a small chunk—or less—of their play time needs to be spent playing *with* us. In many ways, adults are a hindrance to children's play. We tell them they're doing it wrong, we look for "teachable moments," we get busy picking lint off the carpet instead of staying in character . . . we overpower, distract, or bring the wrong vibes to the game, because we're not as invested or interested. Find those few modems of play that feel great, harmonious, and pleasurable together, and don't worry about the rest. As Janet Lansbury writes:

"I really appreciated when Magda Gerber taught me that it is not our job to play with the child. In fact, oftentimes, our play with a child changes the direction of what the child would be doing. And we are very powerful, so she suggested using that power wisely. And that when we are playing "with" our child, that we do so more as an observer from the beginning, a very engaged observer who definitely responds when our child looks to us as an infant, or we see that they're struggling with something, we acknowledge. Maybe they're just looking at us, and we say, "Yes, I see, I notice what you're doing," and we describe what they're doing for them. Children do need us to give them full attention periodically, but not all the time, and not for a long period, certainly not if we don't 100 percent want to be there in that moment."

Magda Gerber also taught us about the concept of "attention during caregiving times." We don't have to feel guilty that we're not getting on the floor and playing, so long as we feel we are truly offering our full presence to our children during caregiving moments such as mealtimes, bedtimes, bathing, dressing. As children get older, it becomes the moments when they're sad and need a cuddle, when they have a nightmare and need to snuggle up in our bed, when we're eating a meal together or tucking them in at night. When there are a few moments of focused presence each day, it's usually enough, because it's more about the quality than the quantity. Rather than distractedly playing with them for hours, we can spend a focused mealtime listening to their stories and then let them play independently as we go about our business. As Lansbury says, "Now, in terms of play time, that's also a wonderful time to give attention, but it's really the icing on the cake and should only be, again, when we really, really want to be there."

Play Pandemic

As I write this final chapter, we are in the midst of the COVID-19 pandemic. Only time will tell how history will write this chapter in the human story, but one concept has come through loud and clear: As families were forced into a lockdown situation, with no outside help, no schools, no daycare, babysitters or even grandparents, we have each received a very powerful demonstration of how our families operate at home.

It has been a time of great anxiety and terrible loss for so many. And as our entire "village" became inaccessible almost overnight, our parenting skills, mindset, and the very design of our homes were put to an extreme test. Could we have manageable—perhaps even beautiful—days in this space, day after day, without a change of scene? Can our children entertain themselves for significant parts of the day while we tend to pressing work and household management (and, dare I mention, self-care)?

Is our home serving as a trusted "co-parent," offering us the play zones our children need daily, to move, to explore their senses, to learn, to sink into flow, and to rest? Or are we being tripped up by mountains of clutter and "stuff" that hasn't earned its place in our precious real estate? Are we trusting our children to educate and entertain themselves with minimal adult intervention? Or are we hovering and helicoptering, causing unnecessary stress to us all?

Many different complex aspects affected parents' experience of the lockdown; some lost loved ones, others lost jobs; some had yards and big houses to roam around, others were in small apartments; some had other adults at home helping them, others were completely alone and lonely. But one thing that helped parents across the globe tremendously was their children's capacity to play. Not only did this make it possible for parents to manage their daily tasks but it was also a crucial refuge for their children's emotional health during a stressful time.

A Play–Filled Life

It's my deepest desire that all children grow up with an environment that supports their most basic natural instinct and their most essential developmental need: to play. And further, it's my passionate hope that all parents know that while parenting is inherently challenging, it doesn't have to be quite *that* hard. Reclaiming play can contribute meaningfully to *enjoying* parenting.

Action Steps

- Infuse your parenting with playfulness as much and as often as possible—take the task of parenting seriously, but never take yourself too seriously.

- Add playfulness by getting into character, using funny voices, becoming contrary, playing incompetent, and switching roles, or simply burst out laughing as you're doing whatever mundane chore you're up to.

- Cut yourself slack and give yourself grace every day: you're okay and it's important to remember that. It's okay that you're too busy sometimes, it's okay that you rarely play *with* your children, and it's okay that you don't enjoy *that* type of play.

- Enjoy this time as much as possible! Now it's time to Reclaim Play!

Works Cited

Chapter 01 – Childhood by Design

- Gilbert, Ben. 2019. "It's Been over Twelve Years Since the iPhone Debuted—Look How Primitive the First One Seems Today." Business Insider. July 22, 2019. https://www.businessinsider.com/first-phone-anniversary-2016-12?r=MX&IR=T.
- Plattner, Hasso, Christoph Meinel, and Larry Leifer. 2016. *Design Thinking Research: Making Design Thinking Foundational.* Basel: Springer.

Chapter 02 – What's the Problem?

- Entin, Esther. 2011. "All Work and No Play: Why Your Kids Are More Anxious, Depressed." The Atlantic. October 12, 2011. https://www.theatlantic.com/health/archive/2011/10/all-work-and-no-play-why-your-kids-are-more-anxious-depressed/246422/.
- MacVean, Mary. 2014. "For many people, gathering possessions is just the stuff of life." Los Angeles Times. March 21, 2014. https://www.google.com/search?q=americans+300%2C000+items+home+toys&rlz=1C5CHFA_enMX880MX880&oq=americans+300%2C000+items+home+toys&aqs=chrome..69i57.7444j0j7&sourceid=chrome&ie=UTF-8.
- Lancy, David F. 2017. Anthropological Perspectives on Children as Helpers, Workers, Artisans, and Laborers. New York: Springer.
- Lukianoff, Greg, and Jonathan Haidt. 2018. The Coddling of the American Mind: How Good Intentions and Bad Ideas Are Setting Up a Generation for Failure. New York: Penguin.
- Martin, Carol Lynn, and Richard Fabes. 2008. Discovering Child Development. Booston: Houghton Mifflin.
- Piaget, Jean. 1962. Play, Dreams, and Imitation in Childhood. New York: The Norton Library.
- Skenazy, Lenore. 2009. Free-Range Kids: Giving Our Children the Freedom We Had without Going Nuts with Worry. San Francisco: John Wiley & Sons.
- West, Anne, and Jane Lewis. 2017. Helicopter Parenting and Boomerang Children: How Parents Support and Relate to Their Student and Co-Resident Graduate Children. New York: Routledge.

Chapter 03 – Why Reclaim Play?

- Clements, Douglas H., and Julie Sarama. 2014. *Learning and Teaching Early Math: The Learning Trajectories Approach.* New York: Routledge.
- Csikszentmihalyi, Mihaly. 1990. *Flow: The Psychology of Optimal Experience.* New York: Harper Collins.
- Dunckley, Victoria L. 2013. "Nature's Rx: Green-Time's Effects on ADHD." *Psychology Today.* June 20, 2013. https://www.psychologytoday.com/us/blog/mental-wealth/201306/natures-rx-green-times-effects-adhd.
- Simpson, James B. 1988. Simpson's Contemporary Quotations. Houghton Mifflin Company, Boston
- Dr. Siegel, Daniel, Mindsight: The New

Science of Personal Transformation, Bantam; Reprint edition (December 28, 2010)

- Eisen, George. 1990. *Children and Play in the Holocaust: Games among the Shadows.* Amherst: University of Massachusetts Press.
- Gerber, Magda. 1998. *Dear Parent: Caring for Infants for Respect.* Los Angeles: Resources for Infant Educarers
- Goodwin, Derek. 1983. *Crows of the World.* St. Lucia, QLD: University of Queensland Press.
- Gray, Peter. 2008. "The Value of Play I: The Definition of Play Gives Insights." *Psychology Today.* November 18, 2008. https://www.psychologytoday.com/intl/blog/freedom-learn/200811/the-value-play-i-the-definition-play-gives-insights.
- International Education Database. 2019. "World Top 20—2019 Rankings." *World Top 20 Project Mission: Educate Every Child on the Planet.* January 1, 2019. https://worldtop20.org/education-data-base-2019.
- Kohn, Alfie. 2006. *Unconditional Parenting: Moving from Rewards and Punishments to Love and Reason* . New York: Simon and Schuster.
- Lokhorst, Gert-Jan. 2018. "Descartes and the Pineal Gland." *Stanford Encyclopedia of Philosophy.* Winter Edition. Accessed May 12, 2020. https://plato.stanford.edu/entries/pineal-gland.
- Marzluff, John, and Tony Angell. 2013. *Gifts of the Crow: How Perception, Emotion, and Thought Allow Smart Birds to Behave Like Humans.* New York: Simon and Schuster.
- Olshansky, S. Jay, Douglas J. Passaro, Ronald C. Hershow, Jennifer Layden, Bruce A. Carnes, Jacob Brody, Leonard Hayflick, Robert Butler, David Allison, and David S. Ludwig. 2005. "A Potential Decline in Life Expectancy in the United States in the Twenty-First Century." *The New England Journal of Medicine* 352:1138–1145.
- Piaget, Jean. 1945. *La formation du symbole chez l'enfant: Imitation, jeu et rêve, image et representation* (*Symbol Formation in Childhood: Imitation, Play and Dream, Image and Representation*). Paris: Delachaux et Niestlé.
- Pirrone, Concetta, and Santo Di Nuovo. 2014. "Can playing and imagining aid in Learning Mathematics? An experimental study of the relationships among Building-Block Play, Mental Imagery, and Arithmetic Skills." *Bollettino di Psicologia Applicata* (*Applied Psychology Bulletin*) 62 (271): 30-39.
- Sarama, Julie, and Douglas H. Clements. 2009. *Early childhood mathematics education research: Learning trajectories for young children.* New York: Routledge.
- Seigel, Daniel J. 2010. *Mindsight: The New Science of Personal Transformation.* New York: Bantam Books.
- Silva, Victor. 2019. "Why Finland's Education System is Successful and How to Apply It at Home." *Built by Me. STEM Learning.* April 1, 2019. https://www.builtbyme.com/finland-education-system-successful-home/.

Chapter 04 – Babies Who Play

- Bauer, Ingrid. 2006. *Diaper free: The Gentle Wisdom of Natural Infant Hygiene.* Penguin.
- Brink, Susan. 2013. *The Fourth Trimester:*

Understanding, Protecting, and Nurturing an Infant Through the First Three Months. Los Angeles: University of California Press.

- Gabriel, Cynthia. 2017. *The Fourth Trimester Companion: How to Take Care of Your Body, Mind, and Family as You Welcome Your New Baby.* Beverly, MA: Harvard Common Press.
- Gerber, Magda. 1998. *Dear Parent: Caring for Infants for Respect.* Los Angeles: Resources for Infant Educarers.
- Issacs, Barbara. 2018. *Understanding the Montessori Approach: Early Years Education in Practice.* Abingdon-on-Thames: Routledge.
- Karp, Harvey. 2015. *The Happiest Baby on the Block: The New Way to Calm Crying and Help Your Newborn Baby Sleep Longer.* New York: Bantam Books.
- Lansbury, Janet. 2013. "RIE Parenting Basics (Nine Ways to Put Respect into Action." *Preschool of the Arts.* December 5, 2013. https://www.nycpreschool.org/blog/2018/4/11/rie-parenting-basics-9-ways-to-put-respect-into-action-by-janet-lansbury.
- Lansbury Janet. 2014. *Elevating Child Care: A Guide to Respectful Parenting.* San Fernando: JLML Press.
- Lansbury Janet. 2019. "Already Exhausted by a Fifteen-Month-Old's Behavior." *Janet Lansbury Elevating Childcare.* January 29, 2019. https://www.janetlansbury.com/2019/01/already-exhausted-by-a-15-month-olds-behavior/.
- Mercer, Jean. 2006. *Understanding Attachment: Parenting, Child Care, and Emotional Development.* Westport, CT: Greenwood Publishing Group.
- Pikler, Emmi, and Anna Tardos.

2018. *Lasst mir Zeit: Die selbständige Bewegungsentwicklung des Kindes bis zum freien Gehen. Untersuchungsergebnsse, Aufsätze und Vorträge aus dem Nachlaß zusammengestellt und überarbeitet.* Berlin: Richard Pflaum Vlg GmbH.
- Rousseau, Margaret. 2012. *The Baby Sleep Training Solution: Get Your Baby to Sleep through the Night.* Atlanta: Parental Insight Press.
- Sluss, Dorothy Justus. 2018. *Supporting Play in Early Childhood: Environment, Curriculum, Assessment.* Boston: Cengage Learning.
- Solomon, Deborah Carlisle. 2013. *Baby Knows Best: Raising a Confident and Resourceful Child, the RIE™ Way.* New York: Little, Brown Spark.
- Wood, Christiane. 2019. *The Literacy of Play and Innovation: Children as Makers.* Abingdon-on-Thames: Routledge.

Chapter 05 – Scheming Toddlers

- Athey, Chris. 1990. *Extending Thought in Young Children: A Parent-Teacher Partnership.* Newbury Park, CA: SAGE.
- Caro, Clare. 2012. "Nature Play UK." *Schemas in Children's Play.* August 8, 2012. http://www.nature-play.co.uk/blog/schemas-in-childrens-play.
- Lindon, Jennie. 2001. *Understanding Children's Play* . Cheltenham: Nelson Thornes.
- Louis, Stella, Clare Beswick, and Sally Featherstone. 2008. *Understanding Schemas in Young Children: Again! Again!* London: Bloomsbury Publishing.
- Mairs, Katey, and the Pen Green Team. 2012. *Young Children Learning through*

Schemas: Deepening the Dialogue about Learning in the Home and in the Nursery. London: Routledge.

- Meggitt, Carolyn, Julia Manning-Morton, and Tina Bruce. 2016. *Child Care and Education*. London: Hachette UK.
- Sufi Whirling Dervishes (video clip). 2013. *PBS Religion and Ethics Newsweekly*. December 13, 2013. https://www.pbs.org/wnet/religionandethics/2013/12/13/february-1-2013-sufi-whirling-dervishes/14517/.

Chapter 06 –
Busy Slayer

- Csikszentmihalyi, Mihaly. 1990. *Flow: The Psychology of Optimal Experience*. New York: Harper Perennial .
- Dillard, Annie. 1989. *The Writing Life*. New York: Harper Perennial.
- Elkind, David. 2006. *The Hurried Child; Growing Up Too Fast Too Soon*. Twenty-fifth anniversary ed. Cambridge: Da Capo Lifelong Books.
- Feiler, Bruce. 2013. "Overscheduled Children: How Big a Problem?" *New York Times*. October 11, 2013. https://www.nytimes.com/2013/10/13/fashion/over-scheduled-children-how-big-a-problem.html?pagewanted=all&_r=0.
- Gibbs, Ryan. 2011. *Idle Time*. Bloomington: AuthorHouse.
- Karp, Harvey. 2015. *The Happiest Baby on the Block: The New Way to Calm Crying and Help Your Newborn Baby Sleep Longer*. New York: Bantam Books.
- Kirchheimer, Sid. 2004. "Overscheduled Child May Lead to a Bored Teen." WebMD. January 1, 2004. https://www.webmd.com/parenting/features/overscheduled-child-may-lead-to-bored-teen#1.
- Michigan Medicine (University of Michigan). 2010. "Television and Children." *Your Child Development and Behavior Resources. A Guide to Information and Support for Parents*. August 1, 2010.
- Nakamura, Jeanne., and Mihaly Csikszentmihalyi. 2009. "Flow Theory and Research." In *Handbook of positive psychology*, by C.R. Snyder and Shane J. Lopez, 195–2006. New York: Oxford University Press.
- Payne, Kim John, and Lisa M. Ross. 2009. *Simplicity Parenting: Using the Extraordinary Power of Less to Raise Calmer, Happier, and More Secure Kids*. New York: Ballantine / Random House.
- Rideout, Vicky. 2015. *The Common Sense Census: Media Use by Tweens and Teens*. Common Sense Media. November 3, 2015. https://www.commonsensemedia.org/research/the-common-sense-census-me-dia-use-by-tweens-and-teens-2015. http://cdn.cnn.com/cnn/2017/images/11/07/com-monsensecensus.mediausebytweensand-teens.2015.final.pdf. January 1. Accessed October 25, 2019. Common Sense Media.
- Sears, William, Robert Sears, James Sears, and Martha Sears. 2008. *The Baby Sleep Book: The Complete Guide to a Good Night's Rest for the Whole Family*. New York: Little, Brown.
- Simpson, Timothy. 2011. *Boredom to Brilliance: Using the Power of Arts in You to Create a Beautiful Life*. Düsseldorf: Satzweiss.

Chapter 07 – Declutter Boss

- Boss, Shira. 2018. "What Your Stuff Is Costing You." *Living on a Budget* (blog). January 3, 2018. https://www.aarp.org/money/budgeting-saving/info-2018/clutter-cost-fd.html.
- Botton, Alain de. 2016. "Brands Must Strive to Fulfill the Emotional Promises of Advertising." *Marketing Week*. February 3, 2016. https://www.marketingweek.com/alain-de-botton-brands-must-strive-to-fulfil-the-emotional-promises-of-advertising/.
- Brunetz, Mark, and Carmen Renee Berry. 2010. *Take the U out of Clutter*. New York: Penguin.
- Davenport, Marie S. 2018. *Declutter Your Mind: How to Free Your Thoughts from Worry, Anxiety and Stress Using Mindfulness Techniques for Better Mental Clarity and to Simplify Your Life*. Ocala, FL: E.C. Publishing.
- Gerber, Magda. 1998. *Dear Parent: Caring for Infants for Respect*. Los Angeles: Resources for Infant Educarers.
- Harrison, Stephen. 2012. *Appreciate the Fog: Embrace Change with Power and Purpose*. Bloomington: Xlibris Corporation.
- Hart, Jennifer L., and Michelle T. Tannock. 2013. "Young Children's Play Fighting and Use of War Toys." *Encyclopedia on Early Childhood Development*. June 1, 2013. http://www.child-encyclopedia.com/play/according-experts/young-childrens-play-fighting-and-use-war-toys.
- Shumaker, Heather. 2012. It's Ok Not To Share. TarcherPerigee
- Hjarvard, Stig Prof. 2013. *The Mediatization of Culture and Society*. London: Routledge.
- Kondo, Marie. 2014. *The Life-Changing Magic of Tidying Up*. New York: Ten Speed Press.
- Payne, Kim John, and Lisa M. Ross. 2009. *Simplicity Parenting: Using the Extraordinary Power of Less to Raise Calmer, Happier, and More Secure Kids*. New York: Ballantine / Random House.
- Schor, Juliet B. 2014. *Born to Buy: The Commercialized Child and the New Consumer Cult*. Avon, MA: Simon and Schuster.
- Toy Association. 2019. *U.S. Sales Data*. Toy Association. January 1, 2019. https://www.toyassociation.org/ta/research/data/u-s-sales-data/toys/research-and-data/data/us-sales-data.aspx.

Chapter 08 – Become a Play Architect

- Meerwein, Gerhard, 2007. *Color - Communication in Architectural Space Hardcover*. Birkhäuser Architecture.
- Davies, Simone, 2019. The Montessori Toddler: A Parent's Guide to Raising a Curious and Responsible Human Being. Workman Publishing Company.
- Cadwell, Louise Boyd, 1997. *Bringing Reggio Emilia Home an Innovative Approach to Early Childhood Education*. Teachers College Press
- Mitchell, David, 2017. *Waldorf Education: An Introduction for Parents*. Waldorf Publications
- Feinberg, Sandra, Keller, James R. 2010. *Designing Space for Children and Teens in Libraries and Public Places*. ALA Editions
- Cole L. Etheredge, Tina M. Waliczek and Jayne M. Zajicek. 2014. *The Impact of Plants and Windows on Building Space Usage and Per-*

ceived Stress of University Students. Journal of Therapeutic Horticulture. Vol. 24, No. 1 (2014), pp. 25-38 (14 pages)

- G. Buchbauer, L. Jirovetz. 1994. *Aromatherapy—use of fragrances and essential oils as medicaments.* Flavor And Fragrance Journal.
- Seong-Hyun Park 1, Richard H Mattson, Ornamental indoor plants in hospital rooms enhanced health outcomes of patients recovering from surgery, J Altern Complement Med, September, 2009

Chapter 09 – Imagination Zone

- Ball, Karlene K., Virginia G. Wadley, David E. Vance, and Jerri D. Edwards. 2004. "Cognitive Skills: Training, Maintenance, and Daily Usage." In *Encyclopedia of Applied Psychology,* by Charles Spielberger. Vol. 1, 387-92. Cambridge: Academic Press.
- Barkley, Russel A. 2012. *Executive Functions: What They Are, How They Work, and Why They Evolved.* New York: Guilford Press.
- Elen, Jan, Elmar Stahl, Rainer Bromme, and Geraldine Clarebout. 2011. *Links Between Beliefs and Cognitive Flexibility: Lessons Learned.* Berlin/Heidelberg: Springer Science and Business Media.
- Gerber, Magda, and Deborah Greenwald. 2013. *The RIE Manual: For Parents and Professionals .* Los Angeles: Resources for Infant Educarers.
- Howe, R. Brian, and Katherine Covell. 2007. *Empowering Children: Children's Rights Education as a Pathway to Citizenship.* Toronto: University of Toronto Press.
- Lindon, Jennie. 2001. *Understanding Children's Play .* Cheltenham, UK: Nelson Thornes.

- O'Connor, Anne. 2017. *Understanding Transitions in the Early Years: Supporting Change through Attachment and Resilience.* London: Routledge.
- Piper, Watty. 1930. *The Little Engine That Could.* New York: Plank & Munk Co, Inc.
- Pitamic, Maja. 2004. *Teach Me to Do It Myself: Montessori Activities for You and Your Children.* London: Barron's Educational Series.
- Premack, David, and Guy Woordruff. 1978. "Does the Chimpanzee Have a Theory of Mind?" *Behavioral and Brain Sciences* (Cambridge University Press) 1 (4): 515-26.

Chapter 10 – Messy Zone

- Bogart, Julie. 2019. *The Brave Learner: Finding Everyday Magic in Homeschool, Learning, and Life.* New York: TarcherPerigee.
- Dweck, Carol. 2007. *Mindset: The New Psychology of Success.* New York: Ballantine.
- Gascoyne, Sue. 2018. *Messy Play in the Early Years: Supporting Learning through Material Engagements.* Abingdon: Routledge.
- Gurewitz Clemens, Sydney. 1991. "Art in the Classroom: A Special Part of Every Day." *Journal of the National Association for the Education of Young Children* 45 (2): XXX-XXX.
- Nicholson, Julie, Linda Perez, and Julie Kurtz. 2018. *Trauma-Informed Practices for Early Childhood Educators: Relationship-Based Approaches That Support Healing and Build Resilience in Young Children.* New York: Routledge.
- Robinson, Ken. 2001. *Out of Our Minds: Learning to be Creative.* Chichester:

Capstone Publishing.

- Shaffer, David R. 2008. *Social and Personality Development.* Belmont, CA: Cengage Learning.

Chapter 11 –
Movement Zone

- Biel, Lindsey, and Nancy Peske. 2009. *Raising a Sensory Smart Child: The Definitive Handbook for Helping Your Child with Sensory Processing Issues.* Revised and updated ed. New York: Penguin.
- Bundy, Anita C., and Shelly J. Lane. 2020. *Sensory Integration: Theory and Practice.* Philadelphia: F. A. Davis.
- Connel, Gill, and Cheryl McCarthy. 2014. *A Moving Child Is a Learning Child: How the Body Teaches the Brain to Think (Birth to Age Seven).* Minneapolis: Free Spirit Publishing.
- Louv, Richard. 2005. *Last Child in the Woods: Saving Our Children from Nature-Deficit Disorder.* Chapel Hill: Algonquin Books.
- Margolis, Aleta. 2015. "Letting kids Move in Class Isn't a Break from Learning. It IS Learning." *Washington Post.* January 29, 2015. https://www.washingtonpost.com/news/answer-sheet/wp/2015/01/19/letting-kids-move-in-class-isnt-a-break-from-learning-it-is-learning/.
- Montessori, María. 1967. *The Absorbent Mind.* Wheaton: Theosophical Publishing House.
- Thompson, Tamara. 2016. *Childhood Obesity.* Farmington Hills, MI: Greenhaven.

Chapter 12 –
Focus Zone

- Bogart, Julie. 2019. *The Brave Learner: Finding Everyday Magic in Homeschool, Learning, and Life.* New York: TarcherPerigee.
- Clopton, Jennifer. 2018. "ADHD Rising in the U.S., but Why?" WebMD. November 20, 2018. https://www.webmd.com/add-adhd/news/20181126/adhd-rising-in-the-us-but-why.
- Csikszentmihalyi, Mihaly. 1991. Flow: The Psychology of Optimal Experience. New York: Harper Perennial .
- Duckworth, Angela. 2016. Grit: The Power of Passion and Perseverance . New York: Simon and Schuster.
- Foley, Denise. 2020. "Growing Up with ADHD." Time. January 1, 2020. https://time.com/growing-up-with-adhd/.
- Gardner, Howard. 2006. Multiple Intelligences: New Horizons in Theory and Practice. New York: Basic Books.
- Green, Simon. 2020. "Scaffolding and Academic Literacies." Scaffolding Academic Literacy with Low-Proficiency Users of English, by Simon Green, 41-71. Leeds: Springer Nature.
- Issacs, Barbara. 2018. Understanding the Montessori Approach: Early Years Education in Practice. Abingdon-on-Thames: Routledge.
- Mason, Charlotte. 2017. Home Education. Vol. 1. Bristol: Living Book Press.
- McSpadden, Kevin. 2015. "You Now Have a Shorter Attention Span Than a Goldfish." Time. May 14, 2015. https://time.com/3858309/attention-spans-goldfish/.
- Pitamic, Maja. 2004. Teach Me to Do It Myself: Montessori Activities for You and

Your Children. London: Barron's Educational Series.

- Schmitz, Stephanie. 2012. The Concept of Scaffolding in Primary English Teaching. Munich: GRIN Verlag.

Chapter 13 – Quiet Zone

- Entin, Esther. 2011. "All Work and No Play: Why Your Kids Are More Anxious, Depressed." *The Atlantic.* October 12, 2011. https://www.theatlantic.com/health/archive/2011/10/all-work-and-no-play-why-your-kids-are-more-anxious-depressed/246422/.
- Gall, Michelle, and William R. Stixrud. 2008. "The Four S's of Adolescent Success." *Independent School Magazine* (NAIS [National Association of Independent Schools]). Summer 2008. Accessed February 20, 2020. https://www.nais.org/magazine/independent-school/summer-2008/the-4-s-s-of-adolescent-success.
- Goodman, Ellen. 1999. "Ads Pollute Most Everything in Sight." *Albuquerque Journal,* no. 27: C3.
- Holguin, Jaime. 2002. "Study Says Kids' Homework Load Bigger." *CBS Evening News.* December 10, 2002. https://www.cbsnews.com/news/study-says-kids-homework-load-bigger/.
- Hutton, Lindsay. 2020. "The M2 Generation: Are Your Kids Too Dependent on the Media?" Family Education. February 12, 2020. https://www.familyeducation.com/life/tv-addiction/m2-generation-are-your-kids-too-dependent-media.
- Kennedy, Rebecca. 2018. "Children Spend Half the Time Playing Outside in Comparison to Their Parents." *Child in the City.* January 15, 2018. https://www.childinthecity.org/2018/01/15/children-spend-half-the-time-playing-outside-in-comparison-to-their-parents/?gdpr=accept.
- Masci, David, and Conrad Hackett. 2018. "Meditation is Common across Many Religious Groups in the U.S." *Pew Research Center.* January 2, 2018. https://www.pewresearch.org/fact-tank/2018/01/02/meditation-is-common-across-many-religious-groups-in-the-u-s.
- Sears, William, Robert Sears, James Sears, and Martha Sears. 2008. *The Baby Sleep Book: The Complete Guide to a Good Night's Rest for the Whole Family.* New York: Little, Brown.
- Stixrud, William. 2018. *The Self-Driven Child: The Science and Sense of Giving Your Kids More Control over Their Lives.* New York: Penguin.
- United States Census Bureau. 2018. "School Engagement Higher for Children Involved in Extracurricular Activities." United States Census Bureau. November 6, 2018. https://www.census.gov/newsroom/press-releases/2018/childs-day.html.

Chapter 14 – Curation Diva

- Toy Association. 2019. *U.S. Sales Data.* Toy Association. January 1, 2019. https://www.toyassociation.org/ta/research/data/u-s-sales-data/toys/research-and-data/data/us-sales-data.aspx.
- Stern, Tom, and Brian Volk-Weiss, dirs. 2017-18. *The Toys That Made Us.* Performed

by Netflix.

- Kirkarian, Heather L., and Daniel R. Anderson. 2011. "Learning from Educational Media." In *The Handbook of Children, Media, and Development*, by Sandra L. Calvert and Barbara J. Wilson, 214-34. Chichester: Wiley-Blackwell.
- Gerber Magda, Dear Parent: Caring for Infants With Respect, Resources for Infant Educarers; 1st edition (January 1, 1998)
- Charlesworth, Rosalind. 2016. *Understanding Child Development*. Boston: Cengage Learning.
- Brooks, Karen. 2008. *Univ. of Queensland Press Amazon.com Casa del Libro Gandhi LibreriaNorma.com Muchoslibros.com Find in a library All sellers » Shop for Books on Google Play Browse the world's largest eBookstore and start reading today on the web, tablet, phone, or eread.* St. Lucia: University of Queensland Press.
- Ellis-Petersen, Hannah. 2016. "Barbie Finally Becomes a Real Woman—with a More Realistic Figure." *The Guardian.* January 28, 2016. https://www.theguardian.com/lifeandstyle/2016/jan/28/barbie-finally-becomes-a-real-girl-with-more-realistic-figure-and-skin-colours.
- Story of This Life. 2018. "Baby Toys vs Random Objects." *Story of This Life* (blog). October 23, 2018. YouTube video, 1:15. https://www.youtube.com/watch?time_continue=3&v=9FizCJdJDec.

Chapter 15 – Strew Pro

- Montessori, María. 1967. *The Absorbent Mind.* Wheaton: Theosophical Publishing House.

- Boyd Cadwell, Louise. 1997. *Bringing Reggio Emilia Home: An Innovative Approach to Early Childhood Education.* New York: Teachers' College Press.
- Burns, O. Claire, and L. Johnny Matson. 2017. "Normal developmental Milestones of Toileting." In *Clinical Guide to Toilet Training Children*, by L. Johnny Matson, 49-62. Baton Rouge: Springer.
- Fine, C. A., & Hines, M. (2002). Sex differences in response to children's toys in nonhuman primates (Cercopithecus aethiops sabaeus). Evolution and Human Behavior, 23(6), 467-479)
- Daly, Lisa, and Miriam Beloglovsky. 2014. *Loose Parts: Inspiring Play in Young Children.* St. Paul: Readleaf Press.

Chapter 16 – Play Guru

- Athey, Chris. 1990. *Extending Thought in Young Children: A Parent-Teacher Partnership.* Newbury Park, CA: SAGE.
- Feuerstein, Reuven, and Ann Lewin-Benham. 2012. *What Learning Looks Like: Mediated Learning in Theory and Practice, K–6.* New York: Teachers College Press.
- Kondo, Marie. 2014. *The Life-Changing Magic of Tidying Up.* New York: Ten Speed Press.
- Montessori, María. 1967. *The Absorbent Mind.* Wheaton: Theosophical Publishing House.
- Steiner, Rudolf. 1996. *Rudolf Steiner in the Waldorf School: Lectures and Addresses to Children, Parents, and Teachers, 1919–1924.* Dornach: Antroposophic Press.
- Tsabary, Shefali. 2014. *The Conscious Parent: Transforming Ourselves, Empowering Our Children.* London: Hachette UK.

Chapter 17 –
Only Children

- Carey, William B. 2004. *Understanding Your Child's Temperament*. New York: Xlibris Corporation.
- Gray, Peter. 2013. *Free to Learn: Why Unleashing the Instinct to Play Will Make Our Children Happier, More Self-Reliant, and Better Students for Life*. New York: Basic Books.
- Hartmann, Corinna. 2019. "Is Only-Child Syndrome Real?" *Scientific American*. January 21, 2019. https://www.scientificamerican.com/article/is-only-child-syndrome-real/.
- Kagan Whelan, Corey. 2015. "Only-Child Syndrome: Real Thing or Unnecessary Worry?" Care.com. August 23, 2015. https://www.care.com/c/stories/4205/only-child-syndrome-a-real-thing-or-unnece/.
- Mose, Tamara R. 2016. *The Playdate: Parents, Children, and the New Expectations of Play*. New York: NYU Press.

Chapter 18 –
Sibling Play

- Parten, Mildred B. 1932. "Social Participation among Preschool Children." *Journal of Abnormal and Social Psychology* 27 (3): 243–69.
- Karyn, Wellhousen, and Ingrid Crowther. 2004. *Journal of Abnormal and Social Psychology*. New York: Cengage Learning.
- Markham, Laura. 2015. *Peaceful Parent, Happy Siblings: How to Stop the Fighting and Raise Friends for Life*. New York: Penguin.
- Shumaker, Heather. 2012a. *It's OK Not to Share and Other Renegade Rules for Raising Competent and Compassionate Kids*. New York: Penguin.
- Shumaker, Heather. 2012b. "Why Gun Play is Still OK." *Huffington Post*. September 29, 2009. https://www.huffpost.com/entry/gun-play_b_1720962.
- Hendrix, Harville, and Helen LaKelly Hunt. 1993. *Keeping the Love You Find*. New York: Simon and Schuster.

Chapter 19 –
Screens

- Akhtar, Allana, and Marguerite Ward. 2020. "Bill Gates and Steve Jobs Raised Their Kids with Limited Tech—and It Should Have Been a Red Flag about Our Own Smartphone Use." Business Insider. May 15, 2020. https://www.businessinsider.com/screen-time-limits-bill-gates-steve-jobs-red-flag-2017-10
- Aristotle. 2000. *Nichomachean Ethics*. Edited by Roger Crisp. Cambridge: Cambridge University Press.
- Bilton, Nick. 2014. "Steve Jobs Was a Low-Tech Parent." *New York Times*. September 10, 2014. https://www.nytimes.com/2014/09/11/fashion/steve-jobs-apple-was-a-low-tech-parent.html?_r=0https://www.nytimes.com/2014/09/11/fashion/steve-jobs-apple-was-a-low-tech-parent.html?_r=0.
- Bushman, Brad J., and L. Rowell Huesmann. 2006. "Short-Term and Long-Term Effects of Violent Media on Aggression in Children and Adults." *Archives of Pediatric Adolescent Medicine* 160 (4): 348–52.
- Christakis, Dimitri A., Frederick J. Zimmerman, David L. DiGiuseppe,

and Carolyn A. McCarty. 2004. "Early Television Exposure and Subsequent Attentional Problems in Children." *Pediatrics* (American Academy of Pediatrics) 113 (4): 708-13.

- Geirland, John. 1996. "Go with the Flow." *Wired.* September 9, 1996. https://www. wired.com/1996/09/czik/.

- Gray, Peter. 2012. "The Many Benefits, for Kids, of Playing Video Games: Think Twice Before Limiting Your Kids' Video Play." *Psychology Today* (blog). January 7, 2012. https://www.psychologytoday.com/ us/blog/freedom-learn/201201/the-many- benefits-kids-playing-video-games.

- Gray, Peter. 2013. *Free to Learn: Why Unleashing the Instinct to Play Will Make Our Children Happier, More Self-Reliant, and Better Students for Life.* New York: Basic Books.

- Hale, Lauren, and Stanford Guan. 2015. "Screen Time and Sleep Among School-Aged Children and Adolescents: A Systematic Literature Review." *Sleep Medicine Reviews* 21 (February 1, 2015): 50-58.

- Holley, Peter. 2014. "Want to Boost Your Brain Power? A New Study Says Video Games Are the Answer. *Washington Post.* November 12, 2014. https://www. washingtonpost.com/news/to-your- health/wp/2014/11/13/want-to-boost-your- brain-power-a-new-study-says-video- games-are-the-answer/.

- Markham, Laura. 2020. "Your Toddler or Preschooler and TV." Aha! Parenting. January 1, 2020. https://www. ahaparenting.com/Ages-stages/toddlers/ toddler-preschooler-tv-computer.

- Lansbury, Janet. 2014. *No Bad Kids Toddler Discipline Without Shame.* Book Jlml Press

- Pinker, Stephen. 2018. *Enlightenment Now: The Case for Reason, Science, Humanism, and Progress.* New York: Viking.

- Rose, Sarah E., Alexandra Lamont, and Nicholas Reyland. 2019. "Watching Television in a Home Environment: Effect on Children's Attention, Problem Solving, and Comprehension." *PsyArXiv* (Society for the Improvement of Psychological Science) (blog). https://doi.org/10.31234/osf. io/8yma9.

- Kim John Payne, Lisa M. Ross, Simplicity Parenting: Using the Extraordinary Power of Less to Raise Calmer, Happier, and More Secure Kids, Ballantine Books; 53651st edition, August, 2010

Chapter 20 – A Play-Filled Life

- Cohen, Lawrence J. 2008. *Playful Parenting: An Exciting New Approach to Raising Children That Will Help You Nurture Close Connections, Solve Behavior Problems, and Encourage Confidence.* New York: Random House.

- Gerber, Magda. 1998. *Dear Parent: Caring for Infants for Respect.* Los Angeles: Resources for Infant Educarers.

- Greve, Werner, Tamara Thomsen, and Cornelia Dehio. 2014. "Free Play Allows Children to Develop the Flexibility Needed to Adapt to Changing Circumstances and Environments—an Ability That Comes in Very Handy When Life Becomes Unpredictable as an Adult." *Evolutionary Psychology* 434-47.

- Hanessian, Lu. 2018. "Dr. Dan Siegel: What Hearing 'Yes' Does to Your Child's Brain."

Mindful. January 11, 2018. https://www.
mindful.org/dr-dan-siegel-hearing-yes-
childs-brain/.

- Hulburt Hamilton, Ruth. 1958. *Song for
  a Fifth Child.* Des Moines: Ladies Home
  Journal.
- Lansbury, Janet. 2018. "It's Really Okay
  to Say 'No' to Playing with Your Child
  (Five Reasons)." Janet Lansbury: Elevating
  Child Care. August 6, 2018. https://www.
  janetlansbury.com/2018/08/its-really-
  okay-to-say-no-to-playing-with-your-
  child-5-reasons/.
- Siegel, Daniel J., and Tina Payne Bryson.
  2012. *The Whole-Brain Child: Twelve
  Revolutionary Strategies to Nurture Your
  Child's Developing Mind.* New York: Bantam.
- Daniel J. Siegel, Tina Payne Bryson. 2016.
  *No-Drama Discipline: The Whole-Brain Way
  to Calm the Chaos and Nurture Your Child's
  Developing Mind.* New York: Bantam.
- Daniel J. Siegel, Tina Payne Bryson. 2018.
  *The Yes Brain: How to Cultivate Courage,
  Curiosity, and Resilience in Your Child.* New
  York: Bantam.
- Thomas, Mindy, and Guy Raz. 2019. "Wow
  in the World + The Story Pirates in Do You
  SEE What I HEAR?" NPR. August 19, 2019.
  https://www.npr.org/podcasts/510321/
  wow-in-the-world.
- Tsabary, Shefali. 2017. *The Awakened
  Family: How to Raise Empowered, Resilient,
  and Conscious Children.* New York: Penguin
  Books.

Acknowledgements

Nina Amir, High Performance Coach and founder of ninaamir.com, thank you for guiding me to sharpen the concept for this book and ensuring its cohesion. Prof. Gabriela Vieyra, head of the school of humanities and education at Tecnológico de Monterrey Campus Santa Fe, thank you for your insightful research and expertise. My deepest thanks to Helga Schier PhD, founder of withpenandpaper.com for your editorial guidance throughout the development process for this book. And thanks to Ellen Leach for polishing my words.

Naama Tobias, old friend and designer extraordinaire, thank you for your typographic genius. Noga Livni, Mary Patan and Guy Levy: thank you all for your dedication to the visual excellence of each page of this book. Ryan Sprenger of New Type Publishing, thank you for making this book a reality and getting into the hands of parents who are hungry to Reclaim Play.

This book couldn't have been written without the unwavering support of my all star, small but mighty team. Tamara Mullenhour, thank you for being a rock: my harshest critic and simultaneously the most enthused supporter. Tracy Lekawa, thank you for being a wizard: taking my outlandish ideas and making them into a practical reality with a supreme attention to detail. Nick Magnuson, thank you for taking the mediocre raw materials I provide you - and alchemizing them to make me look and sound my best. Thank you Rūta, Claire, Hannah and Josie for supporting each of our students with the utmost dedication. Thank you to the thousands of students from over 100 countries around the world who have participated in my programs thus far. It is thanks to your willingness to experiment, to share your wisdom and experience with me (in the forms of hundreds of humbling messages, emails and coaching calls) that I am able to share the concepts of Reclaim Play.

And thank you to my family, extended and immediate, to my friends, near and far, for your extraordinary championing and cheerleading throughout this process.

And thank you, Jer for Reclaiming Play with me.

Reclaim Play
Written and Illustrated by Avital Schreiber Levy

Research: Prof. Gabriela Vieyra
Advisor: Nina Amir
Concept and design: Studio Naama Tobias
Graphic design: Mary Patan, Guy Levy
Illustration inking: Noga Livni
Text Editing: Helga Schier
Copy Editing: Ellen Leach
Publishing and Print Production: Newtype Publishing

Typeset with *Greta* by *Michal Sahar*, *Circular* by *Laurenz Brunner*
and *Alpina* by *Grilli Type*.
Printed and bound in the USA, 2023

Further info can be found at ReclaimPlay.com

About the Author

Founder of HiFam.com, Avital Schreiber Levy believes a life of meaning begins
at home. Her work is dedicated to building unbreakable families: she'll show
you how to make your marriage, your children and your entire family unit
strong and resilient. As a wife and a mother of five herself, Avital blends
ancient wisdom with modern living, her teachings will guide you to design
a family life you love.

This book comes with a free reclaim play guide that
will offer you action steps for each chapter, useful
links to materials or toys you might want to purchase,
meaningful take-away quotes from the book and journal
prompts to help you get the best results from this book.
Get your complimentary resources and more at:

ReclaimPlay.com